Youth Work in the Commonwealth

A Growth Profession

Commonwealth Secretariat

 The Commonwealth

Commonwealth Secretariat
Marlborough House
Pall Mall
London SW1Y 5HX
United Kingdom

Published by the Commonwealth Secretariat
Edited by Allison McKechnie
Typeset by NovaTechset Private Limited, Bengaluru & Chennai, India
Cover image by Andrew Aitchison / Alamy Stock Photo
Printed by Hobbs the Printers, Totton, Hampshire

Wherever possible, the Commonwealth Secretariat uses paper sourced from responsible forests or from sources that minimise a destructive impact on the environment.

Copies of this publication may be obtained from

Publications Section
Commonwealth Secretariat
Marlborough House
Pall Mall
London SW1Y 5HX
United Kingdom
Tel: +44 (0)20 7747 6500
Email: publications@commonwealth.int
Web: www.thecommonwealth.org/publications

A catalogue record for this publication is available from the British Library.

ISBN (paperback): 978-1-84929-173-6
ISBN (e-book): 978-1-84859-965-9

Credits

Lead writer: Dr Brian Belton

Co-writer, baseline design and compilation: Dharshini Seneviratne

Baseline design support: Christopher Jones

Editors: Dharshini Seneviratne, Dr Tim Corney, Dr Robyn Broadbent

Research/analysis and youth consultations: Sionlelei Sina Mario

Research support: Tiffany Daniels

Regional Consultants: Dr Alphonce Omolo (Africa), Ashraf Patel (Asia), Glenyss Adam James (the Caribbean), Dr Brian Belton (Europe and Canada), Dr Tim Corney (The Pacific).

Case Study Contributors:

Dr Shantha Abeysinghe, Sri Lanka

Dr Brian Belton, the United Kingdom

Dr Tim Corney, Australia

Dr Alphonce Omolo, Kenya

Anya Satyanand, New Zealand

Simon Schembri, Malta

Arjun Shekar, India

Dr P Sivakumar, India

Dr John Tan, Singapore

Review Team:

The Commonwealth Alliance of Youth Workers' Associations

Dr Shantha Abeysinghe, Sri Lanka

Dr Jennifer Brooker, Australia

Dr Robyn Broadbent, Australia

Dr Tim Corney, Australia

Francis Kapapa, Zambia

Jane Melvin, United Kingdom

Dr Lee Kwan Meng, Malaysia

Tanya Merrick Powell, Jamaica

Ashraf Patel, India

Anya Satyanand, New Zealand

Simon Schembri, Malta

Dr John K E Tan, Singapore

Andrew Tandeo, Zambia

Youth Division, Commonwealth Secretariat

Layne Robinson, Head, Programmes, Youth Division

Sionlelei Sina Mario, Assistant Programmes Officer, Youth Division

Christopher Jones, Assistant Programmes Officer, Youth Division

Commonwealth Youth Council

Akouyu Alphonse Akohleng Chefor, Cameroon, Membership Committee, Commonwealth Youth Council.

Farzana Akther Chowdhuri, Bangladesh, Member, Commonwealth Youth Council

Country Consultants:

Name	Country
Africa	
Dr Emmanuel M J Tamanja	Ghana
Tonny M Odera	Kenya
Boniface Chibwana	Malawi
Emmanuel Etim	Nigeria
Dr Bernice Hlagala	South Africa
Dr Natujwa Mvungi	Tanzania
Elone Natumanya	Uganda
Francis Kapapa	Zambia
Asia	
Tanvir Mahmud	Bangladesh
Nidhi Srivastava	India
Dr Lee Kwan Meng	Malaysia
Lugma	Maldives
Muhammad Shahzad Khan	Pakistan
Felicia Yong, Gracia Yong, Michelle Ling, Dr John K E Tan	Singapore
Dr Shantha Abeysinghe	Sri Lanka

Name	Country
The Caribbean	
Cleviston Hunte	Barbados
Glenda Diaz-Gordon	Belize
John Roach	Dominica
Glenyss Adam James	Guyana
Tanya Powell	Jamaica
Mary Wilfred	St Lucia
Philcol Jeffers	St Vincent and the Grenadines
Anna Kay Seaton	Trinidad and Tobago
Europe and Canada	
Dr Patti Ranahan	Canada
Anna Dalosi	Cyprus
Miriam Teuma	Malta
Dr Brian Belton	United Kingdom
The Pacific	
Dr Tim Corney, Sushil Ram	Australia, Fiji, Papua New Guinea, Samoa, Tonga, Vanuatu, Solomon Islands
Anya Satyanand	New Zealand
Irene Paulsen	Solomon Islands

Contents

List of figures

List of tables

List of boxes

Acknowledgements

This baseline of youth work in the Commonwealth has been a remarkably collaborative effort. We thank Dr Brian Belton of the YMCA George Williams College for leading on the narrative and for the rich ideas and lively discussions his insightful and focused contributions enable. He was a source of strength and inspiration for the implementation of the baseline.

A special thank you also goes to the five regional consultants for their dedicated work and continued interactions with the Secretariat on ensuring accurate data, and to all the country consultants who worked with regional consultants to make it possible.

We also thank the dedication of members of the Commonwealth Alliance of Youth Work Associations (CAYWA) – Dr Robyn Broadbent and Dr Tim Corney (Youth Workers' Association Australia), Jennifer Brooker, the Professional Association of Lecturers in Youth and Community Work (TAG – Australia), Ashraf Patel and Arjun Shekar (ComMutiny – the Youth Collective, India), Simon Schembri (Malta Association of Youth Workers), Tanya Merrick Powell (Jamaica Professional Youth Workers' Association), Anya Satyanand (New Zealand Youth Workers Association), Dr John Tan (Youth Workers' Association Singapore), Dr Shantha Abeysinghe (Professional Youth Workers' Association, Sri Lanka), Jane Melvin (the Institute of Youth Work UK), Lyn Boyd (the Professional Association of Lecturers in Youth and Community Work- TAG) and Andrew Tandeo and Francis Kapapa (Zambia Youth Workers' Association) for their efforts as reviewers and case study contributors to the work. Others who contributed case studies include Dr Alphonce Omolo, Kenya, and Sue Wallwork of the United Kingdom. This work would not have been possible without their sense of ownership and commitment to the process.

Foreword

More than 60 per cent of the population of the Commonwealth is aged under 30, and young people's unique needs and capabilities, and the importance of their role in national development, have been the central premise of the Commonwealth Youth Programme for over four decades. This is also enshrined in the Commonwealth Charter, which recognises 'the positive and active role and contributions of young people in promoting development, peace, democracy and in protecting and promoting other Commonwealth values, such as tolerance and understanding, including respect for other cultures'.

Youth workers have an essential, but often under-recognised and under-resourced, role in engaging and supporting young people to be these positive and productive citizens who contribute to national peace and prosperity.

With *Youth Work in the Commonwealth: A Growth Profession,* we establish a foundation for discussion, dialogue and policy initiatives to ensure that young people receive the best professional youth work services from practitioners. It sets out key concepts and approaches in professionalising youth work, and assesses the extent of recognition of the profession in 35 member states in Africa, Asia, the Caribbean and the Americas, Europe and the Pacific.

This study is encouraging in its demonstration of significant steps taken in the recognition of the profession in some member states. However, in some contexts, advances in policy statements are often still to be translated to practice, and, in others, existing good practice could be amplified and replicated through distinct policies.

The Commonwealth has been committed to strengthening the professionalism of youth work since the 1970s through the Commonwealth Diploma in Youth Development Work. The Commonwealth Plan of Action for Youth Empowerment (PAYE) also helped establish the foundations of professional youth work by committing to support governments on the education and training of youth workers, facilitating the recognition of youth work by Public Service Commissions and through policy, partnering with youth worker associations in maintaining the ethical and quality standards of the profession, and enabling consultation between professional associations and governments in the shaping of youth work policy. In the recent past, the Diploma has been upgraded to a bachelor's degree by the University of the West Indies in collaboration with the Commonwealth Secretariat and the Commonwealth of Learning. This intellectual property is being made universally available through an online Degree Consortium that aligns with the spirit of sharing and learning that is central to the Commonwealth's vision. Numerous other initiatives to professionalise the sector, including support to strengthen both policy and practice, have been advanced by the Commonwealth.

We have also had the pleasure of working closely with the Commonwealth Alliance of Youth Workers' Associations (CAYWA) in making this publication a reality. This close collaboration has been an encouraging sign of the collective strength of the emerging global entity that is CAYWA, and their shared interest in obtaining recognition for the profession of youth work across the Commonwealth. We applaud their commitment and pledge to continue to work towards the aspirations set by this work, with them.

Katherine Ellis
Director, Youth Division
Commonwealth Secretariat

Message from the Commonwealth Alliance of Youth Workers' Associations (CAYWA)

CAYWA welcomes the comprehensive and critical analysis of youth work in 35 Commonwealth member states undertaken by the Youth Division of the Commonwealth Secretariat. It is a powerful story about the challenges and opportunities for youth work and youth development across the Commonwealth ahead of the 14th Commonwealth Youth Ministers Meeting, 2017.

The baseline is set to benefit professional youth work across the Commonwealth, and tells a broader story about the benefits of youth work to young people and communities. The report provides rich evidence of advancements in the recognition of youth work, and of good practice, and calls for gathering comprehensive evidence of the benefits of building the profession and its relationship to building the personal agency of, and social connectedness in, young people, and youth work's broader benefits to building peaceful, productive and cohesive societies.

The report has a distinct focus on professionalisation of youth work that CAYWA applauds. Currently, CAYWA has 17 member organisations and a connection to a global network of 40 Youth Work Associations. We, as part of the National Youth Workers' Associations forming CAYWA have the pleasure to have contributed to the baseline report that will provide the necessary support for this movement to grow across the Commonwealth.

CAYWA, though in its infancy, has an active membership base that are looking for opportunities to strengthen the ability to learn from each other. CAYWA have adopted the Commonwealth Code of Ethical Practice, which will provide guidance to establishing national associations. It is the ownership of a code of ethical practice that promotes a profession as having distinct boundaries in its practice and makes clear the underpinning principles and values. In the case of CAYWA that would be its commitment to the human rights of young people and young people being a youth worker's primary consideration.

It would be remiss of CAYWA members not to mention that the report also highlights the work that is still to be established. The need for Youth Policies in a number of countries, the importance of Youth Ministries, the promotion of youth work in legislation and/or a Youth Work Act in recognition of what youth work can achieve in relation to young people, is clearly highlighted. The report goes further to highlight which countries do not have a distinct budget line that focuses on young people and youth work as well as youth work training and education.

One of the more serious concerns that is raised in the report is the number of countries that have no vetting of youth workers, either paid or unpaid. Young people and children's safety is paramount, and ensuring that youth work provides safety for young people is the clear responsibility of Governments. Systems that check the criminal history and suitability of people that work with young people are an essential component of the youth work landscape that ensures integrity and community credibility.

Finally, CAYWA looks forward to continuing engagement with the Commonwealth so that we, together, progress many of the recommendations that aim to build the capacity of youth work in the Commonwealth. CAYWA wholeheartedly supports the premise that building the capacity of youth work will be an important 'game changer' in building greater equity and social justice outcomes for young people.

Abbreviations and Acronyms

AIOU	Allama Iqbal Open University, Pakistan
AYAC	Australian Youth Affairs Coalition
AZ	Aġenżija Żgħażagħ (National Youth Agency, Malta)
BOU	Bangladesh Open University
C4YDS	Centre for Youth Development Services, Ghana
CARE	Children-at-Risk Empowerment Association, Singapore
CAYWA	Commonwealth Alliance of Youth Workers' Associations
CCCYCA	Council of Canadian Child and Youth Care Associations
CHOGM	Commonwealth Heads of Government Meeting
CLD	Community Learning and Development, Scotland
CoL	Commonwealth of Learning
CRRP	Criminal Report Review Programme, Canada
CYC	ComMutiny – the Youth Collective, India
CYMM	Commonwealth Youth Ministers Meeting
CYP	Commonwealth Youth Programme
DYW	Development Framework for Youth Workers
ETC	Employment and Training Cooperation, Malta
IYRES	Institute for Youth Research, Malaysia
JPYWA	Jamaica Youth Workers' Association
LG	local government
MAY	Malta Association of Youth Workers
MUT	Malta Union of Teachers
MYC	Malaysian Youth Council
NCS	National Citizenship Service, UK
NCYD	National Centre for Youth Development, Jamaica

NGO	non-governmental organisation
NJC	National Joint Committee, UK
NOS	National Occupational Standards, UK
NSS	National Service Scheme, India
NUSU	National Union of Students, Uganda
NUYO	National Union of Youth Organisations, Uganda
NYWCF	National Youth Work Competency Framework, Singapore
NYP	National Youth Policy
NYA	National Youth Agency, UK
NYKS	Nehru Yuva Kendra Sangathan (youth club collective), India
NYSC	National Youth Services Council, Sri Lanka
ODL	Open Distance Learning
OUSL	Open University of Sri Lanka
PAYE	Commonwealth Plan of Action for Youth Empowerment
PG	postgraduate
PYWA	Professional Youth Workers' Association, Sri Lanka
QCF	Qualifications and Credit Framework, UK
RGNIYD	Rajiv Gandhi National Institute of Youth Development
SAYWA	South Africa Youth Workers' Association
SDC	Social Development Commission, Jamaica
SMILE	Student Mobilisation Initiative for Learning through Exposure, India
TAFE	Technical and Further Education, Australia
TSC	Training Standards Committee, UK
UNFPA	United Nations Family Planning Association
UNICEF	United Nations Children's Fund
UPM	Universiti Putra Malaysia
UWI	University of the West Indies
UYDO	Uganda Youth Development Organisations
YACVic	Youth Affairs Council, Australia
YCC	Youth Consultative Council, Malaysia
YEA	Youth Employment Agency, Ghana

YFU	Youth Farmers' Union, Uganda
YouthWorkWA	Youth Work Western Australia (professional association)
YRIC	Youth Resource and Information Centre, Trinidad and Tobago
YUVA	Youth for Unity and Voluntary Action, India
YMCA	Young Men's Christian Association
YW	Youth work
YWA	Youth Workers' Association, Australia
YWAS	Youth Work Association, Singapore
ZYWA	Zambia Youth Workers Association

Glossary

Asset-based youth work – Youth work that engages young people on the basis that they are assets to society, and are autonomous, and that they have the capability to transform themselves and their environments. The Commonwealth promotes these forms of youth work.

Code of conduct – A code of conduct is typically issued by an organisation but it can be put forward by a professional association. It outlines specific behaviours that are required or prohibited as a condition of ongoing employment/acceptance in the profession. A code of conduct might forbid forms of harassment and intimidation, or viewing inappropriate or unauthorised content on computers. Codes of conduct, to mean anything, are rigorous standards that are usually tightly enforced (sanctions that have teeth). They are put in place largely to avoid scandal, and protect reputation. They also include aspects that can protect colleagues and young people who receive services.

Code of ethics – Generic guidelines that provide direction about values, principles, judgements and choices to influence decision-making and consequent actions. For example, a code of ethics might stipulate that we are committed to anti-oppressive practices. The expectation is that an individual worker, when faced with the option, will make a judgement that will avoid oppressing/harassing/coercing others. In the professional sphere, it is practitioners (and/or those they choose to represent them, i.e. professional associations) who establish and review codes of ethics.

Education and training, youth work – Accredited and non-accredited forms of formal and non-formal education that enhance the knowledge, skills and attitudes of youth workers.

Instrumentalist youth work – Youth work that is geared towards specific pragmatic ends such as ensuring employment and economic empowerment of young people, or sees young people as 'vehicles' of national development. These forms of youth work may or may not include other forms of social and political empowerment and youth engagement strategies.

Intersectionality in youth work – Intersectionality refers to diverse identities/status and how they inform experiences and outcomes. In the youth work profession, this would involve analysing a. the experiences and challenges **of youth workers themselves, in all their diversity,** i.e. by virtue of being youth workers who are women, or those coming from ethnic, religious or sexual minorities, youth workers with disability and so on, and b. the experiences and challenges of **diverse groups of young people that youth work caters for,** such as young women, young people living with physical and intellectual disabilities and young people from religious, ethnic or sexual minorities, high-risk youth groups, and so on.

Just-in-time training – Where the knowledge and skills built meet the immediate needs of professionals. Usually intended for immediate application.

Professionalisation, youth work – Ensuring the recognition of youth work practice, and ensuring that youth workers have the relevant knowledge, skills and attitudes to deliver quality youth work services.

Professional association – A professional organisation that exists to safeguard the quality and integrity of the profession.

Professional care, youth work – Relies on an associative and detached, rather than personal, relationship between the practitioner and young person in the delivery of youth work in caring and secure contexts.

Professional judgement, youth work – Making sound, evidence-based and non-partisan judgements in the delivery of youth work services to young people.

Practice regulation, youth work – Mechanisms and processes in place such as codes of conduct, supervision processes, guidelines for implementation etc. that ensure that practice is regulated and of a high standard.

Professional validation (youth work education and training) – Connects qualifications to the field and helps keep education and training up to date. This ensures that education and training is responsive to changes in contexts and practice and is responsive to young people's ever-changing needs and rights.

Psycho-social care in youth work – Psycho-social models of youth work can refer to youth work that engages with at-risk groups, as in some parts of the Commonwealth. But psycho-social models in asset-based contexts are based on the assumption that young people exist in a psycho-social context and that the development of the human being **requires a clear understanding of the self in relation to the social**.

Rights-based youth work – Youth work that is based on human rights frameworks and advances young people's autonomy and agency. Rights-based youth work supports the realisation of young people's social, political and economic rights as set out in international conventions ratified by governments, and Constitutional rights set down by specific member states.

Supervision, youth work – The exploration and development of reflective practice, and developing the ability to learn from such examination. Support to fellow practitioners in a profession.

Youth empowerment – Enhancing the status of young people, helping them empower themselves to build their competencies and capabilities for life. This involves social, political, cultural and economic empowerment. It will enable them to contribute to, and benefit from, a politically stable, economically viable and legally supportive environment, ensuring their full participation as active citizens.

Youth engagement – Where young people develop sustained connections in their lives. This can occur within themselves, in the immediate world around them, in society and the world. These sustained connections may be emotional, psychological or cognitive, and can be personal or social. Youth engagement is often **reductively**

referred to as young people's involvement in social action (civic action/service, youth-led research etc.). This is not the only form of youth engagement.[1]

Youth for development – This approach sees young people as 'instruments' for broader national development and often fails to perceive the centrality of a young person's own personal and interpersonal needs for self-realisation, empowerment and building social connectedness (the focus of youth work).

Youth participation in youth work – Youth participation in youth work involves young people exercising their agency in defining the nature and quality of youth work services for them, and also in participating in the monitoring and evaluation of the quality of services provided to them. Young people also participate in youth work as peer youth workers (as professionals themselves).

Youth sector – The youth sector comprises the multiple players that focus on social equality for youth and empowerment as their main institutional focus. Generally, youth sector stakeholders include the Government ministry/department for youth at the national and local levels, government youth service implementing bodies, youth-led organisations, youth movements, including students' unions, youth studies and youth work studies delivery departments in universities, colleges and training bodies, youth research institutes, youth workers' associations and other professional bodies in the youth sector.

Youth work – The Commonwealth's working definition describes it as all forms of rights-based youth engagement approaches that build personal awareness and support the social, political and economic empowerment of young people, delivered through non-formal learning within a matrix of care.

Youth work legislation – Legislation that commits to supporting what might be understood as/agreed to be 'best practice' in a profession. Sometimes includes sanctions against unprofessional practice. This may make it probable that the realisation of commitments is justiciable, so that inaction around commitments can be challenged in a country's legal system, but this is often not likely. Legislation may also seek to outline the limits of professional practice and the desired role of practitioners, or control the profession.

Youth work mechanisms and processes – Mechanisms and processes that facilitate the delivery of youth work. These could be the likes of youth clubs, youth engagement spaces, or in detached contexts such as in the street, where processes are based on dialogue, listening and social empowerment. Youth work also occurs in many other contexts such as schools, hospitals and so on.

Youth work policy – Policies that commit to the advancement of youth work as a profession, including commitments to the education and training of youth workers, and the establishment of mechanisms and processes for the delivery of youth work.

Note

1   This definition of youth engagement is derived and adapted from material available in Fletcher, 2013.

Executive Summary

Youth work is defined broadly by the Commonwealth Secretariat as 'all forms of rights-based youth engagement approaches that build personal awareness and support the social, political and economic empowerment of young people, delivered through non-formal learning within a matrix of care'. It is a relational profession built around the skills and competencies of engaging young people to enhance their self-esteem, social connectedness, economic and social productivity, emotional and intellectual maturity, and autonomy, and supporting them in their self-empowerment in caring and supportive environments. Peer youth work involves young people themselves who have built systematic skills and competencies engaging with their peers as youth workers.

The Commonwealth initiated its commitments to the profession of youth work through its support for the implementation of the Commonwealth Diploma in Youth Development Work in the 1970s. The 2007 Commonwealth Youth Ministers Meeting committed to the Plan of Action for Youth Empowerment (PAYE), (Commonwealth of Nations, 2007) the framework which renewed and expanded this commitment to youth development work. The contributions of the Commonwealth to professionalising youth work has subsequently been endorsed by member states including at the Commonwealth Heads of Government Meeting (CHOGM) 2013 which commended 'the Commonwealth Secretariat's ongoing commitment to youth work education and professionalisation' (Commonwealth Secretariat, 2013b, p. 13).

Since then, the Commonwealth has expanded its contributions to youth work education and training through establishing the emerging Youth Work Education Qualifications Consortium and to broader influencing that advances policy and practice commitments to youth work in member states and supporting/encouraging member states to establish youth workers' associations.

Youth work, for us, is a growth profession. It is rapidly evolving and changing, just like young people. It has, throughout its varied and contextualised histories, been a constantly growing practice; varying over time and place and continuing to alter and develop. This has meant that it has been able to remain a relevant social resource. This growth is motivated and created by individuals, groups, communities, nations and societies, who deploy and call on youth workers to adapt and shape their response.

This growth has been necessary in order to respond to the evolving and shifting needs of young people, their personal growth and the requirements, hopes, ambitions and expectations that regions and nations have for their young people.

Youth work also distinctly benefits not only young people, but all of society. The profession has demonstrated great value in providing young people with support to figure out the means of their social, political, ethical, intellectual and physical development. Youth work, when adequately funded and resourced, and when comprehensive training is provided to practitioners, is shown to have greatly contributed to shaping a productive and equitable workforce, enhancing employability skills, and responding sensitively to radicalisation and extreme behaviour – ultimately leading to equitable development outcomes and social cohesion for all. Where mainstream education has faced challenges addressing young people's personal and social development, youth work has met those challenges.

For all this, while youth work is no single thing, neither is it everything. Youth work has core practice principles, but it has needed to be continually emergent and adaptive because the young people it serves, and the social situation they find themselves in, are also continually changing and adapting. Youth works serves no one situation or young person. It has grown and transformed because of its inherent responsiveness; like a butterfly, if you pin it down you will kill it; like the young people it serves, it is becoming more than what it is, looking to be all it might be. But also like young people, while youth work has commonalities in any given circumstance, it is necessarily shaped by local, cultural and social considerations. Youth work is as such a growth profession.

This baseline is an inquiry into the professional identity and multiple practices of youth work, a look at the way in which its professionalisation has been approached in Commonwealth member states, and a preliminary look at how it has begun shaping and benefiting young people's autonomy, self-empowerment and productivity. In an indirect manner, the baseline has also proved a testament to the influence of the Commonwealth in this sphere.

The study was conducted in 35 Commonwealth member states that were considered by regional consultants in relation to the extent of steps taken to professionalise youth work as follows:

Commonwealth Member States included in the Baseline Survey								
Region	**Countries**							
Africa	Ghana	Kenya	Malawi	Nigeria	South Africa	Tanzania	Uganda	Zambia
Asia	Bangladesh	India	Maldives	Malaysia	Pakistan	Singapore	Sri Lanka	
Caribbean	Barbados	Belize	Dominica	Guyana	Jamaica	Saint Lucia	St Vincent	Trinidad & Tobago
Europe and Canada	Canada	Cyprus	Malta	United Kingdom				
Pacific	Australia	Fiji	New Zealand	Papua New Guinea	Samoa	Solomon Islands	Tonga	Vanuatu

It has been a collaborative effort bringing together five regional consultants, 35 country consultants and Commonwealth staff in a bid to assess progress made in ensuring quality youth work delivery for young people through its professionalisation.

While it is difficult to provide quantitative evidence of where youth work is explicitly recognised as a profession due to the varying criteria that govern its practice in member states, not even half the number of member states in the sample had taken what we will term 'significant steps'[1] towards the formal recognition of the profession, if the contributions of all youth sector players[2] are considered. In spite of this, youth work exists in many forms and shapes across the Commonwealth, and benefits the lives of young people in multiple ways.

Out of the 35 countries in the sample, 12 countries (34 per cent) had taken significant steps to professionalise the youth work sector. Only 11 (31 per cent) countries had distinct national-level policies that recognised youth work. Twelve countries (34 per cent) had youth workers' associations that help safeguard the integrity and quality of the profession, and 25 (71 per cent) could claim at least a diploma-level qualification for youth work professionals. In Africa, Asia and the Caribbean, many of the advances have also been directly and indirectly attributed to the Commonwealth's efforts.

The summary charts below for each regions/region groups studied elaborate on:

a. The existence of specific policy commitments to youth work as a distinct professional category,

b. The existence of legislative enactments for youth work in the form of Youth Work Acts,

c. The existence of a professional association for youth workers in order to ensure the quality and integrity of the profession,

d. The availability of qualifications above a diploma level for youth work education and training.

Figure ES.1 demonstrates commitments identified in the survey for the five regions/ region groups of the baseline: there is somewhat of a correlation between policy

Figure ES.1 Regional trends – commitments to professionalising youth work

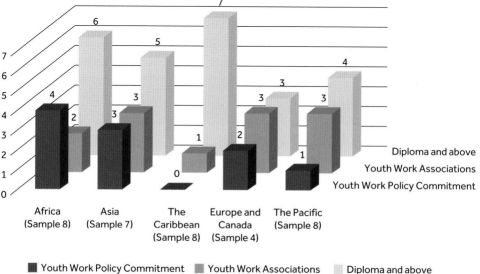

commitment and actioned progress in education and training and the establishment of youth workers' associations, even though in some regions/countries progress in developing commitments to professional practice has occurred despite a lack of supporting legislation and policy.

A breakdown of these across regions indicates the following:

Table ES.1 Commitments to professionalising youth work – Africa (full sample – 8 countries)

Country	Total countries	Ghana	Kenya	Malawi	Nigeria	South Africa	Tanzania	Zambia	Uganda
Policy Commitments to youth work as a profession	4	0	0	✓	0	✓	✓	✓	
Youth Work Act	0	0	0	0	0	0	0	0	
Professional Association	2	0	0	0	0	✓	0	✓	
Degree/Diploma	6	✓	✓	✓	✓	✓	✓	✓ (In progress)	
Masters and PhD	1	0	0	✓	0	0³	0	0	

Table ES.2 Commitments to professionalising youth work – Asia

Country	Total countries	Bangladesh	India	Malaysia	Maldives⁴	Pakistan	Singapore	Sri Lanka
Policy Commitments to youth work as a profession	4	✓ (in draft youth policy)	✓	✓	✓	0	0	✓
Youth Work Act	1	0	0	✓ (draft)	✓ (draft)	0	0	0
Professional Association	3	0	✓	✓ (emerging)	0	0	✓	✓
Degree/Diploma	6	✓	✓	✓	✓	✓	0	✓
Masters and PhD	1	0	✓	0	0	0	0	0⁵

Table ES.3 Commitments to professionalising youth work – the Caribbean

Country	Total countries	Barbados	Belize	Dominica	Guyana	Jamaica	St Lucia	St Vincent and Grenadines	Trinidad and Tobago
Policy Commitments to youth work as a profession	0	0	0	✓ (draft)	0	0	✓ (draft)	0	0
Youth Work Act	0	0	0	0	0	0	0	0	0
Professional Association	1	0	0	0	0	1	0	0	0
Degree/Diploma	7	✓	✓	✓	0	✓	✓	✓	✓
Masters and PhD	0	0	0	0	0	0	0	0	0

Table ES.4 Commitments to professionalising youth work – Europe and Canada

Country	Total countries	Canada	Cyprus	Malta	UK
Policy Commitments to youth work as a profession	1	0	0	✓	✓LG
Youth Work Act	1	0	0	✓	0
Professional Association	3	✓	0	✓	✓
Degree/Diploma	2	✓	0	✓	✓
Masters and PhD	3	✓	0	✓	✓

Table ES.5 Commitments to professionalising youth work – the Pacific[6]

Country	Total countries	Australia	New Zealand	Fiji	PNG	Samoa	Tonga	Vanuatu	Solomon Islands
Policy Commitments to youth work as a profession	1	✓LG	0	0	0	0	0	0	0
Youth Work Act	0	0	0	0	0	0	0	0	0
Professional Association	2	✓	✓	0	0	0	0	0	✓
Degree/Diploma	3	✓	✓	0	✓	0	0	0	✓
Masters and PhD	1	✓	✓	0	0	0	0	0	0

The study highlighted the varied nature of youth work and its existence in diverse contexts through State and non-State delivery. Findings indicated that it was not always State legislation or policy that drives dynamic youth work. Systematic, guided and supervised asset-based youth work was often supported by practice networks, youth workers' associations and education and training institutes. Moreover, commitments to youth work in policy did not always correlate with commensurate investment and implementation of policy.

However, in countries such as Malta, **youth work legislation and policies explicitly paved the way for greater investment in youth work, both for training and practice. The legislative backing for the profession in Malta is in fact broadly seen as the foundation of this cohesive education and training pathways for youth workers and youth work delivery mechanisms in the country.** So, by extension, where effective youth work exists, a State's policy commitments can clearly spread and amplify the quality and impact of this good work.

The above summary findings indicate the extent of the effort that is required in order to establish youth work as a recognised professional practice across the Commonwealth. These supporting policy environments are critical to building a skilled and competent youth work cadre without whom the empowerment of young people will not be a reality.

The primary data for the survey was gathered during 2016 and is a snapshot of a particular point in time. While updates have been made as far as is possible, this report does not claim to be an accurate reflection of all current youth work policy contexts in the Commonwealth. It does, however, offer useful indicative data for further engagement across member states. Additionally, data was often difficult to gather due to non-availability or difficulty of access. Therefore, in some cases, no substantive conclusions could (or should) be made. The paucity of information is a clear indication of the need for meaningful data gathering around youth work at all levels studied in this baseline.

The study has undergone broad-based review for validation through members of the Commonwealth Alliance of Youth Workers' Associations (CAYWA) and the Commonwealth Youth Council (CYC). CAYWA is an Association of Commonwealth associations of the youth work profession that represents a global identity for the advancement of the profession. CYC is a youth-led global platform representing young people within the Commonwealth in order to promote sustainable development, democracy and youth mainstreaming in decision-making processes. The findings and recommendations of this study will critically inform the position of CAYWA and young people as advocates and advisers to the Commonwealth on the professionalisation of the sector in order to provide accountable and quality youth work services.

The baseline is a work in progress and designed as such. It hopes for, invites, and needs addition, further contribution and development by practitioners, researchers, young people, and perhaps you, to become what it can be; and what it can be is, like every succeeding generation of young people, never finished.

Notes

1   For the purposes of this study, 'significant steps' were identified as policy commitments to youth work, existence of professional associations for youth work, and the availability of at least a diploma-level qualification for youth work.

2   The youth sector comprises all players who have youth empowerment/development as a major strategic area of intervention and can include ministries and departments, university departments, professional associations, networks and so on.

3   The University of Stellenbosch has a Theology course specialising in Youth Work. Monash SA has a youth development course.

4   Maldives was a part of the Commonwealth during the time of the study, however has since withdrawn from the Commonwealth.

5   Diploma to commence in 2017 as reported.

6   Certificate courses which are pathways to the Diploma are offered in Fiji, Papua New Guinea, Samoa, Solomon Islands, Tonga and Vanuatu (see Table 9.5).

Chapter 1

Background

1.1 Introduction

This chapter examines a broad Commonwealth definition of youth work and the contexts in which youth work is delivered. It also takes the reader through the role the Commonwealth has played in professionalising the sector. It concludes with the purpose and methodology of the baseline.

1.2 A Youth Work definition and contexts

Youth work is defined by the Commonwealth Secretariat[1] as

> 'All forms of rights-based youth engagement approaches that build personal awareness and support the social, political and economic empowerment of young people, delivered through non-formal learning within a matrix of care.'[2]

It is a relational profession built around the skills and competencies of engaging young people in building their self-esteem, social connectedness, economic and social productivity, emotional, intellectual and ethical maturity, and autonomy,[3] and supporting them in their self-empowerment within caring and supportive environments. Peer youth work involves young people themselves who have built systematic skills and competencies in engaging with their peers.

Youth work practice can be identified around the world in contexts of State provision, provision through voluntary agencies, and the non-governmental sector including faith-based groups. Youth work can be delivered through youth clubs, or in detached spaces where youth workers reach young people in their own natural surroundings.

Youth work is recognised as a distinct profession in some Commonwealth member states through policy and legislation that ensure the delivery of quality practice, including education and training for youth workers. In yet other member states, it is institutionalised through custom and practice, and has created equally rich traditions; in yet others, this recognition is still to become a reality.

Strong youth work can also be identified where there is no distinct policy supporting it. In these cases, policy measures could provide more systemic support to education and training for the profession, and for delivery of youth work services.

1.3 The Commonwealth's role in strengthening youth work practice

The Commonwealth Charter reinforces the core rights-based values of democracy, human rights and the rule of law. It has an explicit asset-based view of young people and recognises 'the positive and active role and contributions of young people in promoting development, peace, democracy and in protecting and promoting other Commonwealth values, such as tolerance and understanding, including respect for other cultures' (The Commonwealth Charter, 2013a).

The Commonwealth understands professional youth work as a key dimension in enabling, ensuring and empowering young people (Harare Commonwealth Declaration, 1992). It considers youth work as integral to participatory nation-building, particularly in the context of the dynamic role that youth workers can play in addressing young people's welfare and rights in a responsive manner. The Commonwealth sees youth workers as ideally placed to provide an interface between young people and decision-making processes at all levels.

The Commonwealth is working to consolidate its previous work in this arena through a rights-based concept of youth work that is responsive to the requirements of young people and their expectations from youth services, while, at the same time, reflecting Commonwealth values and human rights conventions to the fullest. This is the basis of work with member governments and other stakeholders to strengthen mechanisms and procedures to professionalise youth work.

The Commonwealth has been supporting member states to set up education and training for youth workers since the 1970s. The 2007 Commonwealth Youth Ministers Meeting committed to the Plan of Action for Youth Empowerment (PAYE)(Commonwealth Secretariat, 2017), renewing this commitment to youth development work. This was further endorsed at consecutive Commonwealth Youth Ministers Meetings (CYMMs) thereafter.

Action Point 12 of PAYE pledged that the Commonwealth will work with governments to ensure investment in the education and training of youth workers, partner with youth workers' associations to draft codes of professional ethics with express linkages to human rights, and consult youth workers as partners in the policy-making process (Ibid., p. 40).

The Commonwealth's pioneering contribution to professionalising youth work was the Commonwealth Diploma in Youth Development. The Diploma has been delivered in almost 30 Commonwealth member states and continues to be delivered in some. The Diploma received several levels of support from the Commonwealth Youth Programme across the years, including external regional moderation, tutor training, and subsidies for students and for delivery. Later, it was devolved to universities.

Presently, the Commonwealth is in the process of establishing an online, open-source Youth Work Education Qualifications Consortium. It is based primarily, but not exclusively, on a Youth Development Work Degree developed by the Commonwealth Secretariat in partnership with the University of the West Indies (UWI) based in Kingston, Jamaica. The course has been informed by the Commonwealth Caribbean Competency Standards for Youth Development Work developed by the former Caribbean Regional Centre supported by the Commonwealth Youth Programme. The material is to be offered to partners in the Consortium which constitute universities and youth work training agencies from across the Commonwealth and elsewhere.

The Commonwealth also supports governments with technical assistance relating to policy and legislation in professionalising youth work, in building short courses and outcomes frameworks to support 'just-in-time' and refresher training[4] to offset diploma and degree qualifications, and in establishing youth worker associations that are a prerequisite for safeguarding the integrity and quality of the profession, and by extension, safeguarding the quality of services to young people.

Additionally, the Commonwealth supports the global collectivisation of youth work professionals through the emerging Commonwealth Alliance of Youth Workers' Associations (CAYWA), an international association of regional/national/sub-national professional associations dedicated to advancing youth work across the Commonwealth (**Annexure 1**). CAYWA enables the cross-pollination of ideas and collegial support among youth work practitioners across the Commonwealth and beyond, and is developing into a unified global influence providing support to governments and all stakeholders in the youth work profession.

CAYWA's work is informed by the *Draft Code of Ethical Practice for Youth Workers* developed by the Commonwealth Secretariat. Other Commonwealth guidance such as *Professional Youth Work: A Concept and Strategies* and *Establishing a Professional*

Figure 1.1 The Commonwealth's youth work initiatives

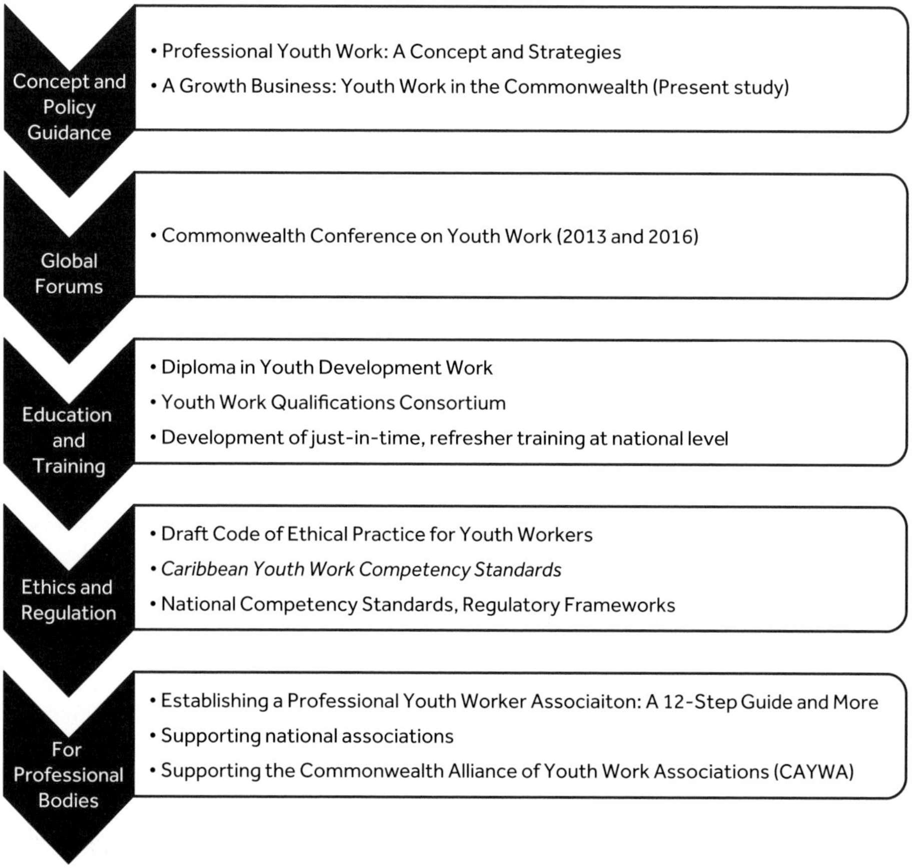

Concept and Policy Guidance
- Professional Youth Work: A Concept and Strategies
- A Growth Business: Youth Work in the Commonwealth (Present study)

Global Forums
- Commonwealth Conference on Youth Work (2013 and 2016)

Education and Training
- Diploma in Youth Development Work
- Youth Work Qualifications Consortium
- Development of just-in-time, refresher training at national level

Ethics and Regulation
- Draft Code of Ethical Practice for Youth Workers
- *Caribbean Youth Work Competency Standards*
- National Competency Standards, Regulatory Frameworks

For Professional Bodies
- Establishing a Professional Youth Worker Associaiton: A 12-Step Guide and More
- Supporting national associations
- Supporting the Commonwealth Alliance of Youth Work Associations (CAYWA)

Youth Worker Association: A 12-Step Guide and More, also continue to be globally instrumental in informing professional associations and stakeholder groups in designing youth work policy and practice.

The Commonwealth also hosted the Commonwealth Conference on Youth Work (2013 and 2016, both in Pretoria, South Africa) that enabled global dialogue, discussion and actioned resolutions around the professionalisation of youth work.

1.4 Purpose of the Survey

Youth Work in the Commonwealth: A Growth Profession establishes a baseline to inform planning and implementation of initiatives to professionalise youth work among Commonwealth member states. It is the product of dozens of practitioners, experts, academics, civil servants and government representatives from across the Commonwealth coming together to explore advances in youth work practice, education and training and legislation and policy. At one level, it provides a catalogue of the extent of recognition of youth work, and at another, an examination of the qualities and rights-based ethos of the various forms of youth work promoted and practised in member states.

The report presents a regional and global analysis. It includes an introduction, encompassing a brief historical overview of youth work as a Commonwealth-wide phenomenon and concepts around the key criteria for professionalism, followed by evidence of advances in professionalising the sector from across member states.

The report is intended to inform practitioners, managers and decision-makers of advancements and gaps in support of professional practice, providing a broad snapshot of youth work in the Commonwealth. As such, it will look to inform youth work practice globally, and help in improving standards and ethical awareness.

There has been no attempt to provide a 'last word' on the subject; neither has there been the ambition to generate an exhaustive encyclopaedia of Commonwealth youth work – that would be an unrealistic goal that would likely be out of date before it could come to press.

The baseline, instead, represents an instrument of orientation to gauge the character and position of youth work throughout the Commonwealth at a given point in time. On the social map of this family of nations, the survey presents a series of trig points for youth work that can help identify the best, most effective paths for future development and investment. It is a general guide to how these might be navigated in the most efficient ways to offer meaningful and impactful support to young people.

The baseline is a work in progress and designed as such. Youth work is a growth business, in a state of constant adaptation and evolution, just like young people. It constantly transforms in order to be responsive to what young people and societies want and need it to be within its frame of practice. In response to this environment, the survey looks to be organic, to have a kind of life. It hopes for, invites, and needs addition, amendment and development by practitioners, researchers and perhaps you, to become what it can be; and what it can be is, like each generation of young people, ever evolving, never finished.

The baseline survey helps identify national strengths and gaps in professionalising youth work, so informing the Commonwealth's decisions as it takes steps to enhance individual youth work sectors and global practice.

While the primary purpose of this baseline was to assess the current contexts in professionalising youth work in the Commonwealth, the means of analysis and dissemination have also acted as a way of creating greater understanding on the dimensions of professionalisation, challenges of such initiatives, and dialogue around improving practice.

In the long term, this data will serve as a starting point for assessing further action in member states to put in place mechanisms and processes to further strengthen the delivery of youth work, and improve outcomes for young people. It will be a critical tool for the Commonwealth Alliance of Youth Work Associations (CAYWA), an association of associations representing the profession, and young people, in advising member states on professionalising the sector.

1.5 Methodology and Data

This is a top-line survey punctuated by a solid conceptual discussion and qualitative data, including case studies.

The baseline is predominantly based on desk research, and relies on secondary data collected through a questionnaire designed at the Commonwealth Secretariat (See **Annexure 2**). The material was generated by staff of the Commonwealth Secretariat and by five regional consultants representing the five Commonwealth regions/ region groups of Africa, Asia, the Caribbean, Europe & Canada, and the Pacific. The consultants worked with 35 country consultants to gather top-line data on the status of youth work.

Secondary data was complemented by in-depth interviews with key stakeholders representing both governmental and non-governmental sectors (**Annexure 3**). In addition, members of the Commonwealth Alliance of Youth Workers' Associations (CAYWA) and other youth work stakeholders contributed case studies of their experiences in enabling the professionalisation of youth work in their countries. All participating Commonwealth member states were notified of the baseline and the involvement of the regional and country consultants in the process.

The Commonwealth may embark on further in-depth research into particularly notable data or good practice that the baseline demonstrates or suggests.

Key dimensions that were surveyed related to

1. The existence of a collectively formulated and owned definition of youth work as a profession,

2. The existence of policy and legislative commitments for youth work as a profession,

3. The professional organisation of youth work practitioners,

4. The existence of a code of ethics and competency standards for youth work and other regulatory frameworks,

5. The existence of qualifications pathways for youth work education and training,

6. The existence of youth-work specific professional validation of education and training,

7. The existence of youth-work specific supervision of practice, and

8. Investments in youth work.

The survey identified the established, or emerging, processes for professionalising the youth work sector (emerging processes are indicated in the tables, but are not represented in the graphs). Some attempts were also made to assess the quality and impact of selected youth work practices in relation to the Commonwealth's rights-based ethos of youth work.

1.5.1 Sampling

Purposive sampling methods were applied in the selection of 35 member states for the survey. Selection was based on relative advances in professionalising the youth work sector given the survey's dimensions.

Table 1.1 illustrates the countries in the sample.

1.5.2 Research team

The survey tool was designed in-house at the Youth Division of the Commonwealth Secretariat with inputs from young people and five regional consultants who consolidated country reports for each region. The report writing was led by an internationally recognised expert in the field of youth work, Dr Brian Belton, supported by members of staff at the Secretariat.

Country-level questionnaire administrators were recruited through a network of scholars, professionals, consultants, youth work practitioners, young people and

Table 1.1 Country sample for baseline

Region	Countries							
Africa	Ghana	Kenya	Malawi	Nigeria	South Africa	Tanzania	Uganda	Zambia
Asia	Bangladesh	India	Maldives	Malaysia	Pakistan	Singapore	Sri Lanka	
Caribbean	Barbados	Belize	Dominica	Guyana	Jamaica	Saint Lucia	St Vincent	Trinidad & Tobago
Europe	Canada	Cyprus	Malta	United Kingdom				
Pacific	Australia	Fiji	New Zealand	Papua New Guinea	Samoa	Solomon Islands	Tonga	Vanuatu

educationists. The majority of the country-level questionnaire administrators were identified by the regional consultants, while others were sourced through the Commonwealth network of consultants and partners. CAYWA members were a strong part of the research and review team.

1.5.3 Use of data

The Commonwealth anticipates that the baseline will support member states to identify the best means of moving forward to ensure that qualified/competent youth workers provide professional youth work support to young people. The report will also provide member states with a preliminary indication of the types of youth work being practised, while highlighting selected innovative and empowering approaches. The focus is primarily on State (or nation-wide)[5] sector activity. However, the document additionally provides good practice examples from non-governmental stakeholders who have been significantly influential in informing youth work cultures across the Commonwealth.

1.5.4 Key findings

Out of the 35 countries in the sample, 12 countries (34 per cent) had taken significant steps[6] to professionalise the youth work sector. Only 11 (31 per cent) countries had distinct national-level policies that recognised youth work. Twelve countries (34 per cent) had youth workers' associations that help safeguard the integrity and quality of the profession, and 25 (71 per cent) could claim at least a diploma-level qualification for youth work professionals.

1.5.5 Limitations of the study

The study, by its very nature, does not set out to represent every aspect of youth work in the Commonwealth. Some limitations are as follows:

1. **Scope:** The scope of the study, while covering 35 countries has been at the level of a top-line survey focusing on State/national practice with selective analysis of qualitative elements of youth work from State/national and non-State sources where examples were made evident. This is not an exhaustive study of all forms of youth work within the Commonwealth, nor does it explicitly study areas such as the impact of youth work on young people's lives, even though other such studies are referenced.

2. **Availability of data:** Data was not always as readily available as had been expected during the design of the baseline. The broad lack of professional status for youth work resulted in difficulties in drawing conclusions; for example, around numbers of practising youth workers, or comparisons of youth worker remuneration. Where data was not available or could not be found, no accurate or responsible inference could be made. There were also situations where data existed, but it could not be accessed by either the country-level questionnaire administrators or the regional consultants. Again, where and when this was the case, no substantive conclusions could (or should) be made. The paucity of data

is a clear indication of the need for meaningful information gathering around youth work at all levels studied in this baseline.

3. **Interpretations of youth work:** Youth work, even where a broad understanding of the profession existed, is interpreted in different ways by different stakeholders, and is based, as in other professions, on different ideologies and goals. The study has attempted to analyse practice against the yardstick of asset-based and rights-based forms of youth work advanced by the Commonwealth.

4. **Interpretations of baseline questions:** While all attempts have been made to harmonise interpretation of survey questions across this wide diversity of researchers, full harmonisation of interpretation has not always been possible and may result in some divergences in responses.

5. **Constant change:** The data in this study is indicative of the status across member states at a moment in time. The legislative/policy status of youth work and commitments to youth work are constantly changing as this report is being written. Therefore data in the report cannot be conclusive.

6. **Intersectionalities:** This refers to implications of intersectionalities such as the experiences **of youth workers** as women, ethnic, religious or sexual minorities, youth workers with disabilities and so on, as well as implications of youth work **delivery to** young people from diverse and minority backgrounds such as young women, young people living with disabilities and young people from religious, ethnic or sexual minorities. Encompassing these intersections is integral to the delivery of professional youth work. While some case studies point to directions in engaging with diversity and difference, this has not been addressed adequately in the baseline largely due to the survey nature of the study. This is an area for further inquiry.

Notes

1   This definition is a reworking of the original appearing in Commonwealth Secretariat 2013b, p. 11.
2   Care is a critical component, though not the only component of youth work due to the need to recognise young people's developmental needs and evolving capacities, and the need to realise their developmental and safeguarding rights.
3   Ability to influence their wellbeing and society's wellbeing.
4   These have included technical and financial support for the development of the Challenger Deep framework in India, support to Sri Lanka's Professional Youth Workers' Association (PYWA) for development of a short course for refresher training, and support for assessor training provided to the Jamaica Professional Youth Workers' Association (JPYWA).
5   There are nation-wide or sub-national youth work practice/regulatory structures/mechanisms that are not necessarily State-led, such as in Australia, or New Zealand.
6   For the purposes of this study, 'significant steps' were identified as policy commitments to youth work, the existence of professional associations for youth work, and the availability of at least a diploma-level qualification for youth work.

Chapter 2

Introduction to Youth Work

2.1 Introduction

This chapter discusses youth work in greater detail and examines the implications of delivering for young people within a rights-based framework. While serving all young people within a framework that sees them as assets, youth work also has a critical place in addressing the needs and rights of young people in difficult circumstances, in preventing extremist thought and action, in creating peaceful societies, and also responding to specific social needs of young people in contact with the law, or engaged in substance abuse.

2.2 The nature of youth work

The Commonwealth's definition of youth work introduced in Chapter 1 indicates the holistic approach of youth work in ensuring young people's development as individuals, as collectives, and as contributors to community, national and global development. This also refers to youth work's unique role in youth engagement, and the facilitation of experiential learning/education and social empowerment.

This is a rights/asset-based approach that avoids perceiving young people as being essentially in deficit. That is, rather than responding to young people as lacking capacity, this approach emphasises, celebrates and looks to maximise and build on the talents and potential of young people. This means that youth workers regard young people as a social asset and resource whose potential can only be fully realised when they are recognised as young citizens with rights and, as such, personal integrity. This also means that young people need to be perceived and engaged as those ready to participate and contribute to making and developing their societies.

Youth workers are situated in the governmental, non-governmental, private and voluntary sectors and work with young people in a range of situations including centre-based contexts (youth clubs, schools, hubs and associations) and in detached settings (sometimes understood as 'outreach', or 'street work') that can take place where young people freely congregate (street corners, parks, bus shelters and so on) of their own volition. Youth work can also take place in hospitals, prisons and other institutions with which young people have contact. Some might argue that many or even all of these constitute 'types' of youth work.

In addition, the international and national NGO sector deploys a workforce variously tasked to meet the needs and nurture the development of young people. These personnel are not always youth workers. However, broadly speaking, many undertake youth-work like roles, including working for the empowerment of young people and promoting their participation in communities and society.

Figure 2.1 Youth work as a global phenomenon

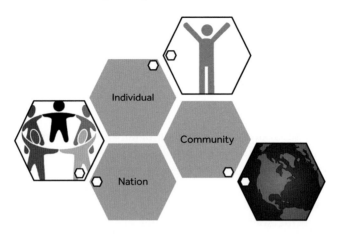

Youth work is premised on the **willing participation** of young people. While this can be contested from a number of standpoints, this is what sets youth workers apart from teachers, justice and prison workers and others who work with young people in contexts where young people are **obliged** to attend agencies, institutions or centres.[1]

In this study, references to youth work constitute the specific practice of engaging with young people through the fostering of empowering and enabling processes. This is reliant on young people's freedom from constraint in making decisions about their attendance, engagement and personal learning, wellbeing and development. This means they are less directed and more encouraged to find their own directions; instructions are displaced by questions while discussion of what is possible takes up the space that can potentially be dominated by attempts to impose didactic forms/ systems of education.

As exemplified in Figure 2.1, youth work's purposes are advanced by **engaging with young people, and focusing on their empowerment as part of enabling processes, within welcoming, tolerant and caring local, national and global environments in which the freedom of expression is maximised.**

The following key tenets of youth work are based on the Commonwealth's *Professional Youth Work: A Concept and Strategies* that sets out the ethos of youth work the Commonwealth advances and supports.

The concept note elaborates these as follows[2]:

a. **Professional care:** The delivery of youth work services in environments providing professional, detached care for young people. This is based on an associative, rather than personal, relationship with young people. Youth workers work **with** young people in order that they might **represent themselves better**.

b. **Building personal awareness and expectation:** Building young people's personal awareness of their strengths and helping them deal with personal challenges, while building their expectation of themselves. This requires that youth workers

Figure 2.2 Key tenets of youth work

are able to support young people to detect interest in/care about their wellbeing and that they might develop the motivation to have expectations of themselves.

c. **Social and political education:** Developing intellectual, personal and ethical means to interact, think critically, and develop in a social context. This can also be extended to mean the development of a collective consciousness among young people in order that they contribute to their advancement and the advancement of their communities, nations and the world. This requires both youth work practitioners, and young people they work with, to develop the ability to take and manage responsibility, as well as deal with the consequences of action.

d. **Making professional judgement:** The youth worker needs to be able to make sound, evidence-based and non-partial judgements based on practice experience around each and every context of their interaction with young people.

e. **A rights-based approach:** Human rights principles and the Commonwealth Charter frame all aspects of youth work advanced by the Commonwealth, including seeing young people as agents in determining the best youth work initiatives for them and foregrounding young people's rights at all times.

f. **Youth participation:** Ensuring that youth work promotes young people's agency and they are enabled to participate in every aspect of decisions around youth work provision, and monitoring and evaluation of youth work outcomes.

However, to simply corral almost any extra-curricular response or practice that encompasses elements of non-formal practice into youth work would overlook the foundation of the nature of professional practice. A solicitor is not a barrister,

Figure 2.3 The place of youth work in difficult/extreme contexts

Contexts of militarised and social conflict	Where there is a lack of access to reproductive and other health concerns	Where young people's political and social participation is curbed
In fragile societies	Where young people do not have access to education	Where young people are in conflict with the law, are misusing drugs etc.

although the former can perform some functions and aspects of the latter's profession, and both share appreciably similar ethical boundaries. Ophthalmologists differ from optometrists and opticians in their levels of training and in what they can diagnose and treat, but they are all interested in eyes. **Because I do a bit of what you do, does not make me you.**

2.3 Youth work for all, especially the marginalised

Youth work, while it serves all young people in the rights-based perception that all youth are real and potential assets,[3] also has its particular functions as a crucial empowering process in difficult or extreme contexts, such as in Figure 2.3.

Youth work taps into something that was evident in traditional societies; the benefits of sociality and association which is the seedbed of basic political consciousness; it informs recuperation (the re-capture of something lost) and recreation (and opportunity to re-create or re-establish the self); youth workers build environments that can facilitate personal and social development, learning, healing and respite.

In the postcolonial Commonwealth, different interpretations and adaptations of youth work have appeared in different contexts and countries. Culture, economics, religion and politics fashioned and transformed provision. Social work was more

Figure 2.4 Social development, learning, healing and respite

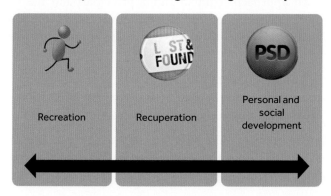

influential in some places than others, while churches', NGOs' and State ambitions for nation-building altered and sometimes necessarily overrode the more broadminded aspects of what might be described as the 'spirit of youth work'.

Notes

1 Qualified youth workers are employed in schools, prisons, hospitals, residential centres and other non-voluntary, statutory circumstances. However, for the most part, the parameters of the roles they assume in these situations are founded on the dominant institutional, organisational or professional frameworks (correction, formal educational functions or social work aims and duties for instance). These practitioners bring youth work skills to largely non-youth work situations in which such approaches might help achieve practical, legal and ethical aims and obligations. Because there are examples of youth workers being employed in non-youth work institutions and agencies does not mean these institutions and agencies are made youth work institutions or agencies, with predominantly youth work related outcomes.

   Youth work may also be understood more as a *fait accompli* than a choice to voluntary participate in situations where no other provision exists; young people use clubs and agencies for the want of any other facility. However, by and large, globally, youth work tradition and theory is underwritten by the recognition of the voluntary participation of young people. To start looking at youth work without this grounding, to claim that practice might encompass a range of adult/youth interaction that is based on obligatory participation, would mean also bringing other defining factors, such as the essential informality of practice, led by and for young people for their personal and collective empowerment, into question. To claim that youth work in young offenders' centres (for instance) might be essentially youth led, for their personal empowerment, is to totally misunderstand the nature of correction and punishment by way of incarceration.

2 These key tenets reflect, and elaborate/ expand on the key criteria for professional youth work set out in the Commonwealth document *Professional Youth Work: A Concept and Strategies.*

3 See for example the work of organisations such as Concerned for Working Children which addresses survival issues through empowerment – http://www.concernedforworkingchildren.org/about/

Chapter 3

Defining Professionalism

3.1 Introduction

It might be difficult to imagine from most perspectives how youth work, some of it undertaken by unpaid volunteers, might be considered professional. One would probably not, given the choice, visit an enthusiastic but unpaid, unqualified, part-time dentist, with no official regulation or recognition by other dentists, for root canal treatment, so why would one send or allow one's child to be looked after by an equally motivated, if relatively ignorant, educational and/or child care worker with only the claim of being a 'specialist'? How do you know that this person even had any background checks assuring that they are not a paedophile, drug dealer, someone connected to extremist organisations or child trafficking?

In fields like youth work, which is emerging as a distinct professional category in much of the Commonwealth, defining what professionalism is, is subject to a broad range of often critical debates. The perceived lack of conceptual clarity is also unhelpful. At the same time, outlining what a profession is, from a global, twenty-first century perspective, is not a straightforward task; there is no single, generally accepted definition of a 'profession'. The term has various meanings, ranging from the strict interpretation of traditional professions like medicine, law and accounting, to the very broad meaning of expertise and competency in any field – e.g. 'professional footballer', or 'professional plumber'.

Even in terms of established professions, for example teaching, defining what professionalism is, or means, is contested. Hargreaves and Goodson (1996) note the absence of consensus with regard to what professionalism means. Fox (1992, p. 2) has it that 'Professionalism means different things to different people' (as cited in Evans, 2008) and that it is doubtful if the notion or epithet 'professional' (or professionalism) has or will be used in only one definite way.

Professionalism according to Hoyle (2001) is connected to the improvement of the quality of service. Sockett (1996) and Evans (2008) argue that professionalism relates to quality of practice and a range of required skills and knowledge. In the literature relating to youth work, a good deal of attention has been devoted to its professionalisation, including the development of the practice of youth work. Because, as a field, youth work is not internationally recognised, its position as a profession or para-profession differs widely according to context (Eisikovitz and Beker, 2001).

The most common definitions approximate to that proposed by Langlands (2005): those occupations 'where a first degree, followed by a period of further study or professional training, is the normal entry route and where there is a professional body overseeing standards of entry to the profession'.

Figure 3.1 Professional practice

1. Acting in the client's interests: members offer professional judgement, objective advice or guidance and act in the best interests of the client.

2. Code of practice: members observe a code of practice or conduct that describes the desired standards of behaviour.

3. High entry standards: in the form of examinations that are not easy to pass and require an initial lengthy period of study.

4. Ongoing competence: maintaining a high degree of competence and expertise involving training and continual professional development.

5. Regulation by an independent body: effective regulation increasingly in the form of an independent body responsible for setting disciplinary procedures and monitoring behaviour.

6. Member accountability: members are subject to an objective form of censure and are accountable to the profession for a breach of expected technical and ethical standards.

7. Enforcement and discipline: the nature of censure is sufficiently punitive to encourage members to maintain standards in line with requirements. This typically includes being named and shamed and potentially barred from the profession and thereby being unable to practise.

The contemporary notion of what it is to be professional has many roots and sources but, given its relatively early industrialisation, the influence of the United Kingdom (UK) on the definition of what it is to be professional has been significant in the Commonwealth context.

For all this, while there is a range of UK legislation that impacts on youth and youth work, and there are regional variations (Scotland, Northern Ireland, Wales, Jersey, Guernsey and Gibraltar for instance); there is no specific, UK-wide Youth Work Act or similar legislation that specifically applies to the professionalisation of youth workers. As in other parts of the Commonwealth, there are polices that apply to young people and, as a consequence, some commitment to youth work. Indeed, Commonwealth member states in the global South have now begun according policy and legislative status to youth work, with concomitant criteria for professional practice, even though implementation is still to take off comprehensively through State or youth-sector-driven initiatives. Conversations between practice advances in some parts of the Commonwealth, and policy advances in others can offer comprehensive solutions to professional practice in many of the member states studied for this survey.

3.2 Professional practice

Deloitte undertook a comprehensive study of professionalism (Deloitte and Touche, 2007), which proposed that the following characteristics have traditionally been considered primary components of professionalism (see Figure 3.1).

Where youth work is relatively well established, the occupation might be said to have most, if not all, of the above components. However, these are not ultimate criteria and interpretations of criteria might differ in different contexts. For example, entry standards (Principle 3) may be determined by non-examination methods, i.e. oral and written assessments.

3.3 Professionalism in organisations

These basic principles of professionalism apply on an individual level. But increasingly, organisations too need to demonstrate professionalism. This might include:

Figure 3.2 Professionalism in organisations

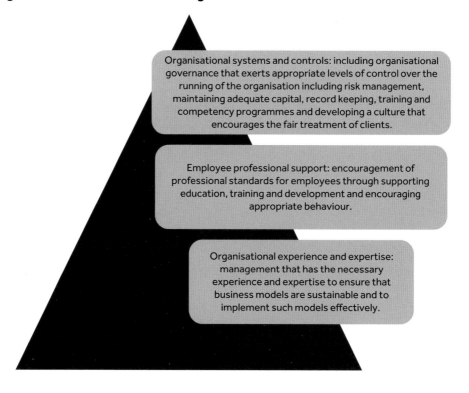

Organisational systems and controls: including organisational governance that exerts appropriate levels of control over the running of the organisation including risk management, maintaining adequate capital, record keeping, training and competency programmes and developing a culture that encourages the fair treatment of clients.

Employee professional support: encouragement of professional standards for employees through supporting education, training and development and encouraging appropriate behaviour.

Organisational experience and expertise: management that has the necessary experience and expertise to ensure that business models are sustainable and to implement such models effectively.

It is uncertain how many youth work organisations comply with the above, although many would strive to encompass these dimensions of organisational professionalism in their practice and operation.

There is no common **practised** foundation for professionalising youth work across Commonwealth member states in spite of the articulations of professional practice and professionalising processes encouraged by the Commonwealth's Plan of Action for Youth Empowerment (PAYE) and other policy guides and the foundational principles set out in the Commonwealth Diploma in Youth Development Work.

This said, practice roles/expectations of practice reflect the standards of what is traditionally thought to be professional conduct/behaviour. Efforts to organise occupational associations such as youth workers' associations are connected to this, although such associations need to be more than debating/friends societies, having the ability to assure the quality and integrity of the profession, and if necessary sanction and bar members of the workforce so ensuring the protection of the service receiver, the young person.

Professional recognition is a two-way street; an occupation needs to act in a professional way, while wider (State) recognition underwrites this. As such, a mutually reinforcing process is required to define any occupation as a profession.

3.4 The baseline's criteria for assessing professionalism and outcomes

The baseline primarily covers eight key criteria which are considered integral to the professionalisation of the youth work sector. **Box 3.1** below outlines these criteria:

The establishment of the eight criteria **is geared towards transforming youth work cultures in order to provide positive experiences and enable the self-empowerment**

Box 3.1 Criteria for professionalism

1. A collectively formulated and understood definition of youth work

This refers to a distinct national/sectoral definition of youth work that informs policies, strategies and programmes that shape the culture and practice of youth work.

2. Legislation and policy that recognises youth work as a profession

This refers to State legislation and policy that provides a clear appreciation of, and underwrites, the professional status of youth work as a discrete, free-standing and distinct profession in its own right. This is distinct from more general youth policies, although these might implicate such recognition. The survey also tries to examine who was involved in shaping legislation and policy as translation of these to practice will depend on relevance, responsiveness and ownership.

(continued)

(*continued*)

3. Existence of professional associations

This refers to the existence of active and representative associations of youth work practitioners. These are bodies that seek and/or have authority over the shape and development of the professional sphere in their context. They are gatekeepers to the profession, and wield influence over qualification and entry to the profession. They may also play a role in advising local and national government on youth work policy as the 'eyes and ears' of youth work on the ground. Fundamentally, they need to be democratically representative and made up of practitioners, or else they risk contradicting some of the central principles of youth work practice. As such they cannot logically be simply commercial or charitable research and/or support agencies.

4. Competency standards, ethical standards and other practice regulators

The dimension is concerned with how the proficiency of youth workers is established and maintained, both in terms of codes of conduct and how the standards of practice are developed and sustained. Ethical principles are understood not to be reliant on personal morality or academic judgement/opinion. Ethical regulation is laid down and reviewed by broad-based practitioner consultation and discussion. This is the outcome of the collective activity of youth workers within and across contexts, sharing and honing the delivery, efficiency and safety of their practice.

5. A Qualifications pathway for youth workers from short courses[1] to PhD

This element looks to identify professionally qualifying routes of entry into youth work. Because of the nature and widespread understanding of professional status in youth work, the basic standard of professional qualification might be taken as degree level and above. Short courses can, in the main, be understood as stepping stones to university entry or 'in-service' training for those already professionally qualified.

6. Professional validation of youth work education and training

This refers to the means, character and relevance of education and training. This requires the constant review of education and training for the relevance of this education to the needs of youth work practitioners in relation to the evolving needs of youth, and contexts that young people inhabit.

7. Supervision of youth work practice

A critical element of professionalisation is the means for professionals to be accountable and responsible practitioners. This logically involves the exploration and development of practice, and the ability to learn from such examination. At the same time, part of the obligation of a community of practice is support to fellow practitioners in a professional (organised and disciplined) manner. The process of supervision encompasses all of the above and is a widely recognised practice in many educational and care professions (most significantly globally in social work).

8. Investment and remuneration

This involves political will and financial and resource investment that underpins youth work as a professional response to the growth and empowerment of young people, in order that their contribution can be recognised and maximised at community, national and global levels.

Figure 3.3 Benefits of professional youth work to young people and society

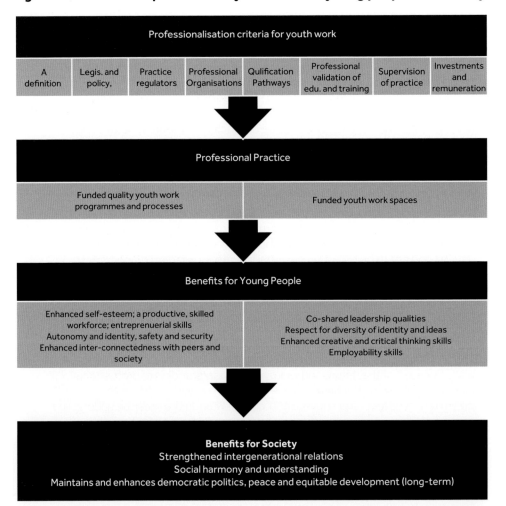

of young people, and the criteria should not be seen as ends in themselves. The measure of success of professional youth work lies in this end goal. Whatever it takes to create systematic, positive cultures is what it takes to create professional youth work in your context.

Figure 3.3 helps articulate upwards from these criteria to a. their bearing on practice, b. benefits for young people, and finally c. for society. While investing in youth work in this way becomes a means of realising young people's rights to adequate support for self-empowerment, it also becomes a means of creating a more cohesive, equal society, in this way contributing to national and global development. The linkages and attributions of youth work to personal empowerment and therefore social development, would, of course, be less visible and direct, than, say, the impact of an immunisation programme, where health outcomes would be clear and direct. However, this does not make the impact any smaller.

These benefits to young people and society are often present, but they may be indirect, and are often hidden. Where robust research is conducted, however, these outcomes are being clearly demonstrated. For example, a study in the United Kingdom which assessed youth work projects with gangs found an over 70 per cent success rate (of these projects, as opposed to social work processes, or justice processes) 'in terms of diverting young people from criminal activity and reintegrating them with effective education and employment. No other intervention has been as effective.'[1] This is a distinct example that demonstrates to policy-makers the benefits of investing in youth work. We need to further build the case through quality research.

3.5 Professionalism exemplified

Of all the baseline's work to attempt to capture data, stories and facts around what professionalism is, the story told in Box 3.2, contributed to us by a youth worker in the United Kingdom, exemplifies how she makes professional decisions in youth work about her ethical/moral practice in relation to legislation and codes of conduct. This case study is also an example of the increasingly challenging circumstances in which youth workers engage with young people. While we all concede that youth work serves all young people, here is an example where a youth worker's professional capacities were stretched in an extreme context. Her reflection on her own dilemmas as a practitioner here is an extraordinary exemplification of what professional practice/reflection is.

Box 3.2 Personal and professional conflict in youth work practice

Sue Wallwork, youth worker, Cambridgeshire, United Kingdom

Conflict I can do, it's in my blood, conflict is comfortably nestled in my very soul and is present in my working day frequently. I think about the conflict that's present in my work life, but you see, from an early age, I had come into conflict with teachers, authority figures and generally society's critical views on why I 'refused' to reach their pre-designed 'full potential' for myself. So, for me, conflict was a negative, it drained you and made you a potential enemy to people due to your ability to use a voice and use it well.

When I entered the working world I initially conformed, desperate to let the internal conflict of emotions rest for a while, to fit into a world previously out of my reach and be accepted was greatly desired.

Reflectively, I'm aware of that short time when the years of low level oppression became too much to bear and I retreated for a short time. I wouldn't be where I'm now if that hidey hole still existed though. I created changes quickly once I thought about what I wanted in life rather than how to survive it. 'The awakening of critical consciousness leads the way to the expression of social discontent

(continued)

(*continued*)

precisely because these discontents are real components of an oppressive situation' (Freire, 1970, p. 18).

I now see those clashes as professional discussions. Conflict in my professional practice is a normal event, I challenge schools, teachers, my own establishment daily and they challenge me. **Handled and approached professionally these are chances to expand your critical professional judgement and not conflicts.** I fear if you see these events as conflict you assume there needs to be a winner and that becomes a saviour complex.

So, conflict is brilliant; it's a chance to grow as a person and a professional, but there is a fine line we walk between of being professional when in fact we are working closely with clients who are unaccepting of authority's interference; thus creating a battle between being honest and being of any use is ever constant. Though the use of the word 'honest' is conflicting as we can only ever be an honest as our roles allow. That's when I start to think that maybe the conflict that troubles me, or has affected me in the past, **has not been as a professional but between my own values and those I hold as a professional.**

Values intermingle, they cross barriers and infuse into other values of acceptance or rejection. Then a young person who has raped three small children makes one think again. Things get a little confusing.

At the base of my own values is family, my children. Within that is my desire to ensure their safety by being protective with my actions. My base need is to give them the opportunity to thrive in their surroundings, to grow up without fear and to have no imaginary limitations of their abilities. In my work I want to ensure children are safe from harm. I do this by encouraging their parents to actively protect them while simultaneously building a child's ability to question their surroundings and strengthen their reliance to thrive 'despite' their hardships.

Realistically, my values are pretty positive; I seek to do no harm and that's as positive as you can get in the scheme of things. I like to think I am wise enough to know the difference between my values and other people's and I try very hard to never fall into a deficit model while working alongside others. **But like everything it's on a spectrum, a child who is injected with heroin or sold for a tenner needs intervention while a child who swears is not, in my opinion, yet my organisation would say they both are.**

Working with the young rapist I struggled with the thought that my professional **actions of accepting him as a young person might create an apparent acceptance of his behaviours.** No resolution was reachable because the situation was so conflicting, so, as a professional I focused on my intervention, but as a person I remained conflicted.

I completed all interactions and set out plans as I would have done with any young person; the reasoning was different though. I would normally meet young people weekly and seek to speak with parents, others, etc. to help widen my view on the situation. I would be interested in their voice and ensure they were the leader of their own changes. I am consciously aware of the possible influence I have over others because of my role, my strength and because of their current position. **I hold my personal values loosely while working, but they are still very much present. I do not expect others to share them, I monitor according to safeguarding legislation and I hold others' actions up against the law, but I do not hold them against my own ethics and values.** I seek the voice, encourage the words, and ensure I offer information to create opportunity to make informed choices.

In the case of this young person I did not seek his voice. This was partly due to the impending court case, partly due to the role I was given and mostly because his words were something I didn't want to hear. I was worried that I couldn't hide behind my professional attitude if he was to share with me any details of his behaviour or desires. Yet I attended every session and when I think back to the reason for this, **I remember I had promised myself that each child would get support no matter what. The fact he was a child still lay heavily within my reasoning to accept the case, because in my mind I was finding it hard to label him a sexual predator, but I also couldn't find in it my consciousness to label him as 'just' a child.** This was proving a large barrier as I believe I was trying to demonstrate acceptance towards a child while not accepting his actions and behaviours, and realistically I don't believe you can when it gets to a certain level.

Perhaps my hope was different in this situation so that altered my approach? Belton (2010, p. 27) noted that creating change, or wanting to, is a way of demonstrating a dislike for that person's values or their behaviours.

My work is not about being right or wrong; it's about never settling with one answer for ever; discuss, explore, and ask questions of yourself. Accept what you bring to the table is more than just your job role and question your ideas and inner values. Realistically I bring everything I am to my job, I just act out professional behaviours. However, when I assess dangers or accept blame I am vulnerable on many levels and not just a professional.

Note

1   Pitts, J. (2007) quoted in Doug Nicholls, *For Youth Workers and Youth Work* (Bristol: The Policy Press. 2012), p186.

Chapter 4

Paradigms of Practice

4.1 Introduction

This chapter is an overview of youth work practice in the very diverse contexts of the Commonwealth. It examines different manifestations of youth work as well as the ideologies and intent that result in different forms of practice, and different outcomes for youth. It also examines synergies between State and non-State youth work – a synergy that the Commonwealth has constantly been concerned with.

4.2 An overview of paradigms of practice

Almost all countries, sometimes even regions, have evolved, refined, adapted and changed received notions of what youth work is, should, or might, be. Often, different forms of youth work take place under the same labels, such as different interpretations of the 'psycho-social' discussed in relation to Canada and the work of the Indian organisation Pravah below.

Other responses are taken to be 'developmental', seeing **particular age groups as relatively 'underdeveloped'**. What appears to be an anthropological slant on occasion comes close to depicting young people as almost a separate species with distinctive (rather than, say, evolving) behaviour patterns and psychological propensities. One fairly prevalent set of techniques and approaches, informal education has fostered a whole body of literature that seems to incline practitioners to act covertly (informally) without the full awareness of those targeted for this 'education',[1] as demonstrated through some of the examples below.

How can this covert education be education? Isn't it indoctrination or propaganda? Such ambitions fly in the face of the ethos and practice of the 'rights of the child'. That aside, this view of youth work assumes the presence of **ignorance on one side (the child/young person)** and **enlightenment on the other (the adult practitioner)**. It is not too hard to discern that such activity appears to be premised on assumptions uncomfortably close to ideas and suppositions that informed colonialism.

Youth work does aspire to promote learning, **but the role of the young person is crucial in this process;** it is they who might teach practitioners about their situation, environment, their wants, needs, issues, problems, hopes and ambitions. Without this knowledge and understanding, the youth worker is ignorant of the position of the young people they are working alongside, with and for. This learning process is based on, and grows out of, conversation (dialogue) between the practitioner and the young person; it is a purposeful, dynamic and open interaction. Figure 4.1 illustrates this.

Figure 4.1 'The dialectic of youth work'

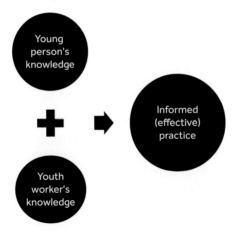

The following examples from across the Commonwealth attempt to look at explicit and implicit paradigms of youth work as articulated through State/national youth work practice.

4.3 A mixed heritage

Youth work, as the practice we might recognise today, has been strengthened by State legislation and action or duties given to local authorities both in the global south and north (most widely during the postcolonial period). At the same time, youth work has been and continues to be used by faith-based organisations and other interests, although not as an end in itself, but as a means to other ends.

State initiatives have blended with the work and the aims of NGOs, while social and community work responses have, more or less, merged with and generated ways of addressing what is usually seen as 'youth problems' and/or the transitional challenges that are perceived to be inherent in people at a stage between childhood and adulthood. Figure 4.2 illustrates these dynamics.

For all this, the social and legal boundaries between childhood and adulthood differ from context to context, in terms of individual perceptions, and sometimes from person to person.

4.4 Uganda: bottom-up initiatives for the recognition of youth work?

As in **Cyprus** and **Canada**, in **Uganda** there is no State recognition of youth work. However, there are possibilities of identifying youth work approaches in existing practice which can be used as a basis for advocating for the importance of recognising youth work as a profession. The structures for youth service delivery in Uganda, as in many other member states, indirectly acknowledge the importance of building youth work competencies in order to maximise the impact of existing youth empowerment structures. This is explored below.

Figure 4.2 State–NGO interactions in youth work

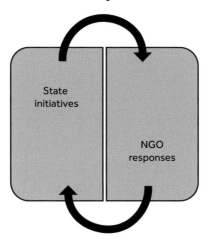

Uganda's National Youth Policy (NYP) (Uganda, Republic of, 2000) defines youth as 'all young persons; female and male aged 12 to 30 years'. It states that 'this is a period of great emotional, physical and psychological changes that require societal support for a safe passage from adolescent to full adulthood'.

The definition does not look at youth as a homogeneous group with clear-cut age brackets but rather as a process of change or a period of time when an individual's potential, vigour, adventurism, experimentation with increased risks and vulnerabilities show themselves in a socially meaningful pattern.

The definition considers the labels 'youth' and 'child' to be mutually inclusive at some stage of young people's lives. It reinforces the definition of a child and seeks to nurture, protect, and ensure their welfare. It seeks to prepare and empower young people to be able to take on socio-cultural, economic, civic, political and adult roles and autonomy. **It also reflects the reality on the ground that the family and extended kinship ties loosen due to different factors, and that many young people have assumed adult responsibilities by the age of 12.** It simply provides a basis for the development and preparation of young people for adult responsibility in the given context.

> Finally, this definition of youth takes into account programmatic issues and is in harmony with a number of operational and strategic definitions of major youth programmes in the country, including factoring in different definitions of youth, including age definitions as they apply to international bodies such as the United Nations and the Commonwealth.

The policy goes on to state:

> The Policy seeks to promote youth participation in democratic processes as well as in community and civic affairs and ensuring that youth programmes are youth-centred. (Uganda, Republic of, 2000, para 5.5)

and

> The Policy advocates for creation of a supportive socio-cultural, economic and political environment that will empower the youth to be partners in development (Ibid., para 5.6)

Here, it can be seen that while Uganda does not have any State recognition of youth work as a profession, **there is State recognition of many of the values and principles the Commonwealth includes in its definition of youth work**. Uganda, as in many other countries in the Commonwealth, does not overtly seek to address the above via State-recognised professional youth work but via 'youth Involvement, participation and leadership' (Ibid., para 8.3) as follows:

- Advocate for increased effective youth representation and participation in key positions of decision-making, leadership and management at all levels of Government and in the civil society,

- Advocate for review of and harmonisation of National Youth Council statute 1993, the Local Government Act 1997 and the Decentralisation Policy to support the Youth Council structures and other Youth Programmes,

- Strengthen and promote Youth Networks at all levels and ensure their integration with Internal Networks,

- Promote and support youth institutions for peace and conflict resolution,

- Advocate for the realisation of the rights of youth with disabilities and ensure their participation in all youth programmes.

Arguably this approach, *as it might theoretically be better implemented by professional youth workers, implicates a youth work/youth participation approach by way of existing or reformed structures and processes.*

The National Youth Council, as is the case in many other member states (**Annexure 4**), is a representative body of local youth councils. The National Youth Council Act states that:

- A village youth council shall consist of every person who has attained the age of eighteen years but is below the age of thirty years and is a resident of the village,

- A parish or ward youth council shall consist of all the members of the village youth committees in the parish or ward,

- A sub-county, division or town youth council shall consist of all the members of the parish youth committees in the sub-county, division or town,

- A county youth council shall consist of all the members of the sub-county, division or town youth committees in the county,

- A district youth council shall consist of the chairperson, vice chairperson, secretary, publicity secretary and finance secretary of each county youth committee in the district; and one male representative and one female representative of each sub-county youth council in the district elected by the sub-county youth council. (Ibid., para 10.4)

The National youth delegates' conference is held once a year and is the main policy-making body of the council. The national youth delegates' conference is made up of:

- the chairperson of every county youth council;

- the chairperson of every district youth council;

- the secretary for women youth at the district level; and

- eighteen students elected by the Uganda National Students Association.

This model of youth participation and action, reflected in several youth council structures throughout the Commonwealth (Annexure 4), **might be understood as far more inclusionary and collaborative than many situations where youth work is recognised in the absence of commitments to such structures.** In principle, it is doing what much youth work sets out to do: empower young people and involve them in decision-making about their own and a wider agenda.

According to how well the Ugandan approach to youth empowerment/participation works (which is similar to other approaches Commonwealth-wide) **a case would need to be made for why and how the development of policies and strategies for professionalising youth work build in existing good practice such as this, and, additionally, learnings that emerge from these experiences, for meaningful, bottom-up policy and legislation.**

4.5 Country X: youth empowerment and party political goals

Policy aims for youth in Country X (a non-Commonwealth member state) are not dissimilar to those of Uganda and others, placing empowerment, participation and the benefit of young people to the fore. However, the youth service in this country might be understood to be more controlled, restrictive and manipulative of youth than in more democratic contexts.

The National Youth Service here was ostensibly established for the transformation and empowerment of youth to support national development. The service claimed to provide young people of the country with a sense of national identity and patriotism. While it aimed to unite people above party lines, it also promoted wariness of foreign influence and intervention in national politics.

An opposing view of this service claims that it **indoctrinates its members towards loyalty to the ruling regime** and even trains them for military operations to enforce its dominance. The government of Country X also had plans to make the programme mandatory for all youths.

According to some reports, members of the youth service are taught exclusively from party political campaign material and speeches.

While the programme collapsed some time back, the government re-established it more recently, claiming it had been re-branded to focus on the development of skills as a way of economically empowering youth. However, conditions in the service training facilities are reported to include poor construction, frequent hunger and sexual abuse of girls and women. It is to be noted though that Country X also has other youth organisations that legitimately empower youth.

So, the aims of services that might at first reading look very much like youth work can have a range of purposes and impacts in practice quite contradictory to how the Commonwealth (for instance) might understand youth work.

4.6 Canada's work with youth: is it youth work?

Some writers have taken the Canadian Child and Youth Care model as being, for all intents and purposes, youth work. However, the scope of practice from the Council of Canadian Child and Youth Care Associations (n.d.) provides a helpful definition of the field:

> Child and youth care practitioners work with children, youth and families with **complex needs**. …. [they] specialize in the development and implementation of therapeutic programmes and planned environments and the utilization of daily life events to facilitate change. At the core of all effective child and youth care practice is a focus on the therapeutic relationship; the application of theory and research about human growth and development to promote the optimal physical, psycho-social, spiritual, cognitive, and emotional development of young people towards a healthy and productive adulthood; and a focus on strengths and assets rather than pathology.

As can be seen, the focus of this work is young people with 'complex needs' rather than the generic response that is fundamental to youth work practice. In 2012 the Office of the Children's Advocate Alberta explained:

> The most common assumption about 'complex needs' is that the term refers to a population of young people experiencing a multitude of issues that cross multiple service sectors (Child Welfare League of America, 2007). A helpful definition that captures this perspective is provided by the CanChild Centre for Childhood Disability Research in Ontario (2004, p.5):

> Children with complex needs [are] defined as children with multiple health/ developmental needs that require multiple services from multiple sectors, in multiple locations.

This definition acknowledges that needs may arise from a number of conditions that affect children's health or development, and asserts that there is value in utilising a 'non-categorical' definition that does not assign responsibility to any single discipline or service sector.

While it is true that some people qualified in child and youth care gain employment in 'youth work-like' posts, perhaps with NGOs or local authorities (as do qualified teachers and social workers) it is evident that this response **is essentially/significantly therapeutic in character and not in the main the generic, empowering approach that is central to youth work**, and specifically the Commonwealth definition of youth work. The latter is underpinned by the contention that youth work is for all young people, focusing on a rights-based approach. Indeed, as in other parts of the world, initiatives in schools and other formal establishment exhibit explicit youth-work like approaches, but they are sketchy and are not named as such.

4.7 Psycho-social 'models': Canadian child and youth care work and Pravah (India)

What is interpreted as psycho-social models of youth work here are discussed through two examples from **Canada** and **India.** The Canadian child and youth care model described above emphasises psycho-social work with young people within youth-in-context strengths/ assets/ resilience models, yet is focused on youth-at-risk rather than all young people. Meanwhile, in other contexts, as in the context of Pravah, an Indian youth work organisation, youth work is seen also as a psycho-social response, but understanding this as a means to recognise that young people exist in a psycho-social context and that the development of the human being **requires a clear understanding of the self in relation to the social** (and vice versa; 'from me to we and from we to me'). In short, this model works to connect the psychological and the social. This, in turn, is placed within a context of a critique of youth-for-development approaches that overlook psycho-social/wellbeing aspects that youth work addresses.

4.8 Youth work in youth development – New Zealand and Zambia

'Youth development' strategies and practice appear to be so close to youth work that they can be understood to be much the same in terms of practice ethos and direction. For example, the Ministry of Youth Development in New Zealand states that 'Youth development means growing and developing the skills and connections young people need to take part in society and reach their potential.' This is elaborated thus:

Youth development is about young people gaining a:

- Sense of contributing something of value to society
- Feeling of connectedness to others and to society
- Belief that they have choices about their future
- Feeling of being positive and comfortable with their own identity.

It's about building strong connections and active involvement in all areas of life including (New Zealand Ministry of Youth Development):

- Family and whanau (extended family)
- Schools, training institutions and workplaces
- Communities (sports, church, cultural groups)
- Peer groups.

This approach is also about young people being involved and having a say in decisions that affect them, their family, their community and their country and putting into practice and reviewing those decisions, which broadly equates to the definition provided by the Ministry of Youth and Sport in Zambia:

> A process which prepares young people to meet the challenges of adolescence and adulthood through a coordinated, progressive series of activities and experiences which help them to become socially, morally, emotionally, physically, and cognitively competent (Republic of Zambia, Ministry of Youth and Sport, 2015, p. 8)

4.9 Economics driving instrumentalist youth work: Bangladesh

Context (economic, social, cultural etc.) tends to drive what youth development/ youth work might be. For instance, in Bangladesh, the Department of Youth Development (DYD) aims to facilitate skills development training, employment and self-employment, and to involve youth in national development. The DYD implements youth policy, sitting within the 'guardianship' of the Ministry of Youth and Sports. The DYD works to encourage self-development and employment, promote involvement in community and national development activities, support youth organisations, involve youth in socio-economic activities and empower youth to become self-employed through micro-credit schemes.

As such, it is evident that while youth development in Bangladesh carries elements of what might be understood to be youth work principles, the emphasis is on economic exigencies via employment.

4.10 Critique of instrumentalist youth work: India

In the global South there is a critique of some youth-for-development models that predominantly respond to young people as instruments to implement wider national development programmes, sometimes at the expense of young people's social, political and ethical development as autonomous beings.

There is a South Asian critique relating to the way orthodox systems can appropriate youth work for their own ends, thus undermining the potential value and importance of youth work that supports young people's broader social, political and economic self-empowerment. Youth for Unity and Voluntary Action (YUVA), a youth work organisation from India, has exemplified this critique of instrumentalism in putting forward its own alternative, transformative definition. YUVA states that the organisation's youth work is:

> framed within a radical theory of impacting larger societal change. It is focused on enabling young people to develop critical thinking and question social and political structures. **YUVA believes youth work is a political act and frames all their work in the rights and social justice frameworks.** (YUVA Youth for Voluntary Action, n.d.)

The organisation The Concerned for Working Children in India, whose core work is in empowering children who work for a living, also takes on a similar position on youth engagement (The Concerned for Working Children, n.d.). These critiques often take youth work more in the direction of reflective thinking/social action that is yet another manifestation of youth work practice.

Similarly, Pravah, a youth work training organisation based in Delhi, and discussed above in relation to their psycho-social model, critiques instrumentalist youth work that perceives young people as instruments in realising national development with little focus on the self-empowerment of young people themselves.

4.11 Diverse contexts, diverse needs

There are consistencies and divergences in the practice of youth work between and across contexts. These multifaceted responses to young people are founded on the solid underpinning of society's care and concern for its young people, their growth and security.

While the above discussions have demonstrated how rich and sensitively-receptive approaches have been developed in youth work, it means that the understanding of, and the perceived need for, professionalisation varies.

The effort to provide cross-national and international views of practice has been tried more than once (certainly in the European context).[2] However even as researchers, theorists, academics, civil servants, voluntary agencies and so on toil at the task of framing a global view of practice, **the ever-shifting realm adapts and responds to social and financial demands, practical limitations, political ambitions and the conscience of the collective**. Much of this movement is unpredictable. At the same time, there are existing traditions to be accommodated that are often struggling, sometimes resisting, to integrate new approaches and reforms in practice. It is then perhaps not surprising that different definitions of youth work, often cumbersome and uncomfortable ones such as 'social pedagogy', are easily misunderstood and quickly become outdated.

Even attempts to obtain a national picture of youth work practice is frequently thwarted by the huge diversity of the practice *within* countries. The following is a perspective from a long-time member of a programme evaluation firm and a professional practitioner:

> Variations in programming and differences in structure are pervasive in all sorts of youth-related programming. Some things fall under Federal responsibility, some come under State or local-level oversight, and some are programmatic (and usually tailored to a specific local population). There are huge cultural differences to account for (regional differences; urban/rural; racial/religious), as well as wildly different access to resources and legislative support.
>
> As someone who works in programme evaluation, I can say from personal experience that assessing youth services in resource-poor, mostly rural areas, wherein racial bias can be built into the system, with a lack of legislative support and faith-influenced culture, is very different from assessing them in a another resource-poor rural area, lacking basic infrastructure, where mobile phones and internet aren't always possible, but which has a concentration of services in isolated

urban centers, sky-high opiate use rates and pockets of very high unemployment. These areas differ from districts with more ethnically diverse populations that also suffer from extreme geographic isolation, but with relatively well-funded behavioral health care. All of the latter contrast with very urban, more diverse populations, with access to services but a high crime rate, etc.

We run into trouble attempting to carry out Federal regulations or determining 'best practice' guidelines that can be reasonably applied to everyone. In a national context that encompasses Arctic to sup-tropical geographic circumstances, hundreds of languages and cultures, regional political divisions, which render resources unpredictable, sheer distance and infrastructure challenges, there are no easy answers.'

This context is perhaps evident within most regions of the Commonwealth but it might resonate more from a pan-Commonwealth perspective. Even within particular countries (for instance, India) this kind of diversity is part of the national profile.

With this in mind, this document has been built, as far as is possible, on pragmatic and concrete perspectives to ascertain the development of professionalisation of practice throughout the Commonwealth and, to some degree, also reflecting contexts within contexts.

The ethos of youth work practice may well take on different persona and be clothed to suit the environment it occupies, but that is how it sustains and advances; how it becomes more than what it has been. The culture of youth work will bend and shape to wider cultural influences; if it failed to do this, one might justifiably worry about its efficacy.

Youth work might perhaps be more of a state of mind and so a set of responses more than any particular set of rules and regulations, standards or guidelines. As a commissioner of mental health services noted:

> Based on my background in youth work, I devised an early intervention model that moved away from the medical model and the constant inappropriate referrals from professionals. Yes, there is a need for some young people to be seen by a qualified therapist and many might need more of a youth work approach (**more people less pills**). Talking to youth workers around the benefits of, say, outdoor activities, could technically be called adventure therapy. Someone to walk alongside them to help deal with life's problems and support young people in developing the skills to manage what life throws at them (at all of us).

> I also worked with one provider to create therapeutic communities around a cluster of schools so the school staff including teachers, learning mentors etc., were not only skilled up but could call upon a qualified therapist to get advice and so on, and only refer to specialists if necessary. It's a model that works well, but needs to be expanded on by colleagues buying into it, albeit slowly. This is where I see youth work being so valuable – I feel a bit like a missionary. I have left youth work but youth work has never left me and I can see where it fits across a whole spectrum of work – it could literally take over the world![3]

4.12 Youth work needs to be inclusive, but is not everything

The above discussions demonstrated the varied forms of work with young people that are defined as 'youth work' across the Commonwealth. That said, youth work can't be everything, because then it would be 'no one thing' (nothing). This presents the complex challenge of the pages that follow. Youth work often seems to be like light: you can see it, you can make it, but you can't bottle it. However, that does not stop us understanding light and its properties.

Notes

1   The literature on IE (informal education) consistently encourages this – it tends to task practitioners to work out how to covertly educate young people. So for instance we set up a table tennis club; we only advertise it as such, but the workers are using this to educate young people in any number of vague ways (for their 'betterment' or 'self-confidence'). There is hardly ever a learning needs assessment for such 'education'; the need is just assumed (deficit model) – this sort of thing is present in most of the literature, but has its root in Jeffs and Smith (2010).

2   See 'Working with young people: The value of youth work in the European Union http://ec.europa. eu/youth/library/study/youth-work-report_en.pdf and 'Mapping Global Youth Work' http://think-global.org.uk/wp-content/uploads/dea/documents/Global%20Youth%20Work%20mapping%20 FINAL%20report%20July%202010.pdf.

3   This demonstrates how youth work skills can complement non-youth work environments and aims.

Chapter 5

A Selective History of Youth Work

5.1 Introduction

The paradigms of practice discussed in the previous chapter have deep historical roots informed by pre- and postcolonial contexts, and synergies across State and non-State youth work. This chapter attempts to place this practice in relation to historical events, youth work domains, and their shaping of youth work.

Youth work and youth workers have responded, adapted and changed according to social demands and contexts over time; this has been the most poignant and effective skill set that youth workers have developed, regardless of academic and State interests to define youth workers as 'educators', 'change agents', 'advocates of young people' or any other individual or particular label that has been applied. However, youth workers are playing all and more of these roles. This is what makes youth workers a unique asset to any society and what keeps the practice relevant.

Different eras and contexts have demanded changes in the way youth work has been delivered and perceived. What we know about history indicates that this will continue to be the case. What youth work was or is likely to be will not be all it will become.

This said, there is an underlying consistency in the general understanding of what youth is, or can be. However, as the Commonwealth definition of youth work stresses, it is something more than nonspecific or generalised work with young people.

5.2 Histories

In the context of the Commonwealth, cultural responses to youth work arose alongside postcolonial, usually State-supported practice. Before this, youth work, like most educational and institutional responses and frameworks in colonised environments, was shaped by colonial influences. The professionalisation of youth work across the Commonwealth largely took place with the independence of nation-states and informed by emerging State structures.

However, this process was never 'instant' or based on any particular model. This can be gathered from looking at how youth work developed in Commonwealth contexts after independence. A few examples are provided here to demonstrate this.

5.2.1 Uganda

Up to the 1960s Uganda lacked an explicit, coherent and comprehensive national youth policy. However, national planning for youth development started at that time, with the Ugandan Government establishing a section of Youth within the Ministry of Culture and Community Development. The Government also established three

Youth Organisations: the National Union of Youth Organisation (NUYO), which was supplanted by the Uganda Youth Development Organisation (UYDO) in the 1970s, National Union of Students of Uganda (NUSU) and Youth Farmers Union (YFU).

NUYO targeted out-of-school young people between the ages of 13 and 30, while the Young Farmers Union (YFU) focused on young people in and out of school in the age group of 10–25 years; the National Union of Students of Uganda (NUSU) looked to serve youth in secondary and tertiary institutions.

These programmes were dependent on substantive investment by the Government and NGOs which looked to address the wide range of social and economic needs of young people. They had a rural focus and worked to provide opportunities for the most disadvantaged out-of-school youth.

Like most sectors, youth services/programmes were hard hit during the period of economic chaos and civil conflict in Uganda during the 1980s. Many young people dropped out of school. For some, education lost meaning. An appreciable number of young people joined the armed struggles and came to be commonly known as 'kadogos' (child soldiers).

There was an increase in rural-urban migration by the young. New diseases like the human immune-deficiency virus (HIV)/acquired immune deficiency syndrome (AIDS) appeared, and those most affected were those between 12 and 30. A great number of households came to be headed by young people as adults were overcome by AIDS, or were lost in the armed struggles.

By the 1990s, the Ugandan Government policy transferred responsibility for youth services to local authorities. This meant that new approaches to youth development were needed. At this point the Government initiated a clear and co-ordinated National Youth Policy to address the developmental needs of young people in an all-inclusive way.

In November 1997 a Youth Policy Committee was organised and tasked to present a framework to guide the process of policy formulation between 1997 and 2000.

5.2.2 South Africa

In South Africa, there is no record of professional youth work before 1969. Prior to that youth work was mainly a church-based pursuit. Sponsored training began in the 1970s. It was also at this point that a national training programme for youth leaders within the Methodist Church was initiated.

By and large, churches were on the side of the anti-apartheid struggle and many community-based organisations developed an increased political and black consciousness. The work of Paulo Freire was popular. Young people were to the fore in the anti-apartheid movement. Many were killed during the struggles for freedom and equality. A lot of youth work was funded by international organisations, while the State mainly funded uniformed organisations.

In the late 1980s, the Youth Practitioners Advocacy Group was established to lobby to forward the professionalisation of youth work. In 1996 120 youth workers attended a conference and produced the 'Hunters Rest Declaration'. This set out a framework for professionalisation that included:

- clear career paths

- a philosophical and education structure for youth work

- desired outcomes

- a code of ethics.

This work ultimately led to the idea of forming a professional association for youth workers and to draft policy documents relating to the development of community-based youth work in the rural areas.

This statement was passed to the Minister of Welfare. Although some of the proposals were not funded, the profession was granted official recognition for the first time.

In 1996, a Youth Commission was established to write South Africa's first youth policy. The consultative process that underwrote this policy was seen as genuine and fully owned.

The Youth Practitioners Advocacy Group became the South African Youth Workers Association (SAYWA) in 1998. It had its own constitution, code of ethics, and standards.[1] It was launched as the first collective voice of professional youth workers (See also Chapter 8).

5.2.3 India

Practices recognisable as youth work have long precedence in India. In the more recent past, in the background of student unrest in the 1960s (replicated in many other parts of the world), the Government looked to develop a programme for an integrated youth service. In 1966, a Planning Commission set up a Working Group tasked with the development of a wide-ranging National Plan for Youth. The Ministry of Education was renamed the Ministry of Education and Youth Services and, in 1969, it called a conference involving youth workers, youth organisations and youth service agencies. The National Youth Board arose out of this process.

Since then, significant progress has been made in the provision of State youth services. The Nehru Yuva Kendra Sangathan (NYKS) is now the largest network of youth clubs in the world, with 200,073 youth clubs across the country served by 623 district youth co-ordinators and 12,000 national youth corps volunteers managed by 29 State-level zonal directors. In a different but related process of encouraging voluntarism among youth, the National Service Scheme (NSS) works with four million young volunteers through chapters in 350 universities, 16,056 colleges, 42 higher education directorates and 1204 higher secondary schools. The Rajiv Gandhi National Institute of Youth Developed (RGNIYD) serves as an education and training agency for youth workers and those in related fields.

Box 5.1 illustrates how the RGNIYD has become a State-sponsored leader in youth work education and training:

Box 5.1 The Rajiv Gandhi National Institute of Youth Development (RGNIYD)'s Mission for Youth Work – India

Dr P Sivakumar
Assistant Professor, RGNIYD

The Rajiv Gandhi National Institute of Youth Development (RGNIYD), Sriperumbudur, Tamil Nadu, is an Institute of National Importance created through Act of Parliament No. 35/2012 under the Ministry of Youth Affairs & Sports, Government of India. The RGNIYD was set up in 1993 under the Societies Registration Act, XXVII of 1975.

The RGNIYD functions as a vital resource centre with its multi-faceted functions of offering academic programmes at postgraduate level encompassing various dimensions of youth development, engaging in research on youth development and co-ordinating training programmes for State agencies and the officials of youth organisation, besides the extension and outreach initiatives across the country.

RGNIYD plays a significant role in supporting the professionalisation of youth work. The Institute has reached all parts of the country to train thousands of youth workers since its establishment. It has adopted and promoted varied models of youth work to create a productive youth work workforce in the country through training/capacity-building programmes, seminars, conferences, extension activities and academic programmes. In order to execute the mandate of RGNIYD and priority areas (education, employment, entrepreneurship, health and healthy lifestyle, sports, social values, youth engagement, politics and governance, social inclusion, etc.) of the National Youth Policy (NYP 2014), it reaches the unreached youth workers in the country with the ultimate objective of realising young people's full potential as contributors to themselves and the nation.

The Government of India has been emphasising India's identity as the 'skill capital of the world'. Youth is the potential of our country, and promoting youth entrepreneurship, etc., is further motivating young people to work for nation building. At this juncture, the role of RGNIYD has become vital in adopting and introducing various programmes in youth work.

Since its inception, RGNIYD has focused on building the capacity of youth functionaries through the National Service Scheme (NSS) and the Nehru Yuva Kendra Sanghatan (NYKS). The thrust areas of capacity-building programmes are building the skills and competencies centred on the principles of youth work.

RGNIYD is very clear in its journey towards creating youth work professionals who can be equipped with scientific knowledge and systematic procedures in engaging with young people and dealing with the problems and issues of youth

(continued)

(*continued*)

in the world in general and India in particular. From the 2016-17 academic years, RGNIYD started offering two programmes exclusively focusing on youth. One is an MA in Social Work with Youth and Community Development specialisation and other is a postgraduate Diploma in Youth Development (PGDYD).

The PGDYD (30 credits) is on offer at five different locations in India. This programme was designed to professionalise youth work, create professionals in youth work and thereby address the problems and issues of youth of this country. It capacitates thousands of learners across the country, which can train and capacitate hundreds of thousands of young people in the country and direct them in a path at right time.

5.2.4 Jamaica

The Garvey Movement of the late 1920s saw Jamaicans working for the development of their communities and their empowerment. This helped to lay the foundation for the nationalist movements of the 1930s. A major feature of the latter was the establishment of the Jamaica Welfare Movement. Under Jamaica Welfare, service groups including community organisations, co-operatives and credit unions took shape.

One major programme under Jamaica Welfare was the Jamaica Youth Clubs Council. The Council was established in 1955 to work with youth groups across the country. It had representatives from the YMCA, YWCA, churches, local government, the civil service, the business sector as well as some co-opted members. In 1973, the restructuring of the Social Development Commission (SDC) resulted in the establishment of a Youth and Community Services Division that was given the responsibilities for all matters related to youth and community organisations. While the SDC and the youth portfolio were shifted from one ministry of government to another, the SDC maintained responsibility for community youth organisations until 2000, when this responsibility was reassigned to the National Centre for Youth Development (NCYD). In 1998, the SDC estimated that there were over 1,600 youth clubs with an average of just under 40 members each. A major feature of the 1980s and 1990s was the increased number of school-based youth organisations and the growing number of youth arms of service clubs.

5.3 The growth of formal state processes and mechanisms

The growth of secular youth work saw ideas related to social justice and themes centred on the empowerment of young people flourish. Following this development, a range of formal training courses, ministries, NGO networks and government advisory bodies began to emerge.

As demonstrated above, in some contexts youth insurgencies and unrest resulted in efforts to engage with young people, not necessarily in youth-centric ways, but as a form of appeasement, for example in Sri Lanka in the 1970s and 1980s (DeVotta, 2004, p. 167). Party politically motivated youth engagement developed throughout the last part of the twentieth century, perhaps most overtly in parts of Asia and Africa, but in more covert/subtle ways in Europe and elsewhere. This kind of motivation, however, cannot be said to be youth work as it looked to empower others, promoting sectional interests, more than seeking to work with young people in order that they empower themselves.

For all this, historically, young people have been the focus of adult philanthropy; attempts to educate, manipulate, indoctrinate, subordinate, control, discipline, reform and liberate. At the same time, young people have been the target of adult concerns about their protection, care and welfare as defined by adults.

Work with young people designed merely to serve the aims of the nation-state, commercial and industrial interests, organised religion, political and military ambitions and secular concerns about everything from the environment to social health cannot be rationalised as youth work, particularly according to the Commonwealth definition. Often, it is downright interference into the personal, group and family life of young people. **Youth work remains, despite every effort to manipulate practice to questionable 'educational' ends or 'betterment', a secular approach that looks to promote human wellbeing by way of forms of association.**

Note

1   At this time, Dr David Maunders from RMIT University in Australia was funded by Australia Aid in partnership with Johannesburg Technicon to establish a course work Masters in Youth Development Work for members of SAYWA.

Chapter 6

Trends in National Youth Work Practice

6.1 Introduction

This chapter outlines baseline findings on trends and approaches in State-led or nationally co-ordinated youth work practices. While the focus will be on State-led youth work, it will also cover other non-State national or major regional policy and programme structures, such as in Australia and New Zealand. These structures are, however, often supported by the State (as in Australia and New Zealand), and they also influence State practice (as in, for example, India). Later chapters will examine the relationship (or lack thereof) between practice, and legislation, policy and regulation.

6.2 State/national responses to youth work

The following tables present some State responses to youth work including through partnerships with non-governmental players, where evidence was shared by countries.

Criteria for identifying a State as engaging in formalised youth work practice (irrespective of the existence of legislation and policy around youth work) were as follows:

- The existence of State-endorsed or nationally endorsed definitions of youth work and/or,

- The existence of systematic youth-work related strategies and programming including through youth clubs, youth parliaments and other youth spaces (with a particular scrutiny of its asset-based nature where possible).

Youth work practice, as discussed above, is diverse, and much that may be considered as youth work might not fit in with the Commonwealth ethos of asset-based youth engagement. However, much work that may not superficially 'look' like youth work, such as social entrepreneurship or employability schemes, may, in fact, have many relational, dialogic aspects built in.

Much of what was observed as youth work practice across the Commonwealth can be described as having features as indicated in Figure 6.1. The arrows in the figure indicate that these are not mutually exclusive approaches and that many of these forms of engagement overlap.

While the Commonwealth recognises all forms of engagement with young people that are empowering as valuable, we promote youth work practices that are relational and dialogic and embraces all tenets of youth work as outlined in Figure 2.2. These approaches can also be developed in more 'instrumentalist' forms of youth work described as directional and traditionally educative, or in more 'activist' forms of

Figure 6.1 Types of 'youth work' practised

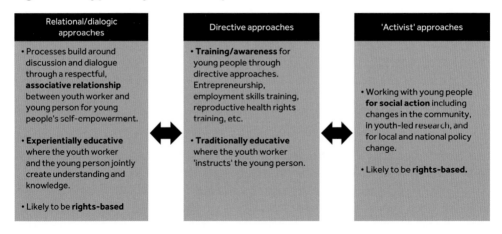

youth work that have a social action focus. While it was difficult to assess nuances of existing practice in a survey-type inquiry, what was reported to us by country consultants as youth work in the specific country contexts is discussed below.

For the most part, however, observations across the regions indicate that the agenda of the State in putting in place what could be potential youth work delivery spaces, such as youth clubs, is not necessarily to foster youth-work like engagement with young people. However, wording such as 'youth empowerment' appears in much of the material defining State practice.

This chapter also makes specific mention of a one-year pilot practice model trialled in India by the Commonwealth Youth Programme in partnership with the Nehru Yuva Kendra Sangathan (NYKS) Punjab/Haryana and the NGO Pravah which attempted to articulate a model of rights-based youth work practice.

A setback to developing and delivering youth work through sustained and resourced structures has been the fact that youth work is often one of the first casualties of rationalising public services. The need for youth work is seen to be less 'urgent' than other core services, and many State structures deliver based on the bare minimum of funding and expertise.

These observations highlight the need for

1. Greater executive-level capacity building on the design and delivery of youth work strategies through State mechanisms, whether policy commitments exist or not,

2. Better conversations between trained field officers and executive staff on the design and delivery of youth work strategies and programmes,

3. Greater State and non-State linkages in building youth work capacities.

6.3 Trends in regional responses

6.3.1 Africa

In Africa, in general, there is little or no prevailing definition of youth work that underpins practice, in spite of some level of policy commitment (see Chapter 7).

In **Ghana**, the Youth Empowerment Agency (YEA) has national, district and regional co-ordinators responsible for the day-to-day running and operations of the agency. The YEA appears to be relatively instrumentally educational in its operation.

In **Kenya**, there are neither youth clubs nor designated 'safe spaces' for youth activities in State-supported programmes. There is no well-defined methodology or standards. Box 6.1, however, indicates a selected non-State example of youth workers amplifying youth work approaches through voluntarism from Kenya and Tanzania:

Box 6.1 Youth work volunteerism in Africa: The case of volunteer business mentors for street youth in Kenya and Tanzania

by Alphonce C. L. Omolo (PhD)
Director Lensthru Consultants Kisumu, Kenya

In Africa, similar to other countries of the world, youth work has an expanded tradition of volunteerism. Volunteerism has remained a strong feature of youth work within the local authorities and the not-for-profit sector. In large sections of traditional African society, the initial volunteer youth educators were grandparents who gave instructions on social and life skills to the youth (who usually spent a night in their grandparents' huts) in the evenings before they slept.

However, with the weakening of traditional family ties, not-for-profit agencies and local authorities have become more dynamic in facilitating youth participation, social and life skills developments, measures to empower youth and role-modelling (Ministry of Youth Affairs, 2006). The spaces where such youth work volunteerism have been practised in Africa are largely in youth sports for development, youth faith-based actions, youth cultural and entrepreneurial movements, local authority youth informal education centres and street youth rehabilitation and reintegration, amongst others. In Africa, the age ranges of youth involved in such youth work practices can be estimated at between 15 and about 25 years for both female and male youth.

This story is a recollection of practice experience during the implementation of measures to empower street youth (Kisumu in Kenya, Moshi and Arusha in Tanzania) to reconstruct their lives and gradually opt for life out of the streets. Street youth can be described as young people who have opted to live and work in the streets rather than their homes (Ennew, 2000 and Panter-Brick, 2004). In both countries, street youth were empowered (by two not-for-profit agencies – Pandipieri and Mkombozi Centres) with skills on small business management,

(continued)

(*continued*)

savings schemes, business licence, business mentorship, grants for small business start-ups and residential options off the streets.

The emphasis is business mentorship which was offered to the youth by community volunteers operating diverse types of businesses in urban centres. Upon deciding on viable businesses and business locations in the streets, and with the support of street educators from the agencies, the young people then identified business mentors who were individuals operating (sometimes similar) businesses within the selected locations. Youth participation and ownership of decisions was a key component of the enterprise whereas the volunteer youth mentors were recruited based on their ability and willingness to provide constant support and follow-up to the youth, including frequent feedback and progress reports to the not-for-profit agency.

While the street educators are trained in social work, teaching, child protection and child counselling and entrepreneurship, amongst other skills, the capacity of the volunteer street business mentors was built through tailor-made training workshops and backstop meetings arranged by the agencies from time to time. This included meetings of all the business mentors to share their experiences, in addition to meeting with all the youth involved in the project so as to address emerging common problems. An example of an outcome from this practice is a street youth who started an arts studio in Moshi in Tanzania where other young artists can bring their art work for display and sale. Another street youth in Kisumu in Kenya established a construction firm where he employs dozens of youth in his various construction projects. Some of the volunteer mentors expanded their business strategies due to the knowledge and skills gained while mentoring the street youth. Thus, the business volunteer mentors gained new tools to respond constructively to different life situations. Furthermore, close collaboration with local authorities in both countries helped in identifying business locations and providing business licences. However, the dynamic nature of such local authorities, their constantly changing functions, leadership and management made it difficult to draw up long-term policies to protect the street youth from any form of disruption by the field personnel of the same local authorities.

A larger part of funding (grants and limited finance from the local authorities) for youth work projects are from erratic sources. Thus, human and financial resources are a key hindrance to the prosperity of unique and high impact models of youth work that involves volunteers from the grassroots (Jenkinson, 2000). This has made it difficult for such projects to achieve a secure sense of sustainability while powering tangible outcomes for the street youth and the business volunteer mentors. Amidst these challenges and lessons learnt, **volunteerism remains a key feature of youth work in Africa that requires distinct recognition when structuring, implementing and reviewing youth work practices.**

Table 6.1 State/national youth work practice – Africa

Country	Asset-based approaches to youth work in State/national settings	Partnerships
Ghana Kenya Malawi Nigeria South Africa Tanzania Uganda Zambia	While national-level government mechanisms exist in some cases for working with young people, evidence of systematic and well-articulated asset-based youth work practices offset by clear guidelines for youth work practice within these national structures was more difficult to identify. Partnerships specifically to strengthen youth work practice as a distinct profession were also not clear, except in the case of Zambia where the professional association reported playing a role.	

In **Uganda**, while youth officers existed at District level in previous administrative structures, the work of this position has now been undertaken by community development officers (CDOs). While it was beyond the purview of the baseline to assess the impact on work with young people themselves, there is still a need for clear definitions, guidelines and practice standards for youth work in Uganda, towards which Uganda is committed to move forward.

State youth work in **Zambia** is centred on Youth Skills Centres. The Government of Zambia engages with ten provincial youth officers in each province working across 19 youth centres across provinces. These youth centres cater for 60 per cent of youths out of the 15.5 million population of Zambia. There are on average two youth centres in each of the six provinces, except one which has four centres, with the rest having only one centre each.

As a means of improving youth service delivery, the government recognises the potential of diversifying partnerships in order to broaden its interventions and to reduce the financial burden on the government budget.

The Zambia Youth Workers' Association (ZYWA) (see Chapter 8) engages with officers in youth work in order to ensure professional practice and to expand on current prevailing practices in the skills centres around skills training – carpentry, mechanical engineering, tailoring, computer skills etc. While these skills are meant to empower youths, very few access any support to start their own ventures.

6.3.2 Asia

In Asia, definitions of youth work are sometimes explicit, and sometimes implicit.

In **Bangladesh**, for example, there is no specific definition of youth work. What is understood as youth work can be gleaned from what is expected in terms of changes for young people in the Youth Organisations (Registration and Operation) Act 2015, which refers to young people's 'physical, mental, moral and cultural development'.[1]

The greatest evidence of attempts at systematic approaches to institutionalise empowering State sector approaches to youth work are from India, Malaysia, Singapore and Sri Lanka.

In **India**, evidence of developing practice is linked to indirect youth policy commitments to the education and training of youth development officers and to the establishment of the Rajiv Gandhi National Institute of Youth Development (RGNIYD). State attempts at mainstreaming youth work are evident in Nehru Yuva Kendra Sangathan (NYKS), known to be the largest network of youth clubs in the world, and the National Service Scheme (NSS), a college-based scheme in India which connects young college/university youth workers to social development. Training specifically directed at youth service officers based on youth work principles was also available. However, the need for more systematic approaches to embedding asset-based youth work practice in State structures was highlighted by stakeholders.

Cases of well-articulated non-State practice significantly influencing national paradigms in India were those such as Pravah's '5th Space' concept, which has a reach across India through 25 members of ComMutiny, the Youth Collective. The 5th Space was also applied in a one-year long trial in India of a youth work practice model by the Commonwealth Youth Programme in collaboration with the Pravah and the Dhanas Youth and Sports Club managed by the Punjab/Haryana office of the Nehru Yuva Kendra Sangathan (NYKS), reportedly the largest network of youth clubs in the world.

Box 6.2 articulates the basic principles of this practice model as highlighted in the publication that was produced by the Commonwealth to document the model, titled *Co-Creating Youth Spaces: A Practice-Based Guide for Youth Facilitators.*[2]

Box 6.2 The Fifth Space – A Youth Work Paradigm from India[3]

By Arjun Shekar, Pravah
ComMutiny – the Youth Collective, Member of the Commonwealth
Alliance of Youth Workers' Associations

In a world where meaning-making has become increasingly difficult, where adults do not know all the rules of the new game, where prediction and control of the future is becoming difficult, there is a need to empower the young to navigate through this. But we cannot empower anyone, they have to empower themselves. All we can do is to create a context and a space that facilitates such an empowering process. Unfortunately, the world is owned and run by adults. For most spaces occupied by young people, the rules have been created by adults and they are expected to follow these without questioning them.

We believe that as a society, traditionally we have 'legitimised' four spaces for young people – those of family, friends, livelihoods/ education and leisure/life-style (which includes sports, religion and recreation). Then, on the margins, there is a 5th space where young people relate to society. In development discourse, this is increasingly being referred to as the space of active citizenship. **However, active citizenship has started to be associated almost solely with social action and volunteering.**

(continued)

We argue that the 5th Space must be repositioned as a space that focuses as much on the self-transformation of youth as it does on transforming society through them. It must be a space that builds on the aspects of understanding the self, developing meaningful relationships and impacting society – all of which are critical to youth development. While impacting society, they impact themselves, and if facilitated properly, these experiences lead to heightened self-awareness, enhanced leadership skills and informed stances on social issues.

Our experience has shown that a thriving 5th Space is a critical element for the all-round development of youth. The skills learnt here are indeed the life skills that can help them to successfully navigate other spheres of their lives, such as the family, friends, work and leisure. The 5th Space has potential to make a positive impact on all the other spaces and society.

Each created space is unique because it caters to young people's individual experiences of identity, thought and understanding. In such 5th Spaces, we focus on co-creating an empowering space with youth, enabling their journey from self to society. As they change the world around them, we also encourage them to observe and reflect on how the world seeps into them and changes them in turn.

The guiding principles in establishing a 5th Space

Ownership is the key

Ownership is not given, it has to be taken. It comes from putting in your own brick when the building is being constructed. Therefore, in youth work spaces, it is imperative to engage in dialogue with young people to decide what to do together. This co-creation of the agenda of the youth club goes a long way in giving them a sense of belonging and they begin to refer to it as 'my space'. Other ways of building ownership are to allow self-expression, democratic decision-making, developing shared goals and common rewards and consequences and, of course, creating a common culture of learning together.

Co-leading the space

It has been found that though young people are wary of adult governance, and scatter at the first sign of being 'bossed around', they do welcome light facilitation and nudges in the right direction. Moreover, there are times when young people are unable to take leadership roles due to lack of experience, capability, or due to existing conflicts among them. In such instances, an external, unbiased facilitator can support by providing guidance and aiding conflict resolution. It works best if young people and the youth facilitator/s create a co-led space. A good youth facilitator lets things self-organise as far as possible by encouraging conversations among young people themselves, and stirs things up with light interventions when young people are avoiding constructive confrontation.

(*continued*)

(*continued*)

Taking young people from what they know to what they don't

Young people need to move from what they are familiar with to spaces they are not, rather than the other way around. Starting with a focus on self and then moving to their immediate group and onwards to society is usually a better route to take than straight immersion into societal issues. Action is taken to learn first about the self and then the world and vice versa.

Learning from acting in the world

We believe experiences help young people to learn better than books alone. Youth citizenship action may not change much immediately in the world outside, but it has the potential for changing a young person from within. This emphasises a combined process of reflection and action, a process we call 'Reflaction'.

A space that is empathic and healing

In a 5th Space, individual feelings of all young people are valued. The culture of the youth club needs to inculcate trust, give them space and provide a non-judgemental environment. The group should be able to sense each other's feelings and empathise, search, confront and co-heal. Everyone should be encouraged to take 100 per cent responsibility to resolve conflict situations. To help them learn how to relate better to each other, the youth club needs to ensure opportunities for emotional release and connecting.

A space that nurtures critical thinking

In a 5th Space, there is a need to go beyond the surface into the depth to recognise the 'social context in which individuals operate and respond'. This would entail critically thinking about the interconnected role of politics, the economy and culture that shapes young people's experiences. Such a 'conscientisation' approach (Freire, 1971) uses consciousness-raising for community education aiming to assist young people to explore the reasons for their political, social and economic disadvantages and powerlessness. This encourages young people to consider their own situation and problems in a broader context that requires both intellectual and emotional maturity which will lead to constructive, non-violent ways to create socially and politically enabling spaces. However, we need to be wary of young people's own tendencies to oppress those with less power which would require the youth facilitator to push within the space to reflectively avoid such tendencies of social forces and look for win-win solutions for all stakeholders.

Valuing the here and now

We are always preparing the young for a life of adulthood. Youth workers should support the creation of spaces to balance the long term with the present. Young people have emotions, needs, desires, and aspirations emanating from their immediate context in the 'here and now'. Sometimes, when we work in the community, we begin to take ourselves too seriously. In the here and now, youth are looking for fun as much as making an impact. It has also been found that fun is one of the most effective ways of learning because it releases feelings that are critical for real learning rather than engaging in a mere intellectual exercise. And, if you want young people to join your club in large numbers, then make sure that you include a lot of fun and inspire everyone to spread joy.

Organic renewal of the space

In order to keep the vibrancy of the space, constant nourishment in the form of new leadership emerging within the youth club is critical. Like a seed that has all the genetic coding required to produce a new plant, the space should be encoded with the ability to infuse all the new people who come in with a will to take ownership and charge of the space. When the founders move on, the space should have the ability to reinvent itself organically in the spirit and the principles of the 5th space.

In **Singapore**, while this policy commitment is to emerge, a youth work supervision framework helps create dialogue among practitioners around reflective and responsive youth work practice.

Sri Lanka's Professional Youth Workers' Association (PYWA), which is independent of, yet collaborates with, the State youth agency, the National Youth Services Council (NYSC), has developed a distinct definition of youth work and is in the process of setting in place strategies and mechanisms to support the implementation of existing youth policy commitments (Chapter 7) to youth work.

The definition of youth work at the Professional Youth Workers' Association, Sri Lanka states that youth work involves

> Appropriate processes conducted by youth workers with the active and willing participation of young people that enables and empowers them through ensuring their emotional, social, ethical, intellectual and physical development, in a caring and secure environment.

In line with this, the new short course developed by PYWA to enhance the practical field skills of youth workers is an indication of ways forward for transforming practice. The State endorsement of the definition and its implications for practice is still evolving.

Youth parliaments, national youth councils and other youth structures operate from sub-national to national level in almost all sampled Asian countries, and there are partnerships with UN bodies and other agencies in some cases to support these processes. However, it was difficult to draw conclusions on how these partnerships resulted in a specific focus on systematic strategies for rights-based youth engagement and youth work approaches in practice in most countries at this survey level. Most engagement with youth was found to be around theme-based work such as

Table 6.2 State/national youth work practice – Asia

Country	Asset-based approaches to youth work in State/national settings	Partnerships
Bangladesh	Focuses on instrumentalist approaches and youth employment initiatives given the country's context.	No clear evidence was provided.
India	Youth worker competencies that enable the creation of programmes and processes for youth empowerment are variable due to the inconsistency of effective training and monitoring on the ground. The State work in Nehru Yuva Kendra Sangathan (NYKS) is done through a network of rural youth clubs, which are autonomous bodies that also have access to modest Government funding. There is much evidence of empowering and asset-based approaches to youth work here, though a systematic approach has yet to be developed. Urban youth are engaged through university chapters under the National Service Scheme (NSS). Today, NSS has more than 3.2 million student volunteers.	The Rajiv Gandhi National Institute of Youth Development (RGNIYD) works with many youth organisations for the education and training of youth workers. The National Service Scheme (NSS) works in partnership with a large number of civil society organisations as students volunteer in different civil society organisations. Partnerships in training and strategic programming include organisations like Pravah, ComMutiny – the Youth Collective (CYC), Yuva, Center for Youth Development and Activities (CYDA), Samvada, Jagori, Breakthrough and Youth Parliament, and collaborations with UN agencies.

Maldives	No information	No information
Malaysia	There are no State-based implementation structures for youth work/youth services. This has been proposed in discussions among youth work stakeholders. It will be further considered in ongoing deliberations in Malaysia on professionalising youth work and through moves to amend Malaysia's Youth Act (Chapter 8 – Asia). Youth work activities in Malaysia are also being carried out by the Ministry's youth and sports officers based at the federal, state and district levels.	The Malaysian Youth Council (MYC) is a non-governmental voluntary organisation that is the sole co-ordinating body for youth and student organisations in Malaysia. It participates in the National Youth Consultative Council (a forum for governmental and non-governmental actors to meet and discuss issues relating to youth development), and plays an active role in the implementation and monitoring of the national youth policy.[4] Youth work aspects of this work are not that clear. The Ministry of Youth and Sports, Malaysia has also been supported by youths represented under the 'Young Friends' or 'Rakan Muda' and '1Malaysia For Youth' or '1M4U' programmes. These three youth representative bodies play an active role in the implementation of youth development activities as espoused in the national youth policy.
Pakistan	State-supported youth work in Pakistan takes on a largely social action focus. There is a general recognition that there is an asset-based focus, combined with a focus on general skill-development programmes.[5] Evidence of actual youth engagement processes are not that clear in the State sector.	Partnerships for youth action were mentioned. A focus on strengthening youth work as a professional category through these initiatives needs to be clearer.

(continued)

Table 6.2 State/national youth work practice – Asia (*continued*)

Country	Asset-based approaches to youth work in State/national settings	Partnerships
Singapore	Evidence of field programmes, processes and spaces for youth work is nascent as national-level initiatives for professionalising the sector have begun only recently (to be elaborated on in later chapters).	Youth sector partnerships were mentioned, but there was no clear partnership for strengthening youth work as a specific professional category.
Sri Lanka	Empowerment and engagement strategies in the State Youth work sector can be improved, but mechanisms such as the Youth Parliament, and certain sub-national to national youth clubs structures, exhibit empowering/ engaging practices, though this is not systematic, or inclusive of the diversity of Sri Lankan youth groups. Systematic programmatic support for youth work approaches is not clear. New policy recognises this limitation and aims to change the situation through capacity-building initiatives.	The clearest State-civil society partnership on enhancing the quality of professional youth work practice is that which exists between the Professional Youth Workers' Association, Sri Lanka and the National Youth Services Council (NYSC).

on reproductive health, but manifestations of skilled youth engagement including approaches to listening, dialogue and co-creating initiatives were not made evident in survey findings, perhaps due to the lack of written, systematic strategies for youth work.

In some cases, good practice was observed to be random, and dependent on specific youth workers rather than based on systematic programming, guidelines and approaches. For example, the education and training of middle-level officers in youth development work, often facilitated through the Commonwealth Diploma in Youth Development Work, has delivered results in some cases, but failed to demonstrate broad asset-based guidelines and approaches.

6.3.3 The Caribbean

According to the baseline, Barbados, Guyana and Jamaica have generally adopted the former Commonwealth definition of youth work as indicated in the Commonwealth Diploma which referred to youth work as concerning the personal and social development of young people in its broadest sense.[6] How well this is linked to the design of programmes and practices is less clear, but indications are given in Table 6.3.

6.3.4 Europe and Canada

Youth work has been relatively well sustained and supported with official recognition at the highest level – for example a Youth Work Act in **Malta**. The Act defines youth work as 'a non-formal learning activity aimed at the personal, social and political development of young people'.

In **Canada,** while the training predominantly caters for youth and child care work with a focus on at-risk groups, professionals also work in recreational/leisure-type settings such as in the YMCA's work with young people, or in boys' and girls' clubs, and Friendship Centres. However, youth work has no official recognition in Canada. Neither is it officially recognised in **Cyprus.**

In **England**, the closest to a national definition for youth work is the National Youth Agency (NYA) definition which states that 'Youth work is an educational process that engages with young people in a curriculum built from their lived experience and their personal beliefs and aspirations. This process extends and deepens a young person's understanding of themselves, their community and the world in which they live and supports them to proactively bring about positive changes. The youth worker builds positive relationships with young people based on mutual respect.' It is still in the process of being significantly endorsed by agencies throughout England.

At a time which has seen a massive drawback on the funding of youth work, many qualified and experienced youth workers have either joined the ranks of the unemployed or taken up careers in other sectors (including employment totally unrelated to youth work, often not needing degree qualification). Others have been deployed to augment a weakened network of social services, becoming what some have called a labour force of 'second class social workers'. Indeed, these workers do

Table 6.3 State/National youth work practice – the Caribbean

Country	Asset-based approaches to youth work in State/national settings	Partnerships
Barbados	The State youth work sector utilises empowering/asset-based approaches, but evidence needs to be gathered. A lack of representation of all youth groups in youth engagement programmes was noted.	While partnerships for youth engagement were highlighted, partnerships for strengthening youth work as a profession were not that clear.
Belize	The Youth Development Policy and the Department of Youth Services (DYS) Strategic Plan articulates the positive youth development approach. More evidence needs to be gathered of its translation to practice through youth engagement programmes.	Partnerships for strengthening youth work as a profession were not clear.
Dominica	The Division uses seven key result areas (KRAs) in its approach to youth development work, which includes youth work facets such as a. training in leadership and youth participation in governance, b. voluntary youth service and participation in groups, schools, club, community-based leisure programmes, specialised programmes for at-risk groups. While this alludes to asset-based youth work, more evidence is required on how this translates to practice.	The Youth Development Division has strong cross-sectoral partnerships as well as strong partnerships within the youth work sector with various non-governmental agencies. These partnerships are strategic and mutual.[7]
Guyana	State-supported youth work in Guyana is to a large extent non-developmental in nature, and is largely carried out from a deficit/youth-in-development perspective. The survey found a largely activity-based list of programmes (sports, crafts, talks, discussion of needs), with little evidence of systematic youth engagement practices, or youth–adult partnerships.Reactive responses were evident, i.e. for teenage pregnancies, suicide and crime, etc.	While partnerships for engagement with youth around thematic areas were found, no explicit partnerships to strengthen youth work as a professional category were clear.
Jamaica	State-supported youth work in Jamaica is predominantly service-driven and is being undertaken by mainly untrained workers; its main focus is on mainstreaming youth in education, training and employment. The practice is still very reactive and reform-oriented in keeping with the general policy response frameworks for youth. No holistic strategy for young people.	No evidence provided.

St Lucia		
St Vincent and the Grenadines	No evidence provided. Proposed commitments to youth work policy in the draft youth policy will change this. State vision and mission statements for youth indicate commitments to promoting their general development, and ensuring full participation in order to achieve a vision of integrating all young people in the programme of nation building (youth-in-development approach); no further practice evidence was provided.	No clear evidence yet of partnerships to strengthen youth work as a profession. No evidence provided
Trinidad & Tobago	The strongest evidence of youth engagement approaches in the Caribbean was found here. The Youth Resource and Information Centre (YRIC) is a unique, innovative youth-friendly facility/space with computers, study areas, meeting/training rooms, and comfortable areas for conversations/discourse. It seeks to empower young people to make informed choices and enhance their personal and development. The Resistance Approach is undertaken in the Youth Development and Apprenticeship Centres (YDACs) target young men 15-17 years old. These centres provide not only technical vocational skills training in a residential two-year programme, but seeks also to provide a holistic approach to the personal development and empowerment of the young men.	The State supports youth-led and youth-serving organisations through grants and subventions.[8] Again, there was no evidence of partnerships for strengthening youth work as a professional category or competency-based youth work delivery as an approach.

not have the powers or protections afforded to social workers, while being expected (albeit informally) to take on what might previously have been understood as social work roles.

Many NGOs in the UK that were once thought to be capable of replacing formerly government-funded services in local authorities (in the light of cuts in central government grants) have been devastated by the financial crisis that hit in 2008 and have yet to come close to recovering. Thus they have not been able to come anywhere near filling the employment gap left by statutory services. Commissioned commercial concerns have been able to take advantage of this situation.

In these public-private initiatives, usually local authorities will look to put whole or parts of services out to tender (this means they do not have the day-to-day responsibilities for plant or employees). A range of commercial and/or community-based enterprises respond and often the most 'value for money' tender is taken, usually after they have agreed to reach targets for areas of practice that can pull down government funds (not related directly to youth work, but considerations like skills, crime, extremism and so on).

However, the conditions of work and salaries for youth workers in many of these commercial/entrepreneurial (not philanthropic) manifestations of youth work have been less than satisfactory. Moreover, work is often temporary, part-time and/or relatively derisory. By no means are all of these organisations 'fly-by-night' agencies, exploiting conditions and circumstances, but some have proved to be.

Considering the UK as a whole, State-funded provision has been significantly redirected. Statutory youth work has historically been part of services provided by local authorities. As such, State funding for youth work has been mediated by way of the overall grants given to local authorities. However, the latter need to meet their collective service obligations (which include housing, policing, highway maintenance and a range of child care and other welfare responsibilities). The legal requirement on any local authority in terms of youth work is minimal, and while youth work is often said by academics and writers to be informal education, no mention is made of this in current UK-wide legislation.[9]

In this sense, there is a kind of vicious cycle of a lack of clarity around the nature and agreed outcomes of youth work, and therefore an inability to agree across the board how success is measured and reported. By extension, youth work has not shown itself to be effective in State eyes – in fact the last big enquiry took youth work to task as a practice for not being able to show evidence of its impact (outside of anecdotal material). Legislated or policy-driven measures in youth work could influence more positive establishment of youth work cultures, and provide greater clarity on what and how progress and impact are measured and reported.

Some local authorities have maintained investment in youth services, but more commonly core budgets have been reduced and in some cases cut almost entirely. As cuts have spread across most local authority services, the impact on statutory youth work has been significant (some say devastating). Box 6.3 illustrates a process that monitors cuts in youth work funding in the United Kingdom.

Box 6.3 Monitoring youth work funding – the United Kingdom

In August 2014 Unison, a UK trade union for public service workers, published a document predicting the impact of cuts to State funding on youth work. The National Youth Agency (NYA) of the UK maintains online updates on local youth work funding cuts.[10] This is a good practice for youth ministries/departments, youth workers associations and other youth development stakeholders in other parts of the Commonwealth in order to keep track of investment in youth work, and lobby for greater investment.

However, initiatives funded by the National Lottery have generated a range of projects which support organisations to continue to provide youth work.

Generally, in terms of impact on the majority of the youth population, the UK's youth work offer has increasingly moved away from directly or indirectly (local authority) State-funded provision to delivery from community and voluntary platforms.[11] However, what funds local authorities have been able to allocate to responses that might be taken to fall into the youth work realm have increasingly been used to commission commercial organisations to deliver services (outsourcing).

The State currently understands youth work as providing preventative services. Many local authorities have linked the Government's 'Troubled Families' initiative with the role of children's services and many youth workers are now effectively working alongside social services and in multidisciplinary teams targeting vulnerable young people within this initiative. Once connected with the Department for Education, youth work is now, in terms of State policy, the province of the Cabinet Office and the Department of Communities.[12]

This said, a good deal of youth work training and education, perhaps partly because of the academic literature (which is often politically and socially uninformed and/or dated) places emphasis on youth work as essentially being informal education. At the same time, it is not unusual for employing organisations to recruit youth workers to undertake or offer non-formal (but also formal) responses to young people (including in schools and colleges). For all this, some charities and NGOs do continue to include some broadly educational tasks in youth worker job descriptions.[13]

For all this, the State is committed to a sizable investment in work with young people via the National Citizenship Service (NCS). While there is some doubt (particularly among youth workers) that this is youth work at all, and they question the claimed outcomes of this initiative, what indicators there are evidence that the NCS overall has provided young people with positive experiences and legacy opportunities.

In **Gibraltar**, a British Overseas Territory, the Youth Service has been a government statutory provision since 1963, run by qualified youth and community workers and locally trained, part-time volunteers and employees. The Youth Service forms part of the Ministry of Family, Youth & Community Affairs. Their mission statement is as follows:

Table 6.4 State/national youth work practice – Europe and Canada

Country	Asset-based approaches to youth work in State/national settings	Partnerships
Canada	The Canadian government does not recognise youth work – people in youth work want to interpret what happens as being youth work – this means that external interpretations contradict internal perceptions.	N/A
Cyprus	None, even though there are some plans to set up initiatives such as ERYCA (youth and information provision) which may be a sign of emerging systematic youth work practice in Cyprus.	No Evidence
Malta	Perhaps one of the richest examples of systematic State-supported youth work structures. Since its establishment Aġenzija Żgħażagħ (Youth Agency) has put in place nationwide administrative structures and operational procedures for the promotion and implementation of youth work practice and youth-related services. The agency has staff located in the Youth Agency and the operation of services are organised and co-ordinated from this single site, which is set in a 'Youth Village', which provides space, facilities and support for young people. A sports facility and a youth residential centre are also being planned for the site. They also develop and implement a wide range of programmes, projects and initiatives focused on youth empowerment, contemporary arts, social drama, literature, local democracy, music, volunteering and further study. New dedicated youth spaces at local community have also been provided, including youth activity centres, youth cafés and hubs. The latter operate in strategic locations. An interactive web portal, 'Youth Information Malta', was set up in early 2011 and is updated on a regular basis while 'Kellimni.Com' provides an online personal support service for young people. There has been a strong focus on engaging with and consulting young people. Their views, concerns and aspirations are valued in the development of practice. This is part of promoting the democratic participation of young people and the development of intercultural and social awareness. Co-operation at European and international level has been consistently prioritised and promoted; this has informed practice and acted as a means to review and energise policy.	The 'Youth Village' provides space, facilities and support for young people and youth NGOs to organise events and initiatives for young people based on youth work models.
United Kingdom	The main State funding for youth work is via the National Citizenship Service, largely supporting certification and skills-based services, rather than youth empowerment processes. The NCS's work through contracted providers may vary from relational services that may be identified as youth work, to less relational, more directive approaches, depending on the contractor. For example, the Essex Boys and Girls clubs have a big contract in that county, and they will take a youth work approach. Other contractors might have a mixture of relational responses, but be more like a cadet corps or school-based project (more directive and outcome- rather than process-related). Most professional associations may not identify much of this work as youth work.	Both voluntary and commercial organisations gain funding to deliver the National Citizenship Service. This makes up the majority of youth work funding of several county authorities.

The Gibraltar Youth Service seeks to promote the social education and welfare of young people up to the age of 25 by adopting a policy of equal opportunities, free from prejudice and developing a curriculum, in partnership with young people, that enables successful personal relationships, awareness to local and global issues, individual self-expression and determination that assists young people in their social and personal development, and encourages them to embrace active and responsible citizenship.

This is elaborated as follows:

Youth work promotes young people's personal and social development, working with them to explore and learn about themselves, others and society, through non-formal educational activities that combine enjoyment, challenge, learning and achievement. Youth work offers opportunities to work in many different ways and settings. From structured, organised activities, like workshops in schools and youth clubs, to informal settings such as street corners and shopping arcades.

Youth work maintains a set of common values and skills; a commitment to the social, personal and emotional development of young people, a sound understanding of the issues that affect their lives and the communities with which they identify. (see https://www.gibraltar.gov.gi/new/youth-services).[14]

This 'social educative' approach, by and large, describes the nature of youth work throughout the Commonwealth and the world.

A significant area of practice in **Canada** for youth work is located within residential settings. These programmes are very expensive and often are entry-level positions with high turnover of staff. Programme costs lead to hiring of 'cheap' staff – often with limited or no youth work qualifications. This happens most often in rural areas where there are limited qualified people available. When people with youth work qualifications are hired into positions in health settings or youth protection, significant shifts in practice occur.

For example, approximately five years ago in a large health centre in Nova Scotia, all child and youth care workers were replaced with licensed practical nurses. This change led to severely 'dysregulated' units where young people were not engaged with effectively. The impact of the change was noticed, and, in the recent past, child and youth care workers were hired back into these positions. In Alberta, the involvement of child and youth care workers on collaborative practice teams has shifted practice to a strengths focus and new numbers suggest that fewer young people are being placed in out-of-home care. In British Columbia, well-paid positions within government mental health and child welfare practice specifically identify child and youth care qualifications as a requirement for the position.

6.3.5 The Pacific

While it is likely that in a number of Pacific contexts there are examples of empowering/asset-based approaches to youth work in the State sector, the evidence gathered mainly pertained to **Australia** and **New Zealand**.

In the context of these two countries, the national youth sector has had intermittent support from State and federal governments. While government continues to be the regulator and primary funding body for the delivery of youth services, youth agencies are more reliant than ever on philanthropic and other sources of funding. New Zealand's national body Ara Taiohi continues to receive a small amount of government support but is principally funded through philanthropy and income generated through membership. The Australian equivalent, the Australian Youth Affairs Coalition (AYAC), has been defunded. Stated-based Youth Affairs Councils and regionally based youth workers' associations in Australia, and the emerging national Association in New Zealand, have also begun to play a role in enhancing and regulating youth work practice. In Victoria, the Code of Ethical Practice (Corney and Hoiles, 2007) introduced in 2007 has over the last 10 years had an important regulatory effect on youth work.

In **Australia**, the national Youth Affairs Coalition drafted the following definitional statement: 'Youth work is a practice that places young people and their interests first. Youth Work is a relational practice, where the youth worker operates alongside the young person in their contest. Youth work is an empowering practice that advocate for and facilitates a young person's independence and participation in society, connectedness and realisation of their rights' (Corney, 2014, p. 10).

In the Australian context, youth services are jointly funded by both state and federal governments. State governments also legislate and regulate the provision of services to young people. While there is no specific act defining or regulating the profession of youth work, state governments do recognise the work and do regulate the work of youth workers in various ways. An example in progressive youth policy is that of the State of Victoria. The current State Government's *Building Stronger Youth Engagement in Victoria* is focused on young people co-designing services with youth workers and their agencies, particularly for the most vulnerable. The Children, Youth and Families Act is the legislation that covers all those who work with young people, children and families in Victoria and is prefaced on the UNHCR Convention on the Rights of the Child. It states that

> For the purposes of this Act, the best interests of the child must always be paramount. When determining whether a decision or action is in the best interests of the child, the need to protect the child from harm, to protect his or her rights and to promote his or her development (taking into account his or her age and stage of development) must always be considered.[15]

Having legislation that locates work with young people in a human rights framework has had important implications for the development of Codes of Practice for youth work (please see case study in Box 10.2).

Youth Work in **New Zealand** is defined through the development of a relationship between a youth worker and a young person. This approach empowers young people, and provides them with the choice to engage for as long as agreed, and in a way that supports their holistic, positive development as rangatahi (young) that contribute to themselves, their whanau (extended family), community and the world.

Table 6.5 State/national youth work practice – the Pacific

Country	Asset-based approaches to youth work in State/national settings	Partnerships
Australia	The Australian Youth Affairs Coalition, formerly government-funded, has the national role of supporting and encouraging quality youth work practice as stated above. However, since being defunded, its capacity to play this role has been significantly reduced.	Australian Youth Affairs Coalition members and State-based youth peak bodies.
Fiji	No official/national definitions or practice guidelines indicated.	No evidence provided
New Zealand	More State recognition needed for youth work as a valid/valued mode of youth development. Great emphasis is placed by the Ministries of Youth and Social Development on the importance of mentoring, which is work that is unpaid and largely carried out by people who do not hold youth development qualifications. The youth work vision is largely carried forward by the National (Non-State) peak body, Ara Taiohi.	Ara Taiohi members
Papua New Guinea	No official/national definitions or practice guidelines indicated.	No evidence provided
Samoa	No official/national definitions or practice guidelines indicated.	No evidence provided
Solomon Islands	Self-regulating code of ethics.	No evidence provided
Tonga	No official/national definitions or practice guidelines indicated.	Solomon Islands Youth Work Association
Vanuatu	No official/national definitions or practice guidelines indicated.	No evidence provided

All Pacific Island nation governments have legislation, policies and programmes focused on or relating to young people. However, as far as could be ascertained, small island states in the Pacific are yet to develop clear, official, nationally endorsed definition or legislation specifically regulating or defining the occupation of youth worker. Sustained State/national practice trends among small island states of the Pacific have been difficult to determine during the course of this survey, even though much exists on the ground as good youth work practice.

6.4 Conclusion

Generally, youth work across the Commonwealth has become increasingly instrumental. More direct and often repressive responses to crime, youth pregnancy, sexual health, drug awareness, training and employment concerns have attracted funding, having found favour in government policy. This has influenced practice. In recent decades, youth work programmes in many instances have shifted to a point where some might suggest (with some notable exceptions), that much of what passes for youth work practice could be taken as forms of surveillance and social control.

This shift can be seen as part of a wider range of responses to produce a relatively cheap, relatively skilled, relatively flexible workforce, perhaps with passing reference to social welfare and health concerns. This approach predictably has some appeal in contexts where young people have the least stake in society, and therefore are seen as posing the biggest threat to social stability.

Nevertheless, the range of associative and dialogical phenomena that the Commonwealth commits to as youth work is being rediscovered, contextualised, developed and redefined. These emerging practices are improving organic, pragmatic approaches that are shaped and delivered by and for young people, and through empowering youth-adult partnerships. These are sometimes found in State delivery structures, including through civil-society-State synergies. A notable example is the work of organisations such as 'ComMutiny – the Youth Collective'[16] and the efforts of youth workers' associations.

The next phase in the development of youth work will likely emerge in the global South, for this is where the majority of the planet's young people live – a situation that is unlikely to change over this century. Old practice frameworks such as social pedagogy, informal education and professionalism shaped by income and status need reassessing and probably replacing. ComMutiny's '5th Space'[17] is a possible precursor of this. If so, youth work has an exciting and dynamic future.

Wherever there is youth work, it becomes embedded within, and shaped by, prevailing cultures, ideas and values. Various motivations for youth work, such as faith-based, philanthropic, political, or State-sponsored approaches all have historically impacted on and influenced the shape and aims of youth work within national contexts. This continues to be the case.

The varied background of youth work reflects the current state of, and in some cases, confusions around current youth work. It is difficult and perhaps somewhat redundant to try to chart a specific or linear history of practice, because it is not and never has been one set of practices or motivations.

For all this, being young is about 'becoming', changing and discovering the new. Youth workers, in order to be effective, need to be aware of this; they are in a 'growth profession'. On the one hand, if youth work stays as it is, if it is too much guided by what others see as the 'traditions' of practice, youth work will be rooted in the past. On the other hand, if youth workers work with and thrives on change, that is perhaps the history that it shares across and between contexts and cultures. The question is, are we ready to change?

Notes

1   This is an unofficial translation of the Act.
2   Available at http://thecommonwealth.org/sites/default/files/inline/Co-Creating_Youth_Spaces_web.pdf.
3   This text originally appeared in a different version as a section in the Commonwealth-Pravah-Nehru Yuva Kendra Document *Co-Creating Youth Spaces – a Field-Based Guide for Youth Workers.*
4   Source: http://www.youthpolicy.org/factsheets/country/malaysia/
5   There are many programmes at the national level with clear empowering, asset-based approaches to youth work in the State sector. For example, the Young Development Fellows programme of the planning commission of Pakistan, Young Parliamentary Associates Programme of iP, Prime Minister Youth Programme, Benazir Bhutto Shaheed Youth Development Programme as well as skills, multiple skills development programmes that are delivered at national and sub-national level.
     Other examples include the Young Parliamentarians Forum (YPF), which is the official body of members of the National Assembly and Senate of Pakistan who are below the age of 40 at the time of their elections and the Punjab Youth Parliamentary Caucus, an official body of members of the provincial assembly of Punjab, which are very vibrant platforms for young people and youth organisations.
6   This has since been fine-tuned to the present definition used in this document and beyond.
7   Key youth work agencies include CALLS, National Youth Council, Social Centre, Child Fund Caribbean, Operation Youth Quake, Girl Guides Association, Scout Association, Cadet Corps, 4-H Local Leaders Association.
8   Some of the organisations which benefit from State funding include: The Trinidad Youth Council and The Tobago Youth Council. Several NGOs also receive financial support to manage programmes on behalf of the State, such as the Child Welfare League which runs the CHOICES Adolescent Mothers' Programme, the Heroes Foundation and the Toco Foundation Gatekeepers Programme.
9   As such, the NYA's position that informal education is the rationale of youth work in England is somewhat out of date; in England the social function of youth work as far as much of the practice and legislation is concerned is part of preventative services.
10 http://www.nya.org.uk/supporting-youth-work/policy/cuts-watch/
11 The funding that local authorities allocate to youth work varies enormously as does the title of departments designated to deliver those services. At the time of writing one London Borough (with a population of just under 400,000) dedicates £10 million to youth work (Children's Services) provision. Another, a 30-minute drive away (with a population of nearly 300,000) has a youth work (Youth Support Services) budget of £250,000. Incidentally, both of these services are due to be cut; in the case of the latter, services will be outsourced, the former will see cuts over the next three years bringing funding down to £3 million.
12 There is no ministry or minister of youth work with UK-wide responsibilities or jurisdiction, and as freestanding practice youth work has no place in the Department for Education. Youth work (as a freestanding practice) is not inspected by the Office for Standards in Education, Children's Services and Skills (Ofsted), although youth work practice can come under inspection scrutiny in colleges, schools (where many youth workers find employment in fields such as 'enrichment') and other institutions/organisations when it is implicated in educational services.
     While regional situations vary (vis-à-vis Scotland, the Province of Northern Ireland, the Principality of Wales, the Crown Dependencies of Guernsey, Jersey and overseas territory of Gibraltar for example), 84 per cent of the population is subject to the deficiency of national government legislation in terms of youth work. In terms of the perception of the UK state, is not essentially an educative practice. It has functions primarily focused on child welfare and care, and although this might implicate issues relating to learning and education, the fundamental role and function of practice is primarily preventative (attending to situations that might be thought to put young people at risk of harm or social disadvantage).
13 In the 2015 Autumn Review, the minister for the Cabinet Office said: 'We will also focus our energies on building the National Citizen Service (NCS) so our young people are more confident and capable.

I'm very proud of the support we give to build civil society and promote engagement, cohesion and responsibility across the country.' This evidences the state view of youth work. This, together with a huge push toward employability within commercial and indirect state-funded youth work (transforming NEETs (those not in education, employment or training) into EET (in education, employment or training), usually by way of commercially oriented organisations, demonstrates state concern for creating and relatively flexible, relatively skilled, comparatively cheap, employment-ready work force.

14 https://www.gibraltar.gov.gi/new/youth-services

15 *The Children, Youth and Families Act*, Victoria State, Australia, p. 21.

16 see http://www.commutiny.in/

17 Society has four 'legitimised' spaces for young people – family, friends, career / career-related education and leisure or recreation. There is on the margins – a 5th Space – a space where young people discover themselves by engaging in social action, a space where they engage in active citizenship, volunteering and much more. The 5th Space can be repositioned as a space to focus as on the self-transformation of young people and at the same time the transformation of society through their activity. The 5th Space can be an area that builds on the aspects of understanding the self, developing meaningful relationships and impacting society – all of which are critical to youth development. While impacting society, young people impact themselves, and if facilitated properly these experiences lead to heightened self-awareness, enhanced leadership skills (such as problem solving, decision-making, team working, dialoguing, etc.) and informed stances and on-ground action on social issues.

A thriving 5th Space can be critical in the all-round development of young people. The skills learnt in the 5th Space are life skills that can help young people 'succeed' in the other spheres of their life, such as with the family, friends, at work and at play. Recognising the oneness between the inner and outer worlds of young people is the key to shifting from a 'youth for development approach' to a 'youth development approach'.

Chapter 7

Legislation and Policy

7.1 Introduction

This chapter addresses State legislation and policy that provides official legitimation of youth work as a distinct profession. This is something additional to more generic youth policy, although youth policies imply the recognition of youth work as a profession. It is this recognition that will ultimately enhance youth work processes and practices as discussed in the previous chapter.

7.2 Legislation and policy for youth work

The Commonwealth has had an ongoing commitment to working with governments to institute enabling policy and legislation for professionalisation of youth work as a means of improving practice and the dissemination of the most effective ideas, approaches and standards relating to the delivery of youth work services. It is the Commonwealth's position that legislative and policy commitments to youth work, as in the case of Malta, or in emerging contexts such as St Lucia, Malaysia, Sri Lanka, South Africa or Zambia, have a distinct bearing on systematic support for realising youth work delivery structures and, ultimately, on the wellbeing of young people. This commitment has been complemented by the Commonwealth's ongoing advocacy to obtain recognition for youth work within public service commissions of member states, as articulated in the Plan of Action for Youth Empowerment (PAYE).

This chapter discusses aspects of State legislative and policy action that can provide the foundation of professional recognition, such as:

a. Generally, the existence of youth policy (which implies support to youth work) and broader legislative enactments such as Youth Acts,

b. Specifically, policies and legislative enactments for youth work including explicit commitments to youth work within youth policies.

Youth policies formulated in the last ten years or so are generally acknowledged irrespective of the end date on the policy. Additionally, it is to be noted that only explicit commitments to youth work that have pragmatic implications for implementing policy, and not mere references to youth work in youth policy, were considered for a positive answer in relation to commitments to youth work.

This report acknowledges that many countries have a specific public sector cadre along the lines of 'youth officers' or 'youth service officers' whose roles and responsibilities often imply youth engagement in enabling and empowering contexts. This too, in essence, can be seen as an indirect policy commitment to youth work.

However, in the absence of professional recognition for youth work, including recognition in public service commissions, and the lack of adequate qualification pathways, these practitioners often receive low priority in terms of status and remuneration, often resulting in high turnover. Greater recognition for the profession will create a higher status, and create a more enabling environment for them to deliver consistently according to collectively agreed, systematic approaches to engaging with young people.

The baseline survey indicates a mixed response to legislation and policy around youth work. Only 11 countries (31 per cent) had distinct national/local government policies that recognised youth work as a distinct profession, and only two had legislated for youth work as a specific profession (one still in draft form). This is perhaps partially due to the lack of political momentum, and partially due to an inadequate understanding of ways in which youth work, as a distinct profession, can contribute to youth wellbeing, and by extension to national development.

From the perspective of youth work practitioners, there has been caution in lobbying for professionalisation because of the implication of narrow qualifications criteria that may exclude certain kinds of youth workers from practice, particularly youth workers from, and serving, marginalised communities who neither have funds, or time, to obtain certified qualifications. A focus on qualifications, they argue, also devalues the finer youth engagement competencies developed in specific localised contexts.

Moreover, in similar professions, such as in children's social work in the United Kingdom, fears have been raised that the accreditation of the profession 'risks being "punitive" to practitioners rather than developing their skills' (CommunityCare, 2016).

These concerns raise pertinent issues, and point to non-constructive tendencies we need to guard against. The Commonwealth's bid to professionalise the sector in no way undermines such concerns of practitioners. It promotes legislation and policy driven by the interests of the profession, the professionals, and of young people, rather than policy that attempts to curb and limit the profession's growth. In terms of broadening the ambit of accepted practice, the Commonwealth has already supported the articulation of competency through assessed practice, as further discussed in Box 9.1: Qualifying through practice: The Caribbean competency framework's criteria.

A snapshot of advances in policy commitments is shown in Figure 7.1. While significant advances have been made in Africa, Asia and Europe, the good work that exists in other regions in relation to education and training, and good practice, has not been reflected in specific state policy commitments. Similarly, countries that indicate policy and legislative commitments need to also examine the extent to which policies are implemented and invested in, and if policy commitments reflect the criteria identified in the baseline for professionalising the sector.

The strongest example of sustained links between legislation and policy and established and systemic structures and processes for youth work practice has been identified in **Malta**, as indicated in the case study in Box 7.2.

Figure 7.1 Regional trends – No. of countries with policy/legislative commitments to youth work as a profession

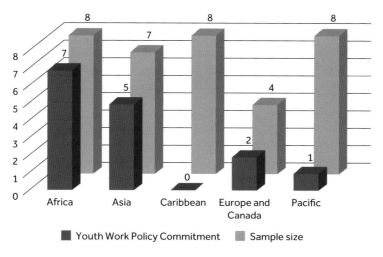

7.3 Regional trends in legislation and policy

7.3.1 Africa

All eight sampled countries have national youth policies, and four countries (Malawi, South Africa, Tanzania and Zambia) explicitly indicate youth work commitments in their policies, including in youth policy. While Malawi and Tanzania have both briefly discussed capacity building for youth workers, South Africa and Zambia have deliberated extensively on the potential legislative framework for youth work. They have taken action in respect of ethical standards, financing and qualifications pathways towards the professionalisation of youth work practice (South Africa National Youth Policy, 2015, p. 18 and Zambia National Youth Policy, 2015, pp. 11, 12).

This activity has been in part motivated by the associations of youth workers in both Zambia and South Africa. These associations have also been involved in dialogue

Table 7.1 Policy/legislative commitments to youth and youth work – Africa

Country	Current youth policy exists	Current youth policy indicates commitments to youth work	Specific youth work policy exists	Youth Act exists	Youth Work Act exists
Ghana	Yes	No	No	No	No
Kenya	Yes	No	No	No	No
Malawi	Yes	Yes	No	No	No
Nigeria	No	No	No	No	No
South Africa	Yes	Yes	Yes (Draft)	Not accessible	No
Tanzania	Yes	Yes	No	No	No
Uganda	Yes	No	No	No	No
Zambia	Yes	Yes	No	No	No

around the development of national youth policy. South Africa, through the efforts of the South Africa Association of Youth Workers (SAYWA), is currently developing a policy for youth work practice.

The National Youth Policy of Ghana (2010) makes no mention of youth work but looks 'towards an empowered youth, impacting positively on national development', implying a role for youth work. The policy makes frequent mention of 'youth development' but does not define what this might be, although it is associated in the document with empowerment.

While the Kenyan National Youth Policy (2007) refers to youth development, empowerment and participation, it does not mention youth work but 'visualises a society where youth have an equal opportunity as other citizens to realize their fullest potential, productively participating in economic, social, political, cultural and religious life without fear or favour (p. 4).' The strategic plan (2007-2012) provided a detailed action plan for the implementation of the eight strategic areas.

The vision of Malawi's 2013 youth policy is 'an educated, healthy, well trained, cultured, vibrant and productive youth'. It lists priority areas – economic empowerment, education, health and nutrition, participation and leadership.

The policy 'strongly advocates' (p. 23) 'Human resource development – training of professional youth workers and youth participation structures and policy-makers in the youth sector'. It also mandates the Ministry of Youth and Sports (p. 26) to 'Develop and provide guidelines for youth development and participation', and 'Build capacity of youth workers, youth participation structures and regulate their professional conduct'.

The policy refers to youth empowerment and participation throughout.

The Nigerian National Youth Policy (2009) aims to

> promote the enjoyment of fundamental human rights and protect the health, social, economic and political well-being of all young men and women in order to enhance their participation in the overall development process and improve their quality of life.

While the policy refers to empowerment and participation it does not mention youth work or youth development.

The South African National Youth Policy 2009-14 made consistent reference to youth work and youth development, starting out by stating (p. 1): 'It is hoped that recognition of youth work as a profession will strengthen capacity while promoting the provision of quality services'.

Empowerment and participation are also key words in the text. The 2015-20 policy provides a similar perspective.

The Tanzanian National Policy on Youth Development (2007) intends to create an enabling environment that builds the capacity of young people and promotes employment opportunities and access to social security. The policy focuses on a number of areas and mentions youth work, (p. 25), pledging to 'Facilitate provision of well-trained and qualified professional staff for youth work at all levels of the community'.

It refers more widely to youth development, empowerment and participation.

The Ugandan Children Act 1997 consolidated the law relating to children, their rights, protections and provisions. The National Employment Policy for Uganda (2011) lists youth employment as a policy priority action area. The National Youth Policy does not mention youth work and refers to youth development briefly just once, but advocates both participation and empowerment.

The core principle of the Zambian National Youth Policy (2006) commits to a holistic, integrated and multisectoral approach to youth development with a vision for 'a nation of skilled, enlightened, economically empowered and patriotic youth'.

Section 4.6 Youth Work includes subsections 4.6.1 'Overall Objective: To professionalise youth work practice in Zambia' and 4.6.2 'Specific Objectives: 1. To regulate youth work practice in Zambia; and 2. To enhance the capacity of institutions offering training in youth work.'

The policy also makes broad mention of youth development, participation and empowerment.

7.3.2 Asia

In Asia, one country has a specific youth work act (in draft),[2] although all but two have a commitment to youth work as part of youth policy. So, with the exception of Singapore and Pakistan there is a field of legislative and policy commitments to youth work in the countries in the baseline sample for Asia.

In Bangladesh a specific section on youth work has been included in the Draft National Youth Policy (2015) with the provision illustrated in Figure 7.2.

Empowerment and participation are also mentioned in the document.

The Indian National Youth Policy (2014) aims to create a productive workforce, promote social values and community service, facilitate participation and civic

Table 7.2 Policy/legislative commitments to youth and youth work – Asia

Country	Current youth policy exists	Current youth policy indicates commitments to youth work	Specific youth work policy exists	Youth Act exists	Youth Work Act exists
Bangladesh	Yes	Yes (draft)	No	No	Yes
India	Yes	Yes	No	No	No
Maldives[1]	Yes	Yes (draft)	No	No	Draft
Malaysia	Yes	Yes	No	No	Yes (draft)
Pakistan	Yes	No	No	No	No
Singapore	No	No	No	No	No
Sri Lanka	Yes	Yes	No	No	No

Figure 7.2 Policy commitments to youth work – Draft National Youth Policy Bangladesh

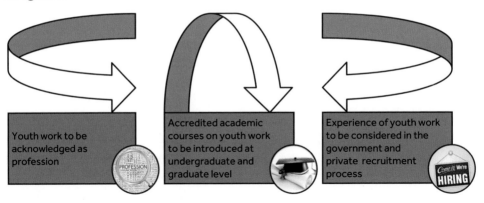

Courtesy: Draft Bangladesh youth policy

engagement, support youth at risk and create equitable opportunities for all disadvantaged and marginalised youth. The policy also aims to provide a framework and guidelines for stakeholders.

While the policy does not explicitly mention youth work, it does recognise the State-supported Rajiv Gandhi National Institute of Youth Development (RGNIYD) as of critical importance in policy advocacy and in its role in capacity building in youth development efforts, and so referring to a central role of the RGNIYD in training youth workers and youth officers (Ministry of Youth Affairs, 2014, p. 65), which it also engages in (see Box 5.1).

In the Maldives, the current National Youth Policy dates back to 2003 and is in the process of review. The policy's vision is that young people are able to contribute to the development of the country and have fair opportunities to develop themselves. The latest progress, the first of its kind in Asia, has been a Youth Work Act, similar to that of Malta in Europe, but information on its implementation has not been received.

The ninth priority area in the Malaysian Youth Policy (MYP) (the 2015 policy due to be implemented in 2018) focuses on building the capacity and competency of youth workers so they, as implementers of policy, might fulfil the needs of youth development and contribute towards strategic development of the country in the future (Malaysian Youth Policy, 2015, p. 12).

The National Youth Policy's objective is 'to establish a holistic and harmonious Malaysian youth force imbued with strong spiritual and moral values'. Its strategies included developing a knowledge base on youth as well as a focus on skill development.

The MYP commits to strengthening the human capital and the potential of youth as drivers for the future strategic development of the country in accordance with the Federal Constitution and Rukun Negara (National Principles). It outlines three policy areas as follows: 'Positive Youth Development', 'From Youth to Youth' and 'Youth are the Nation's Resource and Asset', and it introduced a new youth priority

Box 7.1 Creating platforms for an academically qualified and competent cadre of youth workers: The Sri Lankan Experience

By Dr Shantha Abeysinghe,
Dean, Faculty of Humanities and Social Sciences, The Open University of Sri Lanka.
Member, Board of Directors, Professional Youth Workers' Association (PYWA), Sri Lanka

Youth Work Education and Training

Implementing the Commonwealth Diploma in Youth Development Work was a major milestone in Sri Lanka for enabling youth workers to access the requisite qualifications and skills for youth work practice. This initiative, launched in 1998 as an Open and Distance Learning (ODL) programme, was a collaboration between three key public agencies in the country: The Open University of Sri Lanka, the former Ministry of Youth and Sports, and National Youth Services Council (NYSC) of Sri Lanka, working in collaboration with the Commonwealth Secretariat.

However, offering youth work education and training only in the English medium proved to be a significant limitation that affected students in rural and war-affected areas whose languages of proficiency were Sinhala and Tamil, the two main local languages in Sri Lanka. With the end of 30 years of militarised ethnic conflict in 2009, there was an urgent need to strengthen youth work practice in war-affected areas and this expansion of the offer to local languages met this critical professional need. The Diploma, therefore, was translated into the two local languages to broaden opportunities. According to statistics at the end of 2016, 914 individuals were enrolled in the programme in all three languages.

In line with further strengthening an academically and professionally qualified youth work cadre, the Bachelor of Arts in Youth and Community Development was approved by the Open University of Sri Lanka in 2014 and was further evaluated and approved by the University Grants Commission of Sri Lanka. Part of the degree will be material created through the Youth Work Degree partnership created by the Commonwealth in collaboration with the Commonwealth of Learning and the University of the West Indies.

Towards an evidence-based approach towards youth development work

The first baseline survey of youth work in Sri Lanka conducted in 2011 with the assistance of the Commonwealth revealed that Sri Lanka was the only country which had not formulated a national youth policy in the South Asian Region. It also highlighted the absence of a professional youth work cadre and association of youth workers in Sri Lanka. Based on the findings of this baseline study, a three-day workshop was conducted by the Ministry of Youth and the staff of the

(continued)

(*continued*)

Department of Social Studies of the Open University of Sri Lanka with the support of the Commonwealth Secretariat and Dr Brian Belton – This was another milestone in the development of the youth work sector in Sri Lanka.

This intervention paved the way for a new chapter to strengthen a professionally qualified youth work sector in Sri Lanka.

Moving On: Formal Recognition of Credentials and a Professional Association

The following initiatives were significant among work undertaken as a result of this momentum:

1. The formal recognition of youth work as a professional category in the National Youth Policy of 2014,

2. The establishment and registration of the Professional Youth Workers' Association (PYWA), Sri Lanka in 2014,

3. A range of regional and national workshop led by PYWA on building a relevant and responsive youth work cadre,

4. The development of a short course for continual learning of youth workers by PYWA in partnership with the Commonwealth and India's Youth Collective.

There was no legislation or policy that recognised youth work in Sri Lanka until the Cabinet approved the first National Youth Policy (NYP) in 2014. This recognition became a clear stepping stone towards the work that followed in establishing the Association and promoting professional practice.

PYWA has the capacity to conduct training of trainers (ToT) programmes in all nine provinces in Sri Lanka.

Moving forward: State support and investment

Currently PYWA is in the process of obtaining government support to institutionalise the short course as a complement to the existing diploma and degree qualifications, and to advocate for adequate investment for instituting youth work practice.

Since the Hon. Prime Minister of Sri Lanka is taking the lead role of the Ministry of Youth, both youth workers and other stakeholders of youth are more optimistic concerning government intervention that will support an academically qualified and professionally oriented youth work cadre through the delivery of a quality and responsive youth work programmes for young people in Sri Lanka.

area on professionalising youth work. The MYP is a starting point to structure the current unstructured youth work setting in Malaysia. At this moment, the Ministry of Youth and Sports through its research arm, Institute for Youth Research (IYRES), is studying the framework of youth work practice in Malaysia. The study also examines the possibility of the framework being used as an amendment to the Youth Societies and Youth Development Act 2007 to establish structure and professionalism in youth work in Malaysia.

A Youth Work Act will not be specifically legislated, but a section on youth work will be considered to the amendments of the new Youth Societies and Youth Development Act 2007.

The collaboration in research and development work across youth work practitioners, policy-makers, scholars and researchers strengthen the whole youth development ecosystem in Malaysia.

In 2009, the Pakistan Federal Cabinet approved the national youth policy (2008). However, in 2010 the Ministry of Youth Affairs was dissolved, and responsibility for youth was devolved to the four provinces (Punjab, Sindh, Balochistan, Khyber Pakhtunkhwa) and two territories (Gilgit Baltistan and Azad Jammu & Kashmir). The Punjab province approved its youth policy in 2012, and, at the same time, the Sindh province produced a draft youth policy. Balochistan presented a youth policy in 2015. Khyber Pakhtunkhwa has produced a draft policy, while details of the progress of Gilgit Baltistan and Azad Jammu & Kashmir are available.[3] No specific commitments to youth work were observed.

Singapore has no dedicated youth policy.

The National Youth Policy Sri Lanka (6.5 Professionalisation of the youth work sector) has a fully-fledged articulation of policy commitments to youth work as follows:

> [A]t present youth work is characterised as a top down approach that hardly reflects the developmental needs of young people. This has hampered the evolution of a participatory and development approach to youth work. Youth work could also be characterised as a form of event management where the main youth work programmes are implemented in a uniform manner throughout the country according to an annual calendar. This limits the ability of youth officers to act innovatively at the grassroots level. In general, youth work in Sri Lanka is perceived as a variant of social or charity work, not necessarily as a distinctive professional category. The youth officers are often called to play conflicting roles where they might be seen as involved in political mobilisation at the grassroots levels. This explains the underlying challenge faced by the youth officers in delivering professional youth services. Recruitment to youth service is based on minimal academic qualifications. There are also lack of opportunities for professional education and training for the youth workers.

Figure 7.3 illustrates this.

Figure 7.3   Youth work commitments in youth policy – Sri Lanka

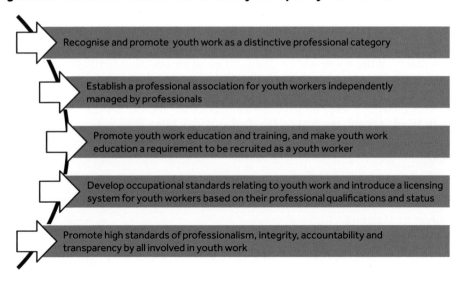

The national youth policy (2014) aims to 'develop the full potential of young people to enable their active participation in national development for a just and equitable society'.

7.3.3 The Caribbean

The youth policies for six of the countries in the Caribbean sample have developed a framework of youth empowerment and speak to the personal development of youth and the role of young people in community and national development. Young people were part of the process and the generation of policy. The Commonwealth Youth Programme's asset- and evidence-based approaches, principles and the Plan of Action for Youth Empowerment (PAYE) are said to have greatly influenced the process.

Table 7.3   Policy/legislative commitments to youth and youth work – the Caribbean

Country	Current youth policy exists	Current youth policy indicates commitments to youth work	Specific youth work policy exists	Youth Act exists	Youth Work Act exists
Barbados	Yes	No	No	No	No
Belize	Yes	No	No	No	No
Dominica	Yes	Yes (draft)	No	No	
Guyana	Yes	No	No	No	No
Jamaica	Yes	No	No	No	No
St Lucia	Yes	Yes (draft)	No	No	No
St Vincent and the Grenadines	Yes (+new draft)	No	No	No	No
Trinidad and Tobago	Yes	No	No	No	No

While most Caribbean youth policies acknowledged youth work and youth workers, specific policy commitments were not directly articulated in the documents provided during the survey, except in St Lucia's draft policy. General commitments do, however, exist.

The National Youth Policy of Barbados (2011) identifies nine areas of priority largely focused on youth development, empowerment and participation. Even though there are no clear commitments to youth work as a profession within the policy, it does state that it agrees with the goals related to youth work and its professionalisation, as stated in the goals of the Commonwealth's Plan of Action for Youth Empowerment (PAYE). The policy mentions youth work and indicates that, locally, youth workers are seen as closely aligned with social workers as the terms were used interchangeably, and refers to social workers specialising in youth. For Barbados, youth workers try to:

> equip young people with core values and effective role models during adolescence to ensure that they can resist the temptation to indulge in anti-social behaviour. Effective youth work is to provide young people with survival kits to help them navigate safe pathways to adulthood.

The National Youth Policy of Belize (2012) centres on three primary goals that focus on empowering and supporting young people to achieve optimal wellbeing, ensuring policies and frameworks are 'multi-sectoral, co-ordinated, cohesive and resourced', creating an 'optimal ecology' of home, school and community that allows young people to grow up to be 'healthy, caring and responsible'.

While making no allusion to youth work, the policy makes consistent referral to youth development. Participation and empowerment are also mentioned.

The mission of the National Youth Policy for Dominica (2004) is

> to create a framework that will ensure that young men and women in Dominica grow up with a sense of belonging and worth and are empowered to participate fully in the social and economic development of the nation.

The policy focuses on six strategic areas.

With regard to youth work the Policy has it that previously youth work was mostly concerned with 'recreation programmes for youth, the traditional model of youth work [as perceived in Dominica]. These developed alongside probationary and youth welfare services' (p. 1).

However

> Youth unemployment and adult reproductive health were the two major concerns for youth work in the 1980s. In response, the government initiated a non-formal youth training programme to assist in job creation among the young. In collaboration with the Ministry of Health, youth centres were established in two areas to attempt to address problems of sexual and reproductive health. Youth volunteerism gained greater importance and as non-government community organisations expanded, the interest in youth work grew also.

Today, unemployment and problems of sexual health still remain major issues and more so since the onset of HIV/AIDS in the latter part of the 1980s. This is compounded with problems of drug abuse and the shift in traditional values and thinking among youth brought on by the revolution in technology and the attending problems of globalisation.

According to the Vin Lawrence Report, 'Youth work in Dominica should supplement the effort of schools and formal training to prepare young people for their life as adults. It should prepare them for future responsibilities of parenthood and family life, enable them to be intelligent consumers and assure their active participation in creating the culture of tomorrow.' Youth services such as sports, education, training, culture, health, employment and recreation therefore should encompass the broad areas of their development. (National Youth Policy, 2004, p. 3)

In spite of these interpretations of youth work, there are no specific policy commitments to professionalising the youth work sector in the Dominica youth policy.

The policy consistently refers to youth development and participation but makes less mention of empowerment.

The Government of Guyana reported in October 2016 that the National Assembly adopted the national youth policy which serves to recognise and respond to the needs of pre-adolescents (age 10-14) and young people (14-35). It was stated in the draft policy that it 'represents a stated commitment to improve the situation of young people in Guyana in a manner that is empowering, inclusive and sustained' (Preface, NYP, 2015). The policy prioritises youth empowerment, identity, political participation and representation along with key youth development components such as education, skills development, employment, entrepreneurship and health. There is no specific mention of youth work.

Jamaica's Ministry of Youth and Culture, National Youth Policy 2015–2030 focuses on nine strategic areas.

The policy states that the Commonwealth Youth Programme's approach will be adopted

which indicates that a new concept of youth development and youth work should promote a positive youth development model rooted in human rights and emphasise the view that young people personify the vibrant hope and potential of any society (Jamaica. Ministry of Youth and Culture, National Youth Policy 2015–2030, p. 4).

The policy makes consistent reference to youth development, participation and empowerment. Again, there are no specific policy commitments to youth work.

In St Lucia, the National Youth Policy (enacted in 2003) is currently being reviewed through technical support provided by the Commonwealth Secretariat. The 2003 Policy aimed to 'provide the youth with a voice, equal opportunities and autonomy, with a view to developing their full potential'.

The draft policy mentions and refers to training of youth workers and indicates that the 'department of youth and sports provides short and long-term training in youth work for persons involved in youth organisations'.

A Strategic Plan for Youth Development was developed in 2008, which formed the basis of the 2012-2017 Development Plan. It focuses generally on the activities of the Ministry of Youth Development and Sports. There are specific commitments to youth work in the strategy.

The older National Youth Policy (1996) of St Vincent and the Grenadines was focused on employment, education, health, culture, sports, participation and representation. It did not mention youth work or empowerment, but made reference to youth development and participation. A new youth policy is underway but reports on progress are pending.

A 2011 report by The United Nations Population Fund (UNFPA) noted a draft National Youth Policy as focusing on education, employment, health, HIV/AIDS, sexual and reproductive health, and gender-based violence. The current status of the draft is unclear.

The National Youth Policy 2012-2017 for Trinidad & Tobago puts forward a vision that sees each young person as having 'a unique purpose to his or her life, based upon naturally endowed skills and competencies and those they may choose to develop over time, and focuses on five strategic goals'. Again, there is no focus on youth work.

7.3.4 Europe and Canada

While all four countries in the European region had legislation and policy relating to young people, only Malta had specific commitments to youth work in the form of a Youth Work Act.

In Canada much of the legislation is made and enacted at province/territory level, but as in Cyprus, youth work is not recognised as a distinct practice at national level; there is no national definition.

The key challenge with respect to youth work policy is that while there may be some support observed in some provinces, it requires a significant investment and existing

**Table 7.4 Policy/legislative commitments to youth and youth work –
Europe and Canada**

Country	Current youth policy exists	Current youth policy indicates commitments to youth work	Specific youth work policy exists	Youth Act exists	Youth Work Act exists
Canada	No	No	No	No	No
Cyprus	No	No	No	No	No
Malta	Yes	Yes	Yes	No	Yes
UK	LG[4]	LG	Scotland and LG[5]	No	No

relationship in order for the profession to be recognised, with a particular political party in place. For example, Alberta has made progress based on the election of a political party with socialist ideals, and a relationship with the Minister of Health who has knowledge of what child and youth care/youth work is. In Quebec, services are divided by language and a regulated profession that is close to youth work – psychoeducation – which is only found in the French sector. Assessing policy for commitments to youth work is challenging as in Canada youth work spans several different legislations – for example, in Nova Scotia, practice is regulated by 13 different legislations for child welfare.

As youth workers are located in various settings – including child welfare, schools, community centres, health and hospitals – the practice setting is regulated with standards, safety guidelines, etc. Therefore, while the occupation is not regulated, the work that youth workers undertake usually is. For example, in Nova Scotia, residential care is regulated and mandates youth work qualifications for staff working in these provincially funded facilities.

A 2010 report from Policy Research Initiative states that very few federal policies in Canada directly address youth rights. Instead, policies at the provincial or municipal level address youth-related issues, including education, health, employment and participation. For example, the province of Quebec has one of the only well-established youth policies in Canada. It has a Quebec Youth Policy and a related Youth Action Strategy, which identifies measurements and indicators for success.

In and across Canada no single national authority has a mandate for youth, but rather several agencies have well-defined youth responsibilities relating to justice and crime, employment and health. Departments and ministries relating specifically to youth exist at the provincial and municipal levels. For example, the province of Ontario has a Ministry of Children and Youth Services. Other provinces, such as Nova Scotia's Youth Secretariat, have one agency responsible for co-ordinating youth interventions across different sectors.

Cyprus has no unifying or over-arching youth policy. Instead, as listed in the 2012 youth policy briefing, Cyprus has a variety of laws that are concerned with youth issues such as No. 33(I) of 1994: Youth Board Law and No. 48(I) of 2001: Protection of Young Persons at Work. According to a 2012 European Commission report, there is also an inter-ministerial Consulting Committee on Youth consisting of representatives from 10 ministries and agencies. Ministries include the Ministry of Labour and Social Insurance, Ministry of Health and Ministry of Justice and Public Order.

Cyprus makes use of broad youth work initiatives (commonly via the European Union). There is no specific definition of youth work and it has no definitive State recognition as an occupation. The people who might be considered to be practising youth work do so as part of their wider occupational role, but have usually been employed to undertake another specialty. This being the case, there is no youth worker association and no minimum qualification for youth workers. There is a tendency for people with a background of psychology to take on youth work-type roles, but people with other degrees undertake similar practices. This said, it is stating the obvious that without recognition youth work cannot be professionalised in Cyprus.

For all this, at the time of writing a process is starting in Cyprus by way of a significant conference focusing on the validation of non-formal and informal learning in that national context. This initiative, motivated by the European Union expectations, is envisaged to last for a two-year period.

Box 7.2 Professional Recognition of Youth Work in Malta – A Brief History

By Simon Schembri
on behalf of Maltese Association of Youth Workers Committee,
Commonwealth Alliance of Youth Workers' Associations (CAYWA)

In February 2014, the Maltese parliament unanimously passed the Youth Work Profession Act, through which youth workers are recognised as professionals (Buontempo, 2014). This makes Malta one of a few states where youth workers are at par with other social and educational professions.

The process for the recognition of youth workers has been a long journey which was initiated by the first group of Youth and Community Studies students graduating from the University of Malta in 1998. This article will have a look at how the academic course in youth and community studies, lobbying and the national youth policies have been instrumental to achieve this result. Furthermore, it will highlight how the setup of Agenzija Żgħażagħ (National Youth Agency) has contributed to the creation of employment opportunities for youth workers.

Up to the early 1990s, youth work provision was mainly provided through church-based youth centres and uniformed groups. In 1993, the Maltese Government through the first National Youth Policy envisaged the need to have trained professionals working with young people (The Ministry for Youth and Theatre, 1993). This led to the introduction of the Institute of Youth Studies, 'later as a programme within the Department of education Studies and now forms part of the Faculty for Social Wellbeing' (University of Malta, para 1).

Azzopardi (1998) states that the Institute of Youth Studies was placed in a unique position because at the time it was the only entity focused entirely on youth issues during a period where there was an increase in the number of services targeted towards young people. The Institute of Youth Studies welcomed its first group of students in 1993 (Azzopardi, 2002, p. 7). The course was set on 3 main concepts: participation; emancipation; and empowerment, concepts which those wanting to work with young people had to adopt in their practice.

The Youth Studies Certificate progressed to a diploma and eventually a BA in Youth and Community Studies by 1998. The first group of students graduating in 1998, inspired by the youth work setup in the UK, decided to setup the

(continued)

(*continued*)

Maltese Association of Youth Workers (MAY). The main goals of the association were to have youth work recognised as a profession, and the setting up of a National Youth Agency. Though qualified as youth workers, most graduates were not officially employed as youth workers but rather performed youth work practice on a voluntary basis with youth NGOs. This consolidated existing youth organisations. A practical example was Zghazagh Azzjoni Kattolika (ZAK), a branch of the Maltese Catholic Action, which was revived during the late 1990s and nowadays is one of the leading youth organisations in Malta with several qualified youth workers working in the organisation.

Some of the work carried out by MAY includes the drafting of the first code of ethics for qualified youth workers, recommendations in the National Youth Policies, providing training courses for youth workers and participation in international fora. A concrete example of the effective advocacy for the youth work profession can be noted in the 1999 National Youth Policy where it declared that the 'government and local councils have to strive to see that youth-oriented services will be managed in collaboration with professional youth workers' (Parliamentary Secretariat for Youth, 1999, p. 24).

At the turn of the millennium, seven Youth Empowerment Centres were set up by local councils in different localities. These were run by part-time youth workers with the aim of providing information and support to young people and local NGOs (Schembri, 2006, p.9). In 2005, the association was enrolled in the Maltese Federation for Professional Associations (MFPA). This meant that though few youth workers were employed, they were considered as providing a professional service to young people even if it was on a voluntary basis.

The next milestone for youth work as a profession was the introduction of youth workers in schools: 'An agreement with the Malta Union of Teachers (MUT) has been established to integrate youth workers in schools both with challenging behaviour students and in extended school settings to support youth participation through student councils' (Teuma, 2009, p. 84). This paved the way to a number of youth work posts being issued by the Ministry of Education and other agencies such as the Employment and Training Corporation (ETC).

All four National Youth Policies published in 1993, 1999, 2003 and 2010 respectively, emphasised the need to set up a National Youth Agency to co-ordinate youth services on behalf of the government. Supporting the need for investment in the youth sector was highlighted by a team of international experts who reviewed the implementation of the Youth Policy in Malta on behalf of the Council of Europe (2004). The report probed the need to increase funding 'to facilitate the creation of more full and part-time youth work posts' (Council of Europe, 2005, p. 41). In February 2011, the Secretariat of Youth and Sport launched the National Youth Agency named Aġenzija Żgħażagħ (AZ). The aim of AZ was to:

- develop action plans for the implementation of the policy;

- co-ordinate, direct and monitor the implementation of such plans as a matter of priority;

- initiate, co-ordinate, monitor and evaluate youth work programmes aimed at young people and facilitate participation and empowerment of youth;

- co-ordinate research work;

- promote a uniform approach amongst stakeholders in the youth field to matters;

- relating to young people;

- make recommendations to stakeholders on issues affecting young people.

(National Youth Policy, 2010, p. 53)

AZ introduced a number of programmes and initiatives such as the 'youth local councils' and 'youth cafés', to cite two examples. All projects are co-ordinated by either full-time or part-time qualified youth workers.

January 2014 marked another milestone for Maltese youth work as the Maltese parliament unanimously passed the 'Youth Work Profession Bill' (MAY, 2014). This makes Malta one of the few countries where youth work is regulated by law. 'Austria, Estonia, Germany, Ireland and Romania have specific legislation that establishes a framework for the provision of youth work' (Youth Partnership, 2008, p. 21). In the comparative analysis, the Youth Partnership (2008, 2009) highlights that existing definitions of youth work focus on providing positive experiences to support young people's personal development and assist them in their transition to adulthood. Similarly, the Maltese Bill defines youth work as

> a non-formal learning activity aimed at the personal, social and political development of young people. It takes into account all strands of diversity and focuses on all young people between thirteen (13) to (30) years of age. Youth workers engage with young people with in their communities and support them in realising their potential and address life challenges critically and creatively to bring about social change' (p. C18).

The Act established that youth work provides learning experiences for youth, sets the base where youth work takes place and indicates the philosophical approach youth workers ought to adopt in their practice. This definition is essential as it guides and provides a common framework for practice for Maltese youth workers. In November 2016, the first group of youth workers were awarded the professional warrant.

This has been a long and fruitful journey for youth workers in Malta. The main objectives set by the first members of MAY have been achieved through the setting up of the National Youth Agency and the Youth Work Profession Act. This does not mean that the journey is at an end but at a crossroad where Maltese

(*continued*)

(continued)

Youth workers need to strengthen and validate their practice by highlighting the impact and benefits of youth work provision. The next steps are to create a collaborative network amongst Maltese youth workers. This is paramount since different forms of youth work provisions are evolving through the different services hence developing new skill sets to work with different groups of young people both in youth clubs, educational institutions and in the streets. This means that youth workers need to invest in their professional development – an aspect which is highlighted in the Youth Work Profession act. These aspects are vital to set youth work standards to establish accountability and a quality service to all young people in Malta.[6]

Malta's National Youth Policy *Towards 2020* provides extensive support for youth work, empowerment and participation. Malta provides the highest form of commitment to youth work through a Youth Work Act and its systematic implementation. Box 7.2 is an elaboration of this exemplary process.

In the United Kingdom, Parliament has devolved responsibility for a range of issues, including education and youth work, to administrations in Scotland, Wales and Northern Ireland. The Department for Children, Schools and Families' Joint International Unit has overall responsibility for representing UK youth policy within Europe and abroad. Ministries with responsibility for youth are as follows:

- England – The Department for Children, Schools and Families (DCSF).

- Scotland – Department of Education and Lifelong Learning, Scottish Executive

- Wales – Department for Children, Education, Lifelong Learning and Skills, Welsh Assembly

- Northern Ireland – Department of Education.

The United Kingdom has an enormous range of policy and legislation relating to young people, and young people are a significant concern in a range of legislation not specifically related to youth. The legislative provision that comes closest to commitments to youth work is a local government legal provision known as 507B which, while it does not explicitly mention youth work, requires local education authorities to provide leisure-time activities for persons aged 13–19, and certain persons aged 20–24. It does not, however, convey minimum requirements and refers to 'activities' and 'training' rather than the nuanced provision that youth work is. However, it has been used to support youth work via English local authorities.

Also regionally (particularly in Scotland, Northern Ireland and Wales, but also in contexts such as Guernsey, Jersey and Gibraltar) legislation impacting on youth and youth work exists. However, in total, these geographical areas include less than 17 per cent of the population of the UK.

As such, across the region and within national contexts, the development of legislation and policy for the professionalisation of youth work is diverse:

- It has been established in Malta.

- It is evolving in Cyprus and Canada (although this is not without challenges).

- In the UK there has historically been an effort to adopt something of the persona and practices associated with profession status. This activity has caused those within and around youth work circles to broadly regard the occupation as professional.

In common with the rest of the Commonwealth, compared to social work or teaching, youth work, as a full-time, paid occupation represents a relatively small (and, due to austerity measures, in the UK shrinking)[7] workforce. It can be regarded as something of a marginal occupation in terms of public consciousness.

At the same time, perhaps with the exception of Malta, youth work practice is broadly understood to be perhaps more closely related to play work, child care and social work than a 'free-standing' response to young people. This is perhaps understandable as youth workers in the region, particularly in Canada and the UK, do often work alongside social workers and in schools, colleges and child care provision.

7.3.5 The Pacific

In the Pacific, while Australia, New Zealand and the Solomon Islands have demonstrated advanced approaches to youth work as established through culture and practice, and instituted through education and training and through youth work coalitions and associations, State commitments to youth work were less evident.

While the Australian national youth policy is not current, all state governments have up to date youth policies and ministries related to affairs of young people. In regard

Table 7.5 Policy/legislative commitments to youth and youth work – the Pacific

Country	Current youth policy exists	Current youth policy indicates commitments to youth work	Specific youth work policy exists	Youth Act exists	Youth Work Act exists
Australia	LG	–	LG	No	No
Fiji	Yes	No	No	No	No
New Zealand	No	No	No	No	No
Papua New Guinea	Yes	No	No	No	No
Samoa	Yes	No	No	No	No
Solomon Islands	Yes	No	No	No	No
Tonga	Yes	No	No	No	No
Vanuatu	Yes	No	No	No	No

to youth work there was no evidence in any Pacific nation, including Australia, of legislation specifically defining or regulating 'youth work' as an occupation or profession, even though some local government policies that facilitate youth work do exist in Australia.

Australia's 2010 'National Strategy for Young Australians' mentions youth workers just once. This strategy is now dated and has not been renewed. The strategy also contains broad elements that can be understood to be congruent with youth work practice. Its vision is that

> all young people grow up safe, healthy, happy and resilient and to have the opportunities and skills they need to learn, work, engage in community life and influence decisions that affect them.

Australia does have national vocational training standards set for the training of youth workers at certificate and diploma levels and does have state-level government regulatory measures and safety standards (e.g. criminal record checks) for all those who work with young people. Broader commitments to shaping and regulating youth work practice have historically been set by youth sector peak bodies, youth councils, youth work academics and youth workers' associations. Youth policies in many states have had limited impact on the shape and delivery of youth work with the exception of Victoria, where legislative commitments to human rights in the Children, Young People and Families Act 2005 led to a rights-based code of ethical practice being developed by the sector (see Box 10.2), and the establishment of an active professional association. Most states, and government-funded Youth Affairs Councils and peak bodies, along with university youth work departments, have largely carried the load of lobbying and encouraging the professionalisation of youth work. This is not unlike the situation in the UK, where peak bodies such as the National Youth Agency (NYA), and to a lesser extent the unions, have filled the gap left by the lack of an effective and broad professional association.

Fiji's National Youth Policy makes no mention of youth work. However, it claims to recognise 'the current status of young people and the potentials they possess for the future'. It further aims 'to enhance their holistic development to become resourceful and effective members of society'.

The policy looks to work 'in tandem' with the Roadmap for Democracy and Sustainable Socio-Economic Development, which has a specific children and youth section.

New Zealand's former youth development strategy titled 'Youth development strategy aoteaoroa' was launched in 2002, but commitments to its implementation have not been clear and are reported to have been largely abandoned.

This strategy expressed a strong understanding of the principles of positive youth development in youth work practice. It had clear commitments to supporting youth workers, as follows:

- encouraging youth work training in conjunction with non-governmental agencies and local authorities,

- promoting youth workers in schools who work as part of youth development programmes,

- ensure training for youth workers in a comprehensive youth development approach,

- creating an infrastructure for community youth workers' training,

- encouraging formal supervision of isolated youth workers,

- encouraging the development of training standards for community youth workers,

- training youth workers working for local authorities in youth development and working with young people,

- encouraging local government to take a leadership role in youth worker networking to support youth development.

It mentions one qualification specifically relating to youth work: the Christchurch Polytechnic Institute of Technology National Youth Work (level 4) Certificate even though in reality, qualifications around youth work are proliferating.

In terms of real strategic initiatives, New Zealand reported a small funding pool (NZ$181,000 nationally) for regional youth work training.

There is no mention of youth work commitments in the Papua New Guinea National Youth Policy.

The vision of the Samoan National Youth Policy (2011) perceives of young people as partners in sustainable community development. The document refers to youth development as a strategy but does not refer to youth work as a career pathway that contributes to youth development.

With regard to the Solomon Islands, *Urban Youth in the Pacific (2011)* had it that the National Youth Policy (2010–2015), and the accompanying strategic action plan, replaced the national youth policy (2000) after a lengthy review and consultation process. Again, while it perceives of young people as partners in development, and refers to youth and wellbeing, there is no explicit mention of the profession of youth work as contributing to this, nor commitments to youth work.

In Tonga, the Secretariat of the Pacific Community supported the development of a youth policy in 2005, which was adopted in 2007 as the Tonga National Youth Strategy (TNYS). The TNYS envisions a strengths-based approach to youth development, but again, does not mention youth work.

Vanuatu has a Youth Development Policy under the Ministry of Youth Development. Its vision is that the young '[avail] themselves of traditional and religious values, along with modern technologies' in support of both person and socio-economic development.

7.4 Conclusions

Generally speaking, the relative professionalism of any occupation is often defined by way of government policy/legislation and or regulation with regards to practice. So

Table 7.6 Policy/legislative commitments to youth and youth work – Cumulative

Region	Total sample size	Has youth policy	Has explicit policy commitments to youth work	Has a Youth Work Act
Africa	8	7	4	0
Asia	7	6	4 + 1 draft	1 (draft)
Caribbean	8	8	2 (draft)	0
Europe and Canada	4	1	2	1
Pacific	8	8	1	0

this is what needs to be assessed, as a first step, in any context, to understand the level and extent to which youth work might be recognised as a profession.

The baseline survey's findings indicate a range of commitments to legislation and or regulation specifically relating to the occupation or professionalisation of youth work. Table 7.6 attempts to provide a general picture of policy/legislative commitments where they were found.

The data indicates a mixed picture around official commitments to youth work. In terms of the actual advancement of youth work practice, however, the clearest correlation between policy and practice was seen in Malta. In countries such as the UK, Australia, New Zealand and India, while relatively advanced approaches to youth work were identified in the practice chapter, empowering and asset-based practice were seen as largely threatened due to the official defunding of structures. In countries such as India, commitments to youth work were seen as emerging.

Countries with clear policy commitments to youth work such as Sri Lanka and Malaysia were still in the process of translating policy to practice, a process which calls for commensurate State investment for the education and training of youth workers, and for establishing mechanisms and processes for youth work practice.

A range of other legislation, policy and institutions of course influence and impinge on the development and shape of youth work as a profession internationally. There is no consistent evidence from across the sampled countries on these. However, legal Acts underpin the work of the National Youth Services Council in Sri Lanka, which has implications for those termed youth development officers.

A provision for the youth work profession is being drafted into the new amendments to Malaysia's Youth Societies and Youth Development Act 2007, and work is currently in progress for a framework on the youth work profession that is being undertaken by the Institute of Youth Research (IYRES) (at the time of writing).

In Canada, although there are no State guidelines or supporting mechanisms and no unified legislation that regulates youth work, efforts have been made to regulate the occupation. However, these vary from one province/territory to another.

Notes

1 Since the conduct of this baseline, Maldives has voluntarily left the Commonwealth. However, due to its progress through a Youth Work Act, the first of its kind in Asia, and its official commitments to youth work, data on the Maldives has been retained in the baseline.

2 This is the Maldives, which has since withdrawn from Commonwealth membership.

3 These can be found on https://www.facebook.com/GBYouthPolicy/ and https://www.facebook.com/AJK-Youth-Policy-532593863423142/about/?entry_pointpage_nav_about_item&tabpage_info respectively

4 In Wales, Extending Entitlement provided the framework for youth support services, bringing together all services, support and opportunities for young people aged 11 to 25. Young People's Partnerships were established in each local authority area to coordinate services for 11-25 year olds.

5 In Scotland, a national youth work strategy was published in 2007, setting out the role of youth work in achieving the broader aims of the Scottish Executive – that young people are nurtured, safe, active, healthy, achieving, included, respected and responsible. The strategy catered for young people aged 11 to 25. In Northern Ireland, the Children and Young People's Unit was set up within government to ensure that the rights and needs of children and young people (up to 18 or 21 for those who are disabled or have been in care) are given a high priority.

    A raft of more recent policy has been applied to the above four contexts within the UK while local authorities and regional assemblies have initiated and dissolved a range of responses. This could consist of one part-time volunteer – although few would go this far but there has certainly been legal action on this that did not find in favour of local authority provision being statutory or legally enforceable. The situation is very much ongoing.

    Northern Ireland, Scotland, Wales each have devoted youth policy and/or youth work strategies. Wales has developed a 2014–2018 National Youth Work Strategy, and Scotland a 2014–2019 National Youth Work Strategy. Both build on civil society consultations and have a transversal approach. Northern Ireland has a youth work policy titled Priorities for Youth

    In a press release on 3 July 2013, it was announced that responsibility for youth policy would be transferred from the Ministry of Education to the Cabinet Office – a cross-thematic Ministry. However, no youth department exists. The Cabinet Office focuses on national programmes, such as the National Citizenship Service, while most youth provisions and services are provided at a local and city level of government. Scotland has a Minister for Children and Young People and Minister for Youth Employment.

6 This case study has been informed by Azzobardi (2002), Buontempo (2014), Ministry of Education and Arts (Malta), (1993), Ministry of Youth Malta (2004), Parliamentary Ministry of Education, Malta (2009), Parliamentary Secretariat for Youth and Sports Malta (2010), Schembri (2006), Teuma (2009), University of Malta (2013), Youth Partnership I (2008), Youth Work Profession Bill, Malta (2012).

7 Austerity considerations, the result of the 2008 economic downturn, do not appear to be as impactful on youth provision in Malta and Canada, although Cyprus has been subject to long-term political, economic and social limitations.

Chapter 8

Professional Associations for Youth Work

8.1 Introduction

This chapter discusses the building of collective professional identities for youth workers and the role of professional associations in upholding the integrity and quality of the profession. This is a means of affirming the Right to Association enshrined in the UDHR and other human rights instruments as it applies to collegiality in the youth work profession. Twelve countries out of the sample (34 per cent) had youth workers' associations that help safeguard the integrity and quality of the profession.

8.2 What is a professional association?

Professional associations provide a resource, a backup and a foundation for professionals who may share common interests and values. Associations are typically created to provide an organised structure to monitor the training and practice of a group of individuals from a specific occupation in order to safeguard the quality and integrity of the profession. Volunteers who are appropriately qualified can sometimes also be members of a professional association.

Professional associations also play a crucial role in defining and regulating the nature of practice, validation, qualification and certification, acting as a gateway to the profession.

The Commonwealth's publication *Establishing a Professional Youth Worker Association: A 12-Step Guide* (Commonwealth Youth Programme Asia, 2012), states that:

> At the foundations of a successful professionalising process lies the collective strength of youth work practitioners participating in defining the parameters of their profession. This could include participatory decisions on required competencies for youth work, establishing parallel qualifications, and assuring the quality of training and practice. Such collective decision making ensures the establishment of a vibrant and responsive youth service that can serve young people optimally. In this sense, collective organisation also precedes other decisions in the professionalising process.

> Professional associations are sometimes formed in order to allow members to reach a common goal whether for legislative, educational, social and/or economic reasons. Out of these bigger goals, professionals can also attain a higher status, influence and authority of the association and its membership.

> Overall, the professional association prioritises its membership through advocacy, capacity building, framing competency standards, establishing Codes

of Ethics, and so on. This includes the representation of marginalised individuals and groups working within the profession.

Professional associations typically 'police' practice. However, sometimes they can take the role of 'deregistering', suspending or striking off those who do not abide by ethical standards, professional codes of practice or cross the moral boundaries of public trust. This being the case, the professional association is;

- **A source of authority** – defining the parameters (limits and extensions) of professional activity,

- **A means of ensuring integrity** – informing and guiding the character of practice,

- **An interpretative body** – promoting recognition and comprehension of what the profession does (its social function) how it operates and who might deliver practice.

Professional associations can have a lot of influence and authority. But very straightforwardly, a professional association is a group of people, coming from similar practice backgrounds, under the auspices of maintaining and developing their shared interests, promoting and seeking to heighten the understanding of their common principles, values, perspectives and skills.

Professional associations can contribute to the following:

- Preserve and advance standards of their vocation

- Engender and sustain ethical practice, building codes of behaviour and professional standards informed by agreed ethical standards

- Inform employers, government, trainers, associated and related fields, clients and the public in general about professional expectations and models of service delivery

- Uphold and expand recognition and status of the profession

- Generate and support relevant professional research

- Provide multidimensional forums/platforms/support networks to share and facilitate the preservation and advancement of best practice

- Frame, influence, advance and inform members about policy, technical and theoretical innovation

- Provide practicing professionals, students of professional practice and those in training with relatively easy access to a database which they can join and make their profession and personal contact details available to other people and potential clients/users/funders and employers

- Offer career information, other learning opportunities

- Offer in-service training and introductory courses/ promotional material for people wanting to begin a career in youth work

- Provide a validating service for other training/education providers and advice to organisations, regional and national government (Commonwealth Youth Programme Asia, 2012, pp. 6–9).

As such, a professional association is a supportive organisation which can be helpful to an individual, but also (and perhaps more importantly) professional associations can help individuals and organisations:

> stay true to and remain consistent with their own values, principles and ethics. When viewed on a broader scale you can see that the effect of the work of professional organisations can have important social impact in terms of promoting best practice, equality and justice (Ibid, p. 8).

More generally, a professional association may:

- Further the interests of its members while promoting public interest

- Make the area of professional practice better understood and available to a wider constituency

- Act as a means of promoting the security and protecting and promoting the position and status of professionals

- Influence local, regional, national and international policy, professional certification, education and training

- Endorse and uphold the integrity of the profession represented (Ibid).

In this way, professional associations can have a considerable reach and an ability to build, strengthen and develop practice, far more than individuals working alone.

Defining a professional association's membership, particularly in contexts where youth work may not even be recognised as a profession, is difficult. This process of identification is important because many people, all over the world, practise youth work without local or national recognition. Sometimes, individuals do not even understand themselves to be youth workers, and fail to completely recognise the complex skills and knowledge they in fact use for working with young people.

Such circumstances curtail the potential political and social influence of youth workers because without a professional identity, an able and committed youth worker risks never being seen to be more than a sort of surrogate social worker, teaching assistant or a kind but relatively directionless 'do-gooder'.

There are two main steps when looking to identify the membership of a professional youth workers' association:

- Ascertain the skills, attitudes, knowledge, clientele, principles and ethics that might together constitute youth work practice nationally, regionally and/or worldwide. At that point the association is in a position to begin to recruit from its designated target group.

- Identify the Constituency: A group of people will need to identify themselves as youth workers. This can be achieved by reviewing potential members' professional concerns, aims, client groups, ethics and principles against the agreed standards (Commonwealth Youth Programme Asia, 2012, p.9).

In many professions, entry to employment is reliant on membership of a professional association. Often, qualifications enabling entry to and promotion within a profession are prescribed and/or wholly or partly validated by these associations.

At the same time, entry to a professional association (and so a profession) is often restricted to those of 'good character'. This is assured by references, peer review and criminal/police checks. It would of course not be protective of potential or actual clients to have a convicted rapist taking on the role of a medical practitioner or a person with a record of serial fraud being welcomed into a fraternity of accountants. Likewise, one would hope that people with convictions involving children and young people would not be able unquestioned to gain employment as a youth worker.

Traditionally, the rationale of professional associations is to assure safe, fair and effective services for the clientele/public. As such, professional associations are more than talking shops, or debating societies. The membership and governance is in the hands of practitioners, not (in the main) interested or concerned lay people or those distant or detached from practice (academics, civil servants and so on). Neither is a professional association a trade union. The latter is primarily concerned with the salaries and conditions of its membership, while the former exists for the benefit of clients; a strong profession is valued because of its service to clients, but a trade union is judged by its members to the extent it preserves and enhances wages and conditions of its members. However, professional associations may in some cases participate in trade-union like activities such as collectively negotiating standard fees or salaries and conditions on behalf of their members. For example, in Australia, the Youth Workers Association (YWA) was instrumental in negotiating the provision of a pay and conditions award category for youth workers (Corney, 2017, pp. 162–172).

In effect, because a professional association is concerned with the status of the profession, it also has an interest in the development and maintenance of the social and/or economic status of practitioners, which might be understood to include salaries (one straightforward indicator of the comparability between like professions – in the case of youth work this might include social work and teaching).

Figure 8.1 Professional associations and trade unions – the focus

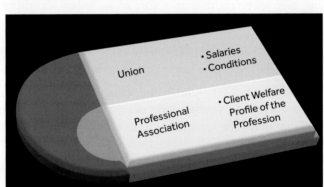

Figure 8.2 Regional trends – No. of countries with national youth workers' associations

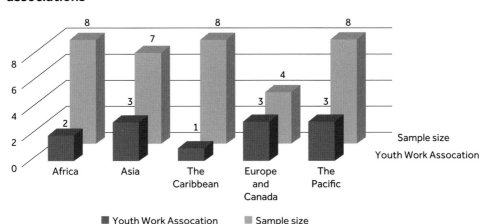

8.3 An overview of youth work associations in the Commonwealth

Commonwealth-wide, the notion of national youth workers' associations is in a state of development (compared to professional organisation in other similar occupations). Nevertheless, while some associations are emergent, others are relatively active, while a few (for example the Maltese Association of Youth Workers) have a fair amount of influence. Out of the sample, 12 countries (34 per cent) had active professional associations for youth workers. Figure 8.2 illustrates existing associations against the sample and demonstrates the need for further action in establishing national associations.

8.4 Regional trends

In the Commonwealth Africa region, South Africa and Zambia could claim existing professional associations for youth workers. At the time of writing, Uganda was clearly demonstrating interest in establishing a professional body for youth work.

Table 8.1 Number & membership of youth work associations – Africa

Country	Number of professional youth workers' associations	Membership
Ghana	0	0
Kenya	0	0
Malawi	0	0
Nigeria	0	0
South Africa	1	1350
Tanzania	0	0
Uganda	0	0
Zambia	1	22

The South African Youth Workers' Association (SAYWA) was formally established and launched in 1998 by the Youth Practitioner's Advocacy Group (YPAG), following six years of advocacy and lobbying for recognition and professionalisation of youth work in South Africa. YPAG was made up of groups of both non-professional youth workers and professionals in the form of social workers, academics, researchers, nurses, teachers/educators, government officials, executives of non-governmental organisations including sports and recreation coaches.

SAYWA continues to revive the Association and the membership is approximately 1350. They are in the process of formalising the provincial as well as student chapters in some institutions of higher learning in South Africa. The membership drive is also to be extended to include community-based technical, vocational education and training colleges (TVET colleges). Activities so far have included

- Developing a contextual analysis of youth work practice,

- Developing a draft youth work policy that is under review,

- Involvement in the development, review and evaluation of the youth policy framework documents and other related policies that now include commitments to professionalise the youth work sector,

- Promoting best practices in working with young people through local and national consultations summits and other interventions,

- Championing the establishment of an oversight body to play an advisory role for the rollout of the B-Tech Diploma for child and youth care at selected universities in South Africa,

- Developing standard practice for the youth sector,

- Involvement in the review and development of the National Qualifications Framework (NQF) levels for youth and community development,

- Drafting a draft code of ethics in collaboration with the National Youth Development Agency (NYDA), provincial and national governments, and NGOs,

- Participating in the development of a draft Bill for the Youth Work Profession for consideration and endorsement by the National Assembly, Parliament.

The Zambia Youth Workers Association (ZYWA) was formed in September 2006 after the realisation of the potential for abuse in an unregulated profession. Some of the key organisations involved in the formation included the Ministry of Youth, the former Commonwealth Youth Programme Regional Centre, Africa, the National Youth Development Council, and a few individuals who constituted the Technical Working group.

The objectives of the association as articulated in its Constitution are:

- To promote, in the interest of youth development and empowerment, the fundamental principles of human rights and fundamental freedoms as enshrined in Articles 2–9 of the African Youth Charter.

- To advance the quality of youth work practice throughout Zambia.

Currently, the association has a membership of 30 on the national electronic register which was officially launched at the 4th General Assembly in November 2016 by the Director of Youth and Sport from the Ministry of Youth, Sport and Child Development. The need for a further membership drive is keenly felt by the Association's committee.

In consultation with relevant Ministry and other stake holders, ZYWA developed its constitution and Code of Ethics in line with national and international provisions including the directions set by the Commonwealth's Plan of Action for Youth Empowerment (PAYE). The Association also launched a report, *A state of Youth Work in Zambia* during its fourth General Assembly which elected the new executive committee in 2016.

In general in Africa, other member states are also appreciating the importance of a professional association and are moving towards organisation.

8.4.1 Asia

In Asia, Sri Lanka and Singapore report existing and operational youth workers' associations, and India indicated that there is a non-traditional association of a collective of practitioners advancing a specific asset-based model of youth work. Malaysia was working towards the establishment of a professional association as a result of commitments to youth work in the country's new youth policy.

India does not have a traditional youth workers' association. However, a group that has been working closely with youth work associations in the Commonwealth is ComMutiny – the Youth Collective (CYC), a group of youth-led organisations that work together to promote youth work processes and methodologies as articulated in the 5th Space previously mentioned – one of the best articulated practice methodologies for youth work in the global South that the baseline has been able to identify.

The development of youth work in Malaysia is at a critical stage. Structures are being put in place for youth worker development, given the political will to invest in the practice. This, together with initiatives such as plans for a professional youth work board that incorporates a number of youth work associations, indicates that the sector

Table 8.2 Number & membership of youth workers' associations – Asia

Country	Number of professional youth workers' associations	Membership
Bangladesh	0	0
India	1	25 (organisations)
Malaysia	1 (emerging)	unknown
Maldives	0	0
Pakistan	0	0
Singapore	1	154
Sri Lanka	1	33

is establishing itself as a profession. The working out of codes of ethics, monitoring and formalised professional development will advance this process.

Since 2011, a series of workshops have been conducted to develop an understanding of the concept of youth work and the functioning of the professional body. A dialogue was also initiated through the Commonwealth's former Asia Regional Centre in 2011, followed by the Commonwealth's support for consultations on competency standards.

Work is progressing in Malaysia on the development of a framework for professionalising youth work. This framework consists of definitions, roles and functions of practitioners in youth work and their professionals, branding, structure, occupational standards, training and education, management, accreditation and certification, as well as a governing Board on Youth Work. A number of specialised professional youth work associations cutting across practice, policy-making, research, teaching and extension will be established and incorporated as part of the structure in the overall framework. This is being done by a multi-stakeholder group as follows, whose plans also include the possible establishment of a professional governing body to monitor processes set by the framework:

- Ministry of Youth and Spots Malaysia (KBS)

- Department of Skills Development, Ministry of Human Resource, Malaysia (MOHR)

- Malaysia Youth Development Academy (Note: the academy is part of KBS)

- International Youth Centre (IYC) Malaysia (Note: KBS linked centre)

- Institute of Youth Research (IYRES) Malaysia (Note: The institute is part of KBS)

- Researchers from University Putra Malaysia (UPM)

- Other stakeholders categorised by the 10 implementer group

In Singapore, the Youth Work Association, Singapore (YWAS), registered since March 2012, was created as a result of ongoing debate for about four years on the distinct difference in competencies between social work practitioners and youth work practitioners. The YWAS was agreed upon following a week-long consultation amongst heads of youth agencies and youth work practitioners and was funded by the Singapore Workforce Development Agency.

The YWAS has a vision for 'a future in which youth work is regarded as a credible and celebrated profession'. Specifically, the association was established to:

- advocate for youth work

- set the benchmarks for quality youth work

- celebrate the joy of delivering youth work

- advance and promote the cause and development of youth work in Singapore.

The work of Singapore's Association includes:

- Promoting and participating in the education and training of those involved in the development, instruction, rehabilitation, support, mentoring, outreach, and care of youths and young people.

- Providing lectures, seminars and courses to contribute to the professional development of the membership.

- Engaging in the exchange of professional and technical knowledge and opinions through the conduct, sponsorship, or encouragement of research and publications, and through distribution of materials, including books papers and reports.

- Providing support for youth development initiatives in schools and the community via teacher/adult training, workshops, seminars and publications.

The YWAS is promoting, advocating for and facilitating the professionalisation and continuing professional development of youth workers in Singapore by:

- Supporting efforts aimed at raising public awareness and recognition of youth work as a profession.

- Maintaining a Youth Work Code of Professional Ethics for the guidance of the Association's members in terms of professional conduct.

- Representing to the relevant authorities and when necessary, the views of the youth workers.

- Facilitating the organisation of in-service training courses and other activities for the development of youth workers.

A challenge seems to be the relative disconnectedness of the professional body from the State youth sector.

In Sri Lanka, the Professional Youth Workers' Association (PYWA) was formally established in 2015 after three years of preparatory work supported by the Commonwealth with the former Ministry of Youth Affairs and Skills Development and diverse youth work practitioners and youth work delivery agencies. The association aims to empower and co-ordinate professional youth workers, based on universal policies, values and guidance through participatory development, continuing education, programme evaluation and monitoring strategies in order to develop a youth work community in Sri Lanka.[1] The Open University of Sri Lanka, and the former Ministry of Youth and Skills Development were critical players in this process.

The minimum requirement for full membership is the Diploma in Youth Development Work offered by the Open University of Sri Lanka, or on consideration by the Committee. Associate membership is permitted based on a competency assessment through PYWA's Core Competency Framework.

In 2016, the Association, with the support of the Commonwealth, and ComMutiny, the Youth Collective, India, developed a short course for youth work trainers and also worked towards the creation of a nationally led youth work training pool for 'just-in-time' training. The creation of the short course has been a clear demonstration of regional collaboration across youth work collectives. Integrating the training course to mainstreaming youth work mechanisms is being advocated by PYWA with the Ministry of Policy and Planning, now holding the youth portfolio.

8.4.2 The Caribbean

In the Commonwealth Caribbean region, Jamaica had an established youth workers' association.

The Jamaica Professional Youth Workers' Association (JPYWA) was launched in 2006 by a group of Youth Development Work Diploma graduates. The organisation very quickly began to respond to the critical need for knowledge and skills among grassroots youth workers and only pursued formalisation of the Association in 2014. The organisation has a strong non-government membership and partner base and works closely with the Government in providing technical support to its youth department. It was established in order to provide

- technical support in youth work and youth development to government and non-government entities,

- basic training for youth workers, and

- advocacy for the recognition and professionalisation of youth work

The association is in the process of developing an accredited training course (level unstipulated) aligned to competency standards, and is training assessors for accreditation with the support of the Commonwealth. It is currently developing a business plan in order to develop enterprise as a form of resource mobilisation to enhance its independence and advocacy capacity.

Table 8.3 Number/membership of youth work associations – the Caribbean

Country	Number of professional youth workers' associations	Membership
Barbados	0	0
Belize	0	0
Dominica	0	0
Guyana	0	0
Jamaica	1	100
St Lucia	0	0
St Vincent and the Grenadines	0	0
Trinidad and Tobago	0	0

8.4.3 Europe and Canada

In **Canada**, nine professional associations relating to child and youth care exist, but there are no associations specifically relating to youth workers (see definition of

Table 8.4 Number/membership of youth work associations – Europe and Canada

Country	Number of professional youth workers' associations	Membership
Canada	9	3700[2]
Cyprus	0	0
Malta	1	30
UK	2	Unknown

Canadian child and youth care above). These associations have a membership around 3700 practitioners.

Although primarily concerned with Provincial matters, there is networking between the associations through the Council of Canadian Child and Youth Care Workers Associations (CCYCW). Since 1986, the CCYCW has been the national networking organisation representing child and youth care professionals in Canada through their provincial associations. The council strives to promote the association movement throughout the nation and through them promote and encourage professional development, advocacy, recognition and networking for child and youth care.[3]

Collectively these provincial youth and childcare bodies can be said to have an appreciable impact on the shaping and development of practice in the child and youth care field.

In Malta, the Maltese Association of Youth Workers (MAY) is perhaps the most integrated and, in terms of being a national regulator of practice, the most influential professional association in the region, and perhaps the Commonwealth.

MAY was founded in September 1998. Soon after, a statute was set up and a code of ethics drafted. Both were approved at a public seminar. Lobbying for professional status commenced around this time. MAY became involved in various tasks within governmental and non-governmental organisations, which included the review of the National Youth Policy, work and training activities for youth workers.

MAY's objectives include marketing the concept of youth work and maintaining quality standards in the profession. The organisation was instrumental in making the Youth Work Profession Act a reality (see the case study in Box 7.2).

The United Kingdom

The idea of a professional association for youth workers has been around for many years in the UK, but it was not until the second decade of the twenty-first century that the National Youth Agency (NYA) initiated a professional membership group, the Institute for Youth Work (IYW); in June 2015 the Institute for Youth Work Council took over management of this body, with the purpose of providing a professional membership organisation for youth work, aiming to drive quality standards.

The IYW is currently working to promote itself and build the network, and to register as a professional body. Membership numbers were not available at the time of writing. However, anecdotally, while at county level there is some support (for instance Essex funds membership for all full-time youth workers) the membership remains, as a proportion of those employed in the field, relatively small, while the organisation is yet to have any influence at a policy-making level or as a gatekeeper to the occupation; it has yet to develop influence on practice or agency over the entry to, suspension or barring from practice. A strategy for a way forward was yet to be shared with the youth work sector at the time of writing.

In addition to the practitioner association, the IYW, the Professional Association of Lecturers in Youth and Community Work (TAG) is a member organisation that represents the interests of academics, educators and researchers in the field of youth and community work in the UK. The association supports and represents over 200 educators at more than 50 institutions and agencies in the UK. They seek to promote an informed understanding of youth and community work in the UK, and across the globe, through connecting membership through conferences, events and sector activity (TAG, n.d.).

Given the above it can be said that regionally in Europe and Canada the situation with regard to national youth worker associations is mixed:

- MAY in Malta is in an advanced position in terms of influence and guardianship of the profession.

- In Canada youth work as a profession has no traction. Associations devoted to child and youth care workers are province-based organisations, maintaining a considerable stake in the development and quality assurance of practice, and in places gatekeeping influence.

- In the UK, the development of a professional association remains at an embryonic stage.

- Cyprus currently has no youth workers' association.

8.4.4 The Pacific

In the Pacific, Australia has two relatively advanced and well-established state (as opposed to national) youth workers' associations in the form of the Youth Workers' Association (YWA) based in Victoria and the Youth Work Western Australia (YouthWorkWA). Both YWA and YouthWorkWA[4] have developed codes of ethics[5] (Corney and Hoiles, 2007). The Australian Youth Affairs Coalition (AYAC), a collective of state-based youth affairs peak bodies and youth work delivery organisations, continues to have an influence on the practice of youth work through its national definition (Corney, 2014, p. 10).

In New Zealand Ara Taiohi (meaning 'pathway to and from young people'), the national peak body for youth development, succeeded in establishing the Professional Association for Youth Development Workers in 2016. It is involved in

- national programme of capacity building and workforce development-youth development champions pathways for all

Table 8.5 Number/Membership of youth work associations – the Pacific

Country	Number of professional youth workers' associations	Membership
Australia	2	400 (YWA)
Fiji	0	0
New Zealand	2	242
Papua New Guinea	0	0
Samoa	0	0
Solomon Islands	1	0
Tonga	0	0
Vanuatu	0?	0

- sector development

- restorative justice at the centre

- self-determination for youth workers regarding the core competencies that define youth development practice

- national work with qualifications providers.

Box 8.1 tells the story of the Association for Youth Workers in Aotearoa (New Zealand)

Box 8.1 The birth of a new association for youth workers in Aotearoa (New Zealand)

By Anya Satyanand, Member

'Tuitui tangata, tuitui korowai' (You should approach the task of bringing a group of people together with the same level care you would employ in weaving a beautiful garment.)

A new step in a long history of youth work

Youth work in Aotearoa has a rich history, an exciting present and a strong future. In 2017, we celebrate the 20th anniversary of the first code of ethics, a significant milestone that the profession is marking by launching a professional association for youth workers.

The history of youth work in Aotearoa is long and proud, and has involved the contribution and leadership of many people, networks and organisations. Youth workers are currently working collectively to build an association that genuinely reflects the aspirations and needs of this very important part of the youth development ecosystem.

Building on the work of our parent organisation, the National Youth Workers Network Aotearoa, in 2016 Ara Taiohi (the peak body for youth development)

(continued)

(*continued*)

launched a pilot association and extended an open invitation to youth workers across the sector to participate in the design of the association. More than 240 youth workers have become founding members, more than six times the number we originally anticipated in a process that has been marked by the enthusiasm of people who have offered their insights, help and energy.

In te reo Māori (the Māori language), the word 'rangatiratanga' means leadership- literally the weaving of people together. The work of constructing this association has been like weaving many different perspectives, different voices, and using the skills of many people.

Why a Professional Association?

Youth workers form a critical part of the workforce needed to support positive youth development for our young people in Aotearoa New Zealand. This professional association will empower youth workers to determine the competencies and ethics that underpin their practice, and to have input into the systems that will enable the profession to grow and develop. We fundamentally believe that youth workers should define the competencies and philosophy that sit beneath the practice of youth work in Aotearoa, rather than a minister or ministry.

International evidence tells us that having a strong national voice on professional issues affecting youth workers is a critical part of a positive youth development ecosystem, along with good policy on young people and decent resourcing to the sector.

In 2017, youth workers working with young people across Aotearoa are more qualified than ever before, but despite this, rates of pay for paid youth workers have declined against the national average wage in the last 10 years. Law changes affecting youth workers and youth development organisations have had significant impacts on youth workers. Youth workers recognise the need for a strong voice to advocate and shape the learning area of youth work and qualifications that sit alongside these.

Philosophy and Models

The philosophy, models and practice of contemporary youth work in New Zealand has been influenced and shaped by Maori practices and knowledge, Pasifika cultures, recreation and outdoor education, and more recently positive youth development models which have been hugely influential in the new millennium.

Youth work in Aotearoa is diverse – from work in schools based on academic and adventure-based learning, to support for gender and sexuality diverse young people, through recreation and culturally based programmes through to church-based programmes and services. These wide-ranging contexts create richness, and despite the broadness of the spectrum, the common ground is a consistent commitment to positive youth development and ethical practice.

> Our Code of Ethics for Youth Workers is an inclusive framework which aspires to hold youth workers who work in a way that is ethical and focused on positive youth development in relationship.
>
> Whāia te iti kahurangi ki te tūohu koe me he maunga teitei 'Aim for excellence in everything you do: if you bow your head, let it be to a lofty mountain.'

The Canterbury Youth Workers Collective (a member group of the above national association) has established registration and compliance processes and a code of ethics.

In the Solomon Islands, moves towards the establishment of the Youth Workers' Association of the Solomon Islands (YWASI) was begun in 2012 and the Association is soon to be launched. The group active in its formation has spearheaded several activities such as engaging experts to assist in drafting a code of ethical practice, initiating youth worker exchange programmes (2013–2014) and lobbying government to establish National Youth Workers Awards (2015–2016) to recognise outstanding contributions by individual and organisations in youth work – a lobby that has succeeded, with the Ministry taking this on board. The most recent is the policy consultation (2016–2017) on the review of the National Youth Policy to include youth work.

8.5 The Commonwealth Alliance of Youth Workers' Associations (CAYWA)

A commitment to establish CAYWA was made by over 10 representatives of national associations and other youth work stakeholders during the 2015 Commonwealth Conference on Youth Work. The interim committee for the association was in the process of consulting globally on the Constitution at the time of writing. Generally, it aspires to be a global professional entity, along the lines of other Commonwealth professional bodies, that represents the interests of the profession and professionals in regional and global contexts of policy and dialogue.

8.6 Conclusion

The status and progress of national professional youth worker associations is mixed. One or two associations are in advanced positions in terms of influence and guardianship of the profession, maintaining a comparatively significant stake in the development and quality assurance of practice, and in places gatekeeping influence.

Elsewhere, the development of professional associations remains at an embryonic stage, often being little more than a title and a set of intentions.

Notes

1   Sr.9.1: Article of PYWA.
2   This membership is made up predominantly of child and youth care workers and counsellors; as outlined above this vocational group might not be understood to be youth workers as defined by the Commonwealth.

3 http://www.cyccanada.ca/
4 http://www.youthworkwa.org.au/site-content/Code-of-Ethics-Youth-Workers-WA.pdf
5 The Youth Workers Association, and Youth Workers, Western Australia. With no National Framework for Youth Workers, the Australian Youth Affairs Coalition has provided a discussion paper regarding the ethics and values of Youth Work as a profession. See Australian Youth Affairs Coalition (2014).

Chapter 9

Qualifications Pathways

9.1 Introduction

This chapter provides an overview of youth work practitioner education and training, from some of the most prominent short courses directly linked to developing the skills of youth development workers and youth workers, to accredited qualifications providing professional recognition. This is meant to be an indicative snapshot of the state of the potential for service development, delivery enhancement and quality maintenance, rather than exhaustive catalogue of learning/educational opportunities. Out of the sample, 25 countries (71 per cent) could claim at least a diploma-level qualification for youth work professionals, due in great part to the support provided through the Commonwealth for the establishment of the Commonwealth Diploma in Youth Development work within university structures more than two decades ago.

9.2 A qualifications pathway for youth workers from short courses to PhD

The offer with regard to youth work training and education is in a constant state of transition and flux. Programmes and training courses emerge, evolve, alter and cease to exist, reflecting the wants and needs of communities, nations and job markets. The following should thus be read with that in mind and be seen collectively as an indicator relating to the growth and position of youth work in any given context and across the Commonwealth.

Unlike social work and teaching in many contexts, youth work is undertaken worldwide across a variety of employment (and non-employment) situations (full-time, part-time, temporary, paid and voluntary) by people from a diversity of backgrounds, a variety of experience and qualifications (which can range from none at all to doctorate level).

There is no international consensus about pathways to qualification in youth work. Indeed, it is hard to identify a definite route in any country. However, this chapter is concerned with the state and circumstances of education and training towards professional qualification.

There is some international agreement about what it is to be a qualified doctor, lawyer, social worker, nurse, teacher, accountant and so on, and so in youth work. This allows qualification transfer and practice across national boundaries where this training and qualifications are recognised. Clearly, practice contexts require adaptations (and maybe further qualification) and cross-border protections of professional boundaries which are maintained by governments, unions and professional associations. Yet, practically, a qualified Ugandan nurse is likely to be able to function effectively in a Canadian hospital, having the foundational knowledge and attitudes requisite to nursing; an Indian lawyer might well be able operate at least adequately within the English (or Scottish) legal system. Shared professional contexts, while different, are rarely alien to qualified practitioners.

The Commonwealth Diploma in Youth Development Work, which has evidently (and quite powerfully) been deployed Commonwealth-wide for many years, is an example of a global qualification that has been adapted and delivered in varying contexts across Commonwealth member states. The legacy of the shared knowledge and understanding it has provided is evident in most contexts. The emerging Commonwealth-supported Degree in Youth Development Work delivered by the University of the West Indies, and soon to be administered worldwide through educational institutions, is a further indication of ongoing trends in such cross-border initiatives.

Having said that, it has been questioned if there is ever likely to be agreement across national boundaries in relation to qualifying as a professional youth worker. In this context, it becomes critical to ensure that qualifications, and the theories and practice underpinning them, serve context-specific needs.

9.3 What is a professional qualification?

Worldwide, there is no entirely agreed definition of what a professional qualification is. However, taking a broad international/cross-profession perspective, there are parameters for a professional qualification. For instance, it is generally taken to be a high level of vocational training. As such, a purely academic programme would not, for the most part, be appropriate, as there needs to be evidence of competence, which logically can only be attained through practice experience.

Qualification refers to passing examinations and/or assessment. Those qualifications conferring professional status usually also designate the professional with a range of qualities beside their general expertise. So, when an individual becomes professionally qualified, frequently following a course provided by and/or approved by a professional body, they are perceived to demonstrate their knowledge of the relevant subject matter, or 'body of knowledge' relevant to that profession. They are then examined on their ability to use this knowledge in a responsible and (for the client) useful way. As such their values, attitudes and moral fibre; in essence, their competence to practice, are underwritten by the professional qualification.

The profession's qualification marks and assures the acquisition of professional knowledge, conduct, and therefore status. Professional qualification often requires undergraduate-level study and assurance of vocational expertise at a similar level.

As such, professional qualification is a form of regulated education and training, directly geared to the practice of a profession. It comprises a training course or courses complemented by professional practice in an appropriate field and context, which usually includes probationary or professional practice requirements, the structure and level of which are largely determined or sanctioned by professional bodies/associations (Chapter 8) and sometimes employer and university representatives.

Universities, colleges and training providers often deliver courses approved by these bodies and in some cases university departments and staff themselves, maybe accredited/approved by the by the professional associations.

In some areas of work, for example in nursing and teaching, studying approved courses is understood generally to be essential and it is compulsory to register with a specific professional body if a licence to practice is required. With some professions, this licence is a self-regulatory measure of the profession. For others, it is a legislative requirement of government. Therefore, qualifications accredited by a professional body carry a stamp of approval and can have positive benefits for prospective professional employability.

The above notwithstanding, some professional qualifications may be obtained by other routes. For instance, they may be awarded after a number of years of practice, rather than through undertaking formalised training and/or study and passing of examination(s). An example is the Caribbean Competency Standards for Youth Development work, discussed in Box 9.1.

However, all credible and effective professional qualifications focus on developing the skills, intellectual capacity and judgement one needs to be effective in a specific industry, occupation or vocation/calling. Essentially, professional qualifications generally require on-the-job experience, and are, broadly speaking, awards for the achievement of vocational competence of a high level.

Box 9.1 Qualifying Through Practice – The Caribbean Competency Frameworks' Criteria

The Caribbean Competency Standards for Youth Development Work clearly denotes in its assessment criteria that 'the major consideration in any [competency] assessment process must be the attainment of the required standard of performance rather than how the competencies may have been acquired … Within the Youth Development Work sector there may be a number of learning pathways. These learning pathways encompass the formal training systems as well as knowledge and skills gained solely from workplace experience. The certifying body must be conscious of the multiple ways that persons have gained workplace competence and as a consequence, the assessment process should be non-discriminatory in acknowledging that competence.'[1]

The Competency Standards acknowledge the following forms of competency acquisition

a. Training

b. Workplace experience

c. Recognition of Prior Learning (RPL)

d. Recognition of Current Competency (RCC)

e. Related learning experiences

Many sectors have some sort of specific professional qualification. Lawyers, doctors and accountants study for professional qualifications. One can also gain professional qualifications in areas such as advertising, marketing, sport and banking. Often, people study while working full-time. As a result, many professional training courses are offered on a part-time basis or through distance learning.

9.4 A professional qualification in youth work

Given the above, what might a viable, robust, reliable and reputable professional qualification in youth work look like? It would differ significantly from academic programmes such as those titled 'youth studies' and so on, and would focus more on practice and the impact of practice on young people, similar to the impact of social work or teaching.

If it is taken that a professional youth work qualification might demand degree-level study (and certainly the oldest courses, and the ones with most distinction and reputation, have been embedded in undergraduate programmes for the last couple of decades), then it will need to have a significant field practice element and include those from the field in the design, development and process of the programme. See the example in Box 9.2.

Box 9.2 Youth work education and field engagement

By Dr Brian Belton
Senior Lecturer, Youth Work, YMCA George Williams College

The 'field component' in youth work training provides students with the opportunity to undertake practice and test theory in an appropriate placement; that is, a context that can provide exposure to 'real life' youth work, practice support, guidance, management and assessment, from (ideally) a professionally qualified and experienced practitioner.

Such situations offer student practitioners the potential not only to test theory, but to develop their own theory in the light of practice. In this way, theory becomes validated (or otherwise) by practice, while practice can become informed by theory, and give rise to further theory.

However, the crucial aspect of this exposure to fieldwork is the examination of the student's response; looking at how they exercise and develop their knowledge, skills and attitudes, and how they exercise and hone their professional judgement. A youth worker who is unable to operate without constant instruction, make swift, safe, and so efficient, judgements when managing clients, volunteers and other colleagues, cannot be said to be professional in any meaningful way. Given this, arguably, the only way the student can make the transformation from student practitioner to professional is within the crucible of the field.

(continued)

(*continued*)

At the YMCA College, such placements are part of 'continuous assessment' of the student. The line manager's report relating to the student's performance in the field is considered alongside their supervisor's assessment of learning (relating to their ability to review and examine their practice) and the tutor's assessment (which is concerned with 'in-college' performance and academic and group interaction). Finally, the student's self-assessment brings all of these elements together, providing a 360-degree view of the student as a developing professional.

Practice placements and ongoing assessment of this type are not unusual in many professional fields. Indeed, it is hard to understand how someone can be regarded as professional without being exposed to the judgement of practice peers (line managers and supervisors); professional qualification being synonymous with being adjudged to be fit to practice by one's fellow practitioners (not just remote academics). At the same time, someone who is not called on to make professional judgements as part of their training is going to be hard pushed to do it the first day out of school. In short, this person is left vulnerable because they are unprepared and not acclimatised to the trials of the practice situation.

At the YMCA College employers are also involved in examination boards, taking particular interest in the student's capacity to operate as a professional with young people on a day-to-day basis. One of the most common criticisms of newly qualified youth workers is that they often are unable to adapt to the practice situation (that is, they are qualified, but cannot do the job). Not unusually, this reflects a lack of ongoing assessment in and development via a significant field component. Currently at the YMCA College students are expected to undertake 360 hours of practice in each year of study.

Field practice assessment as described above was a strong component of the Commonwealth Diploma in Youth Development, and its function and processes are laid out in the Diploma's Tutor Manual.

Such qualifications have both academic and professional requirements; students need to pass assignments and exams as well as fulfil professional criteria premised on competencies broadly agreed on by experienced practitioners, employer representatives, and where possible, professional bodies. Exam boards may also include representatives from the field (employers and experienced professionals). Ideally, those teaching the academic side of things will themselves have a professional background in the field and be subject to ongoing professional development via training, helping to keep their knowledge up to date, and therefore relevant.

9.5 Accredited courses

A range of pre-graduate programmes and other accredited courses were detailed in the regional baseline surveys but these findings were not exhaustive. The survey focused specifically on the education and training of youth workers and not on general youth studies programmes. In some regions, the details of many apparently available courses were not accessible. At the same time, the number and range of options and variations, as well as differences of opinion within contexts about whether a particular course constitutes a youth work qualification, make the generation of a potential Commonwealth-wide directory of youth work qualifications an onerous task. Added to this, the recognition, shape and content of pre-graduate programmes internationally is in a constant state of flux. The recent 'Post-16 Skills Plan' is just one example from the UK context (Department for Business and Skills/Department for Education, 2016).

However, the regional surveys did identify a representative selection of such programmes and courses. These are included partly to provide a vista on the character and range of training and education available, but also to demonstrate the diverse understanding and opinions of what training and education for professional youth work looks like across the Commonwealth.

The Commonwealth Diploma in Youth Development Work is still independently delivered by some universities. As such, creating a pathway to progress towards a degree through the Commonwealth's Youth Work Qualifications Consortium was seen as a means of further increasing the quantity of practitioners and enhancing interest and enrolment. In many countries, the diploma has been discontinued or administrators were having difficulty maintaining enrolment and completion rates since the discontinuation of Commonwealth subsidies for delivery and tuition (which resulted in increased fee structures for the course in most universities). However, strategic planning and marketing, and adapting to local contexts, including addressing language needs, has enabled yet other universities to continue the course.

Figure 9.1 illustrates a generally high rate of qualifications from diploma and above in Africa, the Caribbean, Europe and Canada, with greater room for improvement in Asia and the Pacific. The Caribbean specifically benefits greatly from the University of the West Indies, the regional university for the Caribbean, offering both the diploma and degree in youth development work.

Figure 9.1 Regional trends - No. of countries with youth work education and training, Diploma and above

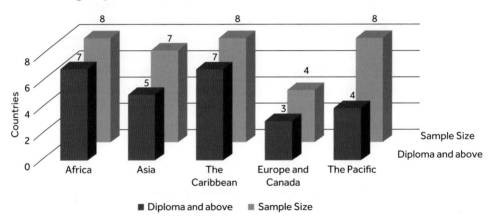

The following assessment attempts to distinguish youth development work/youth work courses from general, more academically oriented Youth Studies courses as far as is possible in a context where numerous courses in human science, youth development and youth work were reported. Other programmes, for example child and youth care (there are around 30 of these in Canada) have been included as they demonstrate education and training around a strength-based approach to engaging with youth, even though the focus is still youth at risk rather than all youth. All courses in this section are reported to carry credits.

Where courses were known not to be exclusively youth work courses, the specific name has been indicated as far as is possible.

9.5.1 Africa

In Africa, Diploma programmes are offered at the University of Ghana, the University of Nairobi, Kenya, Bunda College of Agriculture, Malawi, University of Abuja, Nigeria, The University of South Africa and Makarere University, Uganda. Certificate studies are delivered at the University of Nairobi, Kenya, and a Basic Technician Certificate in Youth Work is offered at Mwalimu Nyerere Memorial Academy, Tanzania. The Certificate and Diploma courses at Nairobi are offered in youth in development work and referred to as Adult Education, Community Development and Youth Work courses.

Most of the certificate and diploma courses in Africa are based on the Commonwealth Diploma in Youth Development Work, and are largely offered as distant learning courses. The curriculum has, in some cases, been revised and adapted to attract more students. The students are mainly individuals who have gained employment in the youth work sector, but without practice skills. Some challenges in maintaining enrolment rates were reported.

In Abuja, Nigeria, the course is the only accredited course with core content credits for youth development work. The course is not widely publicised and enrolment has dropped because it is no longer driven by subsidies from the Commonwealth which allowed for low or no student fees and therefore higher enrolment. Similar experiences have been shared by other countries such as Kenya.

South Africa has the most number of accredited courses in relation to youth development work.

The Basic Technician Certificate in Youth Work offered at the Mwalimu Nyerere Memorial Academy in Tanzania is mainly to equip students with skills in youth leadership, general knowledge of youth work in developing nations, attributes of mobilisation and organisation, and active participation in the political, socio-economic life of their country. The course is also meant to develop their management, communication and psychosocial skills.

In Zambia, the Certificate and Diploma in Youth Work being offered at King George College are not accredited yet. As noted in a recent report commissioned by the Zambia Youth Workers' Association (Zambia Youth Workers' Association, 2016 p. 6):

> This means that the country is not yet investing enough in youth work education and training, consequently the youth work has and continues to develop as a

Table 9.1 Accredited courses – Africa

University/Institution	Short	Certificate course	Diploma	BA	MA	PhD	Other
Ghana							
University of Ghana, Legon							
Kenya							
University of Nairobi		✓	✓				
Malawi							
Africa University of Guidance, Counselling & Youth Dev. (AUGCYD)					✓		
Bunda College of Agriculture			Youth & Dev				
Catholic University of Malawi				Youth Dev			
Nigeria							
University/Institution	Short	Certificate Course	Diploma	BA	MA	PhD	Other
University of Abuja			✓				
South Africa							
University/Institution	Short	Certificate Course	Diploma	BA	MA	PhD	Other
University of South Africa			✓				
University of Venda				✓			
Nelson Mandela Metropolitan University				✓			
Durban University of Technology				✓			
University of Stellenbosch							Theology specialise in Youth work / Youth Dev Course
Monash South Africa							
Tanzania							
University/Institution	Short	Certificate course	Diploma	BA	MA	PhD	Other
Mzumbe University							
Mwalimu Nyerere Memorial Academy MNMA		✓					
Open University of Tanzania			✓				
Uganda							
Makarere University			✓				
Zambia							
University/Institution	Short	Certificate course In process*	Diploma In process*	BA	MA	PhD	Other

*In the process of accreditation

voluntary practice rather than a professional field informed by the academic disciplines. This also means that the profession of youth work has no academicians to teach youth work and undertake research. Consequently, youth work tends to be generalised into other traditional disciplines (e.g. sociology, social work and education) rather than as a distinct programme with its own professional criteria.

None of the qualifications above have so far been recognised as a minimum entry to youth work practice, nor have competency frameworks been developed for assessing levels of qualification.[2]

9.5.2 Asia

The Diploma in Youth Development Work at the Bangladesh Open University (BOU) was initiated in collaboration with the Commonwealth Youth Programme.

In India, in addition to the above, it is apparent that non-youth work courses also include modules around working with youth such as the Bosco Institute of Social Work's Master of Social Work programme, which includes as reading a paper titled 'Working with Youth' as part of its specialisation.

The RGNIYD offers interdisciplinary doctoral programmes on youth studies which involve elements of youth work/youth engagement. Research has been broadly classified into the following areas: Youth Empowerment, Career Counselling, Gender Studies, Local Governance, Life Skills Education and Development Studies. All the areas suggested for research are interdisciplinary in nature.

In Malaysia, the Masters and PhD in Youth Studies offered in Universiti Putra Malaysia is largely a youth studies programme, but it has some components on youth work, i.e. international youth work, professional youth work, principles and practice of youth work, which are essentially postgraduate studies related to youth work. The Commonwealth Diploma in Youth in Development Work being currently run by Universiti Putra Malaysia (UPM) is the primary basic professional qualification in youth work. Besides Universiti Putra Malaysia, Universiti Malaysia Sabah also established the youth and community psychology academic programme both at Bachelor and Masters levels. This is the academic pathway.

However, another two qualifications pathways, i.e. TVET (technical, vocational education and training) and professional qualifications pathways are being proposed and under consideration. The TVET pathway will be more practice-based, the academic pathway will be more theoretical and concept-based, while the professional pathway will be a combination of both. Nonetheless, these pathways are not finalised yet, and are undergoing more detailed discussions at present.

In Pakistan, the Allama Iqbal Open University (AIOU) runs a postgraduate diploma based on the Commonwealth Diploma in Youth Development Work.

In Sri Lanka, the Commonwealth Diploma in Youth Development Work has been offered by the Open University of Sri Lanka (OUSL) since 1998. While it was initially taught only in English, since 2011 it has been offered in the local languages of Sinhala and Tamil. The modules of the diploma have also been translated into the two

Table 9.2 Accredited courses – Asia

University/Institution	Short	Certificate Course	Diploma	BA	MA	PhD	Other
Bangladesh							
Bangladesh Open University	-	-	✓	-	-	-	
University of Dhaka/ Development Studies, Population Science	-	-	-	✓	-	-	
India							
	Short	Certificate Course	Diploma	BA	MA	PhD	Other
Rajiv Gandhi National Institute of Youth Development,	-	✓	✓	BSc in Youth Work to be launched in 2017–18	MA Social Work (Youth and Community Development)	-	Interdisciplinary doctoral programmes with Youth studies/youth development work
Centre for Youth Development and Activities (CYDA) in collaboration with Tata Institute of Social Sciences (TISS), Mumbai	-		-	Diploma in Youth Development and Social Change–part time course	-	-	-
YUVA and Centre for Lifelong Learning, Tata Institute of Social Sciences, Mumbai	-		-	Diploma in Youth Development and Social Change	-	-	-

	Short Course	Certificate Course	Diploma	MA/PG Dip	PhD	Other
Samvada&Baduku Community College Regional (kannada)	–				–	Youth Work for Inclusive & Sustainable Development
Abhivyakti Media Centre in collaboration with TISS(Nashik)						Youth and Media
Pakistan						–
Bangladesh			✓			
Pakistan						
Allama Iqbal Open University (AIOU)				✓ (PGDip)		
Malaysia						
Universiti Putra Malaysia			✓	✓		
Universiti Malaysia Sabah			✓	✓		
Maldives						
To start a diploma-level youth workers course in 2017.						
Singapore						
No accredited courses for youth workers.						
Sri Lanka						
Open University of Sri Lanka			✓	Upcoming		

languages. Special attention is provided for the delivery of courses in the Northern and Eastern provinces of Sri Lanka, which were directly affected by the country's recently ended 30-year military conflict.

Since the withdrawal of the Commonwealth subsidies for tuition, the government has succeeded in creating full scholarships for youth workers with the support of UNICEF, and the National Youth Services Council, which enrols its youth service officers in the programme. Over 70 full scholarships have been awarded to NYSC staff, and youth parliament and youth club leaders (peer youth workers).

9.5.3 The Caribbean

The diploma delivered in the Caribbean is once again the Commonwealth Diploma in Youth Development Work. The BA is the Commonwealth-support Degree in Youth Development Work designed by the University of the West Indies for the Caribbean region.

Table 9.3 Accredited courses – Caribbean

University/ Institution	Short Course	Certificate	Diploma	BA	MA	PhD
Barbados						
UWI, Open Campus			✓	✓		
Belize						
UWI Open Campus			✓	✓		
Dominica						
UWI			✓	✓		
Guyana						
Jamaica						
UWI Open Campus			✓	✓		
St Lucia						
UWI Open Campus			✓	✓		
St Vincent and the Grenadines						
UWI Open Campus			✓	✓		
Trinidad and Tobago						
UWI Open Campus			✓	✓		

9.5.4 Europe and Canada

In Canada, child and youth care studies are provided by a broad range of universities, as illustrated in Table 9.4. Similarly, there is a broad and varied number of under- and postgraduate routes to qualification in the United Kingdom; a plethora (likely many dozens) of pre-graduate pathways (apprenticeships, level 1 to 3 and so on) that provide different levels of accreditation to practice. These include Youth Support Worker courses like the QCF Level 3 Certificate in Youth Work Practice and QCF Level 2 Certificate in Youth Work Practice that are designed for those working in a supporting role to professionally qualified workers (often this is not an individual's

Table 9.4 Accredited courses – Europe and Canada

University/Institution	Short	Certificate Course	Diploma	BA	MA	PhD
Canada						
University of Victoria				✓	✓	✓
Vancouver Island University			✓	✓		
Douglas College			✓	✓		
University of the Fraser Valley				✓		
Selkirk College			✓			
Grant McEwan University				✓		
Lethbridge College			✓			
Mount Royal University				✓		
Red River College			✓			
Ryerson University				✓	✓	
Humber College			✓	✓		
George Brown College			✓			
Algonquin College			✓	✓		
Centennial College			✓			
Cambrian College			✓			
Confederation College			✓			
Durham College			✓			
Fanshawe College			✓			
Georgian College			✓			
Lambton College			✓			
Loyalist College			✓			
Niagara College			✓			
Sault			✓			
Seneca			✓			
Mohawk College			✓			
Sheridan College			✓			
St Clair College			✓			
St Lawrence College			✓			
Fleming College			✓			
Brock University Child & Youth Studies with CYCW option				✓	✓	
Trent University Child & Youth Studies				✓		
Nipissing University				✓		
Concordia University					✓	
Oulton College			✓			
Nova Scotia Community College			✓			
Mount Saint Vincent University Child & Youth Studies				✓		

(continued)

Table 9.4 Accredited courses: Europe and Canada (*continued*)

University/Institution	Short	Certificate Course	Diploma	BA	MA	PhD
Keyin College (private institution)			✓			
Holland College (private institution)			✓			
Malta						
University of Malta				✓	✓	
UK						
Anglia Ruskin University				✓	✓PG.Dip	
Bradford College				✓		
Cardiff Metropolitan University,				✓	✓	
Centre for Youth Ministry				✓	✓	
Coventry University				✓		
Cumbria University				✓	✓Grad.Dip	
Durham University					✓	
Edgehill University					✓	
Edinburgh Napier University				✓	✓	
Glyndwr University				✓	✓	
Goldsmiths College, University of London				✓	✓	✓
Greenwich University				✓		
Leeds Beckett				✓	✓PG.Dip	
Liverpool Hope University					✓	
London Metropolitan University				✓		
Manchester Metropolitan University				✓		
Middlesex University				✓		
Moorlands College				✓	✓PG.Dip	
Nazarene Theological College				✓		
Newman University				✓	✓	
Oasis College of Higher Education				✓	✓Grad.Dip.	
Open University				✓		
Open University Scotland				✓	✓PG Dip	
Ruskin College				✓		
Sheffield Hallam University				✓	✓Grad.Dip.	
St Helens College				✓		

(*continued*)

Table 9.4 Accredited courses: Europe and Canada (*continued*)

University/Institution	Short	Certificate Course	Diploma	BA	MA	PhD
Teesside University				✔ (BSc)		
Ulster University				✔ (BSc)		
University College Plymouth St Mark and St John				✔	PG.	
University College Birmingham				✔	✔	
University of Aberdeen				✔	✔PG.Dip	
University of Bedfordshire				✔		
University of Bolton			✔			
University of Brighton			✔			
University of Chester			✔			
University of Derby			✔			
University of Dundee			✔		✔ (MSc)	
University of East London			✔	✔		
University of Edinburgh			✔		✔ (MEd.)	
University of Gloucestershire			✔	✔		
University of Huddersfield			✔	PG.Dip		
University of Hull			✔	Yes		
University of Northampton				Yes		
University of Manchester			✔			
University of South Wales			✔	PG.Dip		
University of Sunderland				✔		
University of West of Scotland			✔	✔ (MSc)		
University of Wales Trinity Saint David			✔	✔		
University of Worcester			✔			
York St John University			✔			
YMCA George Williams College	✔	✔	✔	✔	✔	

main career and they may do this work in the evenings in addition to their main job). In Wales, the Agored Cymru level 2 & 3 qualifications are used by many local authorities. Higher National Certificates (HNC) and Professional Development Awards (PDA) are also available. See also for example the OCN Northern Ireland specifications for various relevant qualifications at Open College Network Northern Ireland (OCN NI), 2015.

The number and range of these certificates and professional development awards are too extensive to list here, but some examples are provided below. Most of these can be found on the National Youth Agency website: http://www.nya.org.uk/careers-youth-work/getting-qualified/. To give an example, in the Oasis College Offer a level 2 certificate and level 3 diploma, the Certificate of Credit in 'Youth Work Practice' looks at the principles, purpose and values of youth work, the role of the youth worker, informal learning and the promotion of equality, and also involves modules on reflective practice. The course is taught over three days and requires 40 hours of youth work practice. In another example, Northern Highland College delivers a certificate programme (Youth Work SVQ2). This is a practice-based qualification, and assessment takes place in the workplace using a portfolio. This course is a requirement for employed youth support workers and takes up to one year to complete. The course 'is based on standards developed collaboratively by the Scottish Social Services Council (SSSC), TOPSS (England), Skills for Care, Care Council for Wales, the Northern Ireland Care Council and Skills for Health'.

In the **United Kingdom** and **Malta** an undergraduate degree or postgraduate diploma/degree are usually considered the standard required for professional qualification. There are no professionally qualifying courses available in Cyprus.

The UK list was compiled via the most recent data from the National Youth Agency, the Youth Council for Northern Ireland, Community Learning and Development, Scotland and Education Training Standards, Wales.

It should be noted that in Scotland, what is broadly recognised as youth work in the rest of the UK is referred to as 'community learning and development'.

9.5.5 The Pacific

In the Pacific, the Commonwealth Diploma in Youth Development Work was previously offered across the Pacific and is currently being offered by the Solomon Islands National University, and Divine University in PNG. The National University of Samoa and the University of the South Pacific were reported to be enrolling around 2010. Some Pacific universities also offer modules of the diploma as part of other development courses. The Australian Pacific Technical College, funded by Australian aid, delivers the cert 4 in Youth Work in Fiji, PNG, Samoa, Solomon Islands, Tonga and Vanuatu; this qualification is also a pathway to the Diploma.

The Youth Workers' Association (YWA) Australia has developed a framework to endorse courses for professional validation, which has already been undertaken by the Victoria University youth work degree (Annexures 5–7). With reference to international recognition and validation, the Victoria University course has also been recognised by England's Youth Work Institute.

9.6 Short courses (usually non-accredited)

Non-accredited courses are problematic in terms of tracking and development, basically because they are unaccredited. However, some non-accredited courses

Table 9.5 Accredited courses – the Pacific

University/Institution	Short	Certificate Course	Diploma	BA	MA	PhD
Australia						
Victoria University (Footscray)		Cert IV			✓	✓
Royal Melbourne Institute of Technology (Melbourne)		Cert IV	✓	✓ Bachelor Social Science (YW)	✓	✓
Australian Catholic University (Melbourne)			✓		✓	✓
Edith Cowan University (Perth)				✓	✓	✓
Tabor College (Adelaide)				Bachelor Social Science (YW)		
TAFE colleges nationally		✓		Diploma in Youth Work		
Fiji						
Australian Pacific Technical College		✓				
New Zealand						
Weltec				✓		
Unitec				✓		
Workforce Development		✓	✓			
Praxis		✓	✓			
Careerforce		✓	✓			
Auckland University of Technology			✓		✓	
Papua New Guinea						
Divine University			✓			
Australian Pacific Technical College		✓				
Samoa						
Australian Pacific Technical College		✓				
Solomon Islands						
National University			✓			
Australian Pacific Technical College		✓				
Tonga						
Australian Pacific Technical College		✓				
Vanuatu						
Australian Pacific Technical College		✓				

are tied to competency assessment (for example, the outcomes framework in India associated with the 'Ocean in a Drop training'). For all this, the reports, claims and impressions about the reliability, validity, viability and existence of many non-accredited courses differ. At the same time, the appropriateness, content, quality and scope of such courses vary considerably. However, some of the more distinctive and robust of such programmes were identified by the baseline surveys.

While there are non-accredited courses that are still seen as viable for competency building in the global South, and are indeed doing remarkable work in enhancing the skills of youth workers, in Canada and the UK, for example, courses are not considered viable unless they are accredited. All courses in the latter case have to be aligned to qualifications and credit frameworks – more details of this is provided in the charts themselves.

While these courses are not designed to offer entry into the profession per se, they support the development of a minimum set of competencies for youth workers, such as in India, Sri Lanka and other similar contexts. In Sri Lanka, the short course recently developed by the Professional Youth Workers' Association, for example, is meant to enhance youth engagement skills and is broadly seen as a complement to the Diploma.

In fact, many professional associations have noted that if professionalising initiatives are to make a significant mark on youth work, and by extension on the lives of young people, then they must place a greater focus on 'just-in-time' continual learning and recognise the capacity needs of youth workers, including those in the diverse forms of voluntary youth work.

The following descriptions of short non-accredited courses are meant to be indicative, and are not comprehensive. The focus is on courses that primarily cater for youth workers. While many theme-based courses that cater for youth workers among a multitude of other trainees were highlighted in the surveys, these have not been included here.

9.6.1 Africa

In a Pan-African context, the Centre for Youth Development Services (C4YDS) offers a Professional Certificate in Youth Development Practice (PCYDP) with modules offered in partnership with the University of Minnesota, Extension Centre for Youth Development (USA), the College of Community and Organisation Development (CCOD) in Ghana, and the Youth Interventions Programmes Association (YIPA) in the USA. This is a seven-month online training course offering professional certifications to youth development practitioners (Zambia Youth Workers Association, 2016, p. 6).

In Zambia, the Certificate and Diploma in Youth Work being offered at King George College are accredited yet not. This issue is on the agenda of the Zambia Youth Workers Association (ZYWA).

Table 9.6 Non-accredited courses – Africa

Country	Name of course and target trainees (youth workers, youth work managers, policy-makers, etc.)	Training institute
Pan-African	Professional Certificate in Youth Development Practice (PCYDP)	Centre for Youth Development Services (C4YDS)
Ghana	No information	No information
Kenya	Youth Leadership, Entrepreneurship (tailor-made workshop at request of youth workers)	University of Nairobi
Malawi	Youth Inclusion & Engagement including for youth workers	National Youth Council
	Advocacy, Monitoring & Evaluation including for youth workers	Malawi Institute of Management
	Leadership, Resource mobilisation & Project management including for youth workers	Exploits University
	Youth leadership for youth and youth workers	Africa University of Guidance, Counselling & Youth Development (AUGCYD)
	Social entrepreneurship for youth, including for youth workers	
	Guidance & counselling for youth, including for youth workers	
Nigeria	No information	No information
Tanzania	Empowering Youth Workers on Youth Entrepreneurship Promotion (TOTs).	Eastern and Southern Africa Management Institute
	A sustainable management of National Youth Development Loan Fund	National Micro Finance Bank, NMB
South Africa	Theology and Youth Work course	University of Stellenbosch
Uganda	No information	No information
Zambia	No information	No information
	Certificate & Diploma in Youth development Work for youth workers	King George College

In South Africa, the University of Stellenbosch offers a Theology and Youth work course which is not accredited. Although this is applied in youth work in the faith-based agencies, it can also be applicable in secular agencies. However, the fact that it is offered at an institution of higher learning makes it visible to potential and practising youth workers.

9.6.2 Asia

Table 9.7 Non-accredited courses – Asia

Country	Name of course and target trainees (youth workers, youth work managers, policy-makers etc.)	Training Institute
Bangladesh	Several training courses-Youth workers' training & motivation, youth organisations' development training, etc.	Sheikh Hasina National Youth Centre
	The UN Youth Advisory Panel members are provided several trainings	The Secretariat, UN Theme Group on A&Y
	Training for government youth officers	Central Human Resource Development Centre (CHRDC)
India	**1: A one-month comprehensive, responsive and customised capacity-building programme** for UNV volunteers, National Service Scheme (NSS) programme officers and NYKS programme officers working with youth clubs, universities and college youth collective structures. This is also being converted into a training manual.	RGNIYD in partnership with VSO/UNDP India
	2: 10-day professional development programme for NYKS officers.	RGNIYD in partnership with VSO/UNDP India
	3: Ocean in a Drop: A learning journey varying from 10 days to six months for youth workers/youth facilitators. The course content includes four themes: systems thinking, deep self-awareness, youth development, instruction design and facilitation skills. Nearly 2,000 youth facilitators have been trained through this programme. Youth development organisations, both national and international and government and private sector organisations have also accessed this training.	Pravah

(continued)

Table 9.7 Non-accredited courses – Asia (*continued*)

Country	Name of course and target trainees (youth workers, youth work managers, policy-makers etc.)	Training Institute
	2. Re-Strategising Teen Clubs under Adolescent Health and Development Project: This is an APV (Adolescent Peer Educator/peer youth worker) programme. Since 2007, UNFPA has been partnering with NYKS to implement a programme with adolescents by creating spaces/processes where they can build their capacities and take leadership and responsibility. As part of the re-strategisation, 1,860 Teen Clubs were supported with peer educator training.	Pravah
	3. SMILE Youth Facilitators training – Student Mobilisation Initiative for Learning Through Exposure. SMILE is a programme that supports youth development. Over 100 young leaders emerge from this journey every year, of which 30-50 are trained to be youth facilitators of the next journey as they graduate.	Pravah
	Change Looms-Learning and Leadership Journey is a leadership support program that encourages, recognises and supports young change leaders who have started social change initiatives with a focus on youth development. The programme offers opportunities for intensive personal and organisational development and has created a large community of youth-led organisation and youth workers in the country.	Pravah
	Youth Leadership Building Course and Youth in Media course. It covers topics similar to the TISS course, but in a more experiential and less academic manner. Conducted in Hindi and Marathi. Can be for youth workers as well.	YUVA (Youth for Voluntary Action) and Anubhav Shiksha Kendra(ASK)
	Short courses for youth workers	Vishva Yuva Kendra
Malaysia	Preparatory service course for officers of the Ministry of Youth and Sports Malaysia	Malaysian Youth Development Academy

(*continued*)

Table 9.7 Non-accredited courses – Asia (*continued*)

Country	Name of course and target trainees (youth workers, youth work managers, policy-makers etc.)	Training Institute
Maldives	Advanced level courses were conducted by Ministry of Youth and Sports	
Singapore	Currently, apart from the Singapore Workforce Skills Qualification (WSQ) certification, there is no comprehensive training programme that prepares individuals to serve as youth work practitioners, other than for those working with youth at risk, which are run by the Workforce Development Agency (WDA) and Social Service Institute (SSI). These include • Collaborative Skills for Effective Youth Programmes • Delivering Impactful Training to Youth • Engaging Reluctant Adolescents Effectively • Engage Youth-At-Risk through Effective Outreach Programme • Engaging Youth-At-Risk through Effective Strategies and Techniques • Helping Youths Cope with Anger • Working with Youths on Sexuality Issues	Social Service Institute
	Short Youth Work Supervision Training A five-day foundation training programme conducted by the Youth Workers' Association, Singapore (YWAS). The course prerequisite is minimum three years of practice in youth work. It covers the following: • Understanding the Singapore youth work context for Supervision, Coaching and Mentoring. • Relationship building and contracting • Skills and interventions in Supervision • Developmental Stages in Supervision • Ethics and Values in Supervision • Strengths-Based Peer Group Supervision • Dealing with unconscious elements and dynamics in Supervision (including the drama triangle, Parallel process and Transference/Counter-transference). • Reflective Practice • Review and Evaluation in Supervision • Mentoring and Coaching tools for professional practice	Youth Workers Association Singapore (YWAS) with Children-at-Risk Empowerment Association (CARE), Singapore.

(*continued*)

Table 9.7 Non-accredited courses – Asia (*continued*)

Country	Name of course and target trainees (youth workers, youth work managers, policy-makers etc.)	Training Institute
Sri Lanka	**Ocean in a Drop** (Professional Youth Workers' Association, Sri Lanka, 2016), based on India's 5th Space Training, in collaboration with the Commonwealth, ComMutiny, the Youth Collective, and Pravah to build core youth engagement competencies of field-based youth workers.	Professional Youth Workers' Association (Sri Lanka)
Pakistan	Multiple theme-based courses on peace and tolerance, human rights and youth engagement were identified run by Centre for Human Rights Education, Centre for Civic Education, Community World Services Asia, National Commission on Human Development, Channan Development Trust, Centre for Peace and Development Initiatives, Individual Land Pakistan, School of Leadership Pakistan, Oxfam Novib Pakistan, Youth Parliament of Pakistan and UNFPA. The extent of training in youth work approaches within these courses needs to be further studied.	

9.6.3 The Caribbean

Table 9.8 Non-accredited courses – Caribbean

Country	Name of course and target trainees (youth workers, youth work managers, policy-makers, etc.)	Training institute
Belize	A leadership manual and a manual for enterprise development exists which supports the (non-accredited) training of many, including youth workers.	CUSO International Department of Youth Services (DYS).
Guyana	Youth Participation and Involvement	Department of Culture, Youth and Sport
Dominica	Multi-Disciplinary Leadership Course (six months) targeting youth workers, youth leaders & community leaders. Basic and Advanced Counselling Seminars targeting youth workers, youth leaders and community leaders.	Youth Development Division

(*continued*)

Table 9.8 Non-accredited courses – Caribbean (*continued*)

Country	Name of course and target trainees (youth workers, youth work managers, policy-makers, etc.)	Training institute
Jamaica	Youth Focus Facilitation/Basic Youth Development Work	Jamaica Professional Youth Workers Association
St Vincent and the Grenadines	No clear evidence of training for youth workers to enhance youth work skills.	
Trinidad and Tobago	No clear evidence of training for youth workers on youth work skills.	–
	Some preventative work, but clarity of strengthening youth work through these not clear.	Ministry of Sport and Youth affairs RAPP – PAN American Foundation

9.6.4 Europe

Table 9.9 Non-accredited courses – Europe

Country	Name of course and target trainees	Training institute
Cyprus	Youth Worker Development (youth workers/ youth trainers)	Cyprus Youth Council
	SOHO – European Training Course for EVS Support People International training course (SOHO: Sending Organisation-Hosting Organisation EVS: European Voluntary Service)	National Agency for Erasmus+ Cyprus (Youth Board of Cyprus)
	Empowerment of the Members of the Boards of the Youth Clubs of Cyprus (some youth workers)	Cyprus Youth Clubs Organisation
Canada	Most courses delivered within Canada need accreditation to be viable.	
UK	The reputation of the Qualifications and Credit Framework (QCF) has meant that most courses delivered within the United Kingdom need to be accredited to be viable. The framework provides a standardised alignment of qualifications.	The register is managed by Ofqual (a government organisation) and can be found at http://register.ofqual.gov.uk/.

9.6.5 The Pacific

Table 9.10 Non-accredited courses – Pacific

Country	Name of course and target trainees (youth workers, youth work managers, policy-makers etc.)	Training Institute with address, email and phone numbers
Australia	There are a large range of various short courses delivered by youth NGOs across Australia. Such as: Youth Mental Health First Aid	Nation Not for Profit Mental Health First Aid (NFP MHFA)
Fiji	No information	No information
New Zealand	MentorPlus Mentoring Matters	New Zealand Youth Mentoring Network
	Code of Ethics Basic Training Ethical Champions	Ara Taiohi
	Supervision	The Project Team
Papua New Guinea	No information	No information
Samoa	No information	No information
Solomon Islands	No information	No information
Tonga	No information	No information
Vanuatu	No information	No information

9.7 Qualifications and competencies of teachers of youth work

In a number of contexts, youth work programmes are taught as interdisciplinary programmes and faculty often comprises those from other related disciplines such as sociology/psychology, etc., with very few of the teachers themselves having youth work qualifications. This is the reality of an emerging academic discipline in many parts of the Commonwealth that is still making a mark in academia, particularly in the global South. While it is unsure what proportions of academic staff teaching on youth work courses have a background or training in youth work, it seems that the lack of developmental training or specific education in relation to teaching roles is widespread.

Part of the comprehensive support provided to member states during the full implementation of the Commonwealth Diploma in Youth Development Work under the direct aegis of the Commonwealth was the provision of tutor training support and external regional moderation which provided youth work teachers with teaching assessment support and updated resources relating to the teaching of youth work. This process has been abandoned in most cases, barring a few exceptions.

Teacher training for teaching youth work and related to the field was practically absent in the present context except for evidence of induction programmes in developing a theoretical base, skills development and supervision in South Africa, training of supervisors in Singapore, and the continuation of the tutor training model established by the Commonwealth in Sri Lanka.

In Europe and Canada, further education (pre-graduate) courses generally demand that teachers are teacher trained; however, while this is desirable at higher education (under- and postgraduate) level, it is not as a general principle demanded, as experience in the field or related fields is often seen to compensate. There are many hundreds of in-service-training options in Canada and the UK but few specifically for those involved in training professional practitioners.

Australia identified specific training pertaining to Technical and Further Education (Cert IV – Technical and Further Education (TAFE) (Training and Assessing) University Level – Masters or PhD.[3] Additionally, the Youth Workers' Association endorsement of training courses requires that they have teaching staff who are qualified in youth work at minimum degree level and are full members of the professional association.

9.8 Practice assessment

As outlined above, a professional qualification has a vocational focus, therefore students are usually required to undergo continuous practice assessment throughout their studies. Part-time students might well be employed in the field as unqualified practitioners and will often use their employment to fulfil practice requirements. Full-time students will more typically use placements in the practice field for the same purpose. These placements will need to be quality assured to make sure they are able to offer a practice environment that can accommodate the professional requirements of any given programme; the practitioner will need to be able to use the placement to demonstrate that they have appropriate professional expertise. Therefore, an under-11s football club or a Sunday School (for example) is unlikely to have this type of scope.

There is a range of ways practice can be assessed but all involve producing **evidence** of practitioner learning from practice:

- students' work can be observed at regular intervals and reports generated

- students can explore and share their practice with study peers and course tutors

- placement- or employment-based line managers might write reports

- supervisors working with students might write assessments of the student's learning in practice

- students can write self-assessments of their learning.

The most respected professional training will include several or all of the above. However, without any continuous assessment of practice, which generally demands evidence of hundreds of hours (not unusually between 200 and 400) of practice over

Figure 9.2 The assessment of professional qualification

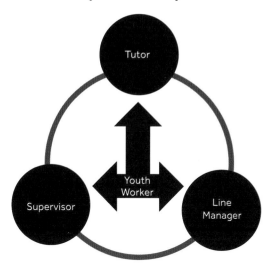

an academic year, it is hard to see how any programme can be understood to be a professional qualification.

While there are a number of variations, a number of assessments (independently produced and presented) can provide a 360-degree perspective of evidence of appropriate professional learning and development:

- The tutor assessment, which might be based on seminar/tutorial discussions of practice, including case studies

- The supervisor assessment, which could be made up of evidence, drawn from the practice situation, gleaned from a number of one-hour supervision sessions (usually 8 to 12) over an academic year

- The line manager's assessment, based on evidence from the practitioner's day-to-day practice

- The practitioner's self-assessment, which presents evidence from all aspects of the programme and effectively makes the case for their advancement on the programme or graduation.

Figure 9.2 illustrates the relationship of tutor, line manager and supervisor in enhancing youth work.

The only individual in this framework to see all the evidence is the practitioner (the exam board will of course also be privy to all the assessments).

While practice assessment was not surveyed in the baseline, anecdotal evidence indicates that practice assessment exists, even though its quality across regions and universities may vary.

9.9 Conclusion

Across the Commonwealth, there are a vast number of accredited and unaccredited qualifications directly or indirectly relating to youth work. At the same time, governmental requirements for recognition as a youth worker range from none at all to undergraduate qualifications.

While there is a broad and diverse number of pre-graduate pathways (from apprenticeships, to undergraduate certificates and diplomas), not all of them provide accreditation to practice.

9.9.1 Undergraduate programmes

The generation of a general perspective on undergraduate programmes presents a challenge and the data above attempted to cover what was evidenced.

Of course, employment opportunities impact on the demand for programmes of study; if there is insufficient demand, colleges and universities may choose to suspend or scrap programmes. Austerity economics in a number of national contexts has seen the demise of many youth work qualifying programmes, while some universities have altered their offer, developing variations such as 'youth work studies' and 'child and youth development' – sometimes without the continuous assessment of practice that is often a prerequisite for professional qualification.

However, it is unclear how many of the courses included in the figures above might reflect professional standards as outlined above. The regional baseline surveys did not include details of programme requirements, staffing, safeguarding and vetting procedures or details of the presence or otherwise of continuous practice assessment (for instance). Anecdotally, at least some programmes are little more than academic courses, in the main staffed by academics with little or no background in youth work. Professional status is sometimes granted on the basis of little more than a paper exercise, while supervision is largely underutilised and/or not altogether understood.

In the past, the Commonwealth Diploma in Youth Development work had rigorous guidelines relating to practice assessment, which were part of the training of tutors. However, this support is no longer provided, and there is little evidence that all universities maintain the same rigour in terms of practice assessment and so on. It seems that organisational funding constraints and general austerity have meant that a lot of this attention to detail has been lost in the delivery of qualifications.

This said, the cost of running a bespoke professional course is necessarily high (relative to, say, a straightforward academic programme). Supervisor time and training is costly, as is the finding and maintaining of placements. Academic courses need to be augmented with professional input and review, which has administrative and other on-costs.

Given that youth work is largely unrecognised in more than a few national contexts, certainly with regard to professional status, occupational rewards might not be comparable to other recognised professional occupations, both in terms of salaries and secure employment. Even in contexts where youth work is well established, employment in the field is hard to find. By and large youth work is seen as a 'non-essential' service and as such is among the first sectors to be dispensed with in times of austerity.

9.9.2 Postgraduate studies

The regional baseline surveys revealed two coursework Masters programmes outside of the European region. In the European region there are 33 qualifying postgraduate routes available, 32 in the UK, one at the University of Malta and one at Concordia, Canada.

Doctrinal studies are available in the UK; for example Goldsmiths University offers an MPhil that can lead to a PhD in Community & Youth Work. This course is based on a research project. Candidates are assessed on a thesis and viva voce (oral assessment). Cardiff Metropolitan University offer a postgraduate diploma in Youth and Community Work. This is designed for people working in youth work, who wish to gain a professional qualification. Two separate placements are required. The core modules are the Principles and Practice of Youth and Community Work, Management in the Youth and Community Sector, The Community Context of Practice, The Social Context of Practice. Informal lectures and small-group discussions are the main method of teaching, as well as self-study. This is a two-year part-time programme.

The Africa University of Guidance, Counselling & Youth Development (AUGCYD) Malawi has recently applied to the Commission for Universities in Malawi to have its doctoral degree on Youth Development Work accredited, upon which they will start offering the course.

Higher degrees might provide opportunities to develop advanced critical thinking and engagement and research/advocacy skills. They can also be helpful to those who have not gained professional recognition at undergraduate level and may improve prospects and mobility in terms of promotion and the job market.

Relatively few universities will offer doctoral studies in youth work, although it could be a subject area within a humanities or education department if an appropriate supervisor could be identified.

However, for those with non-qualifying degrees, coming from purely academic undergraduate backgrounds, postgraduate study can be a relatively swift and cost-effective route to professional qualification.

Notes

1 Commonwealth Youth Programme Caribbean Centre, 2012.
2 In all cases, where the title of the degree indicates an interdisciplinary or combined course, the full names are stated.
3 Minimum qualification that must co-exist with youth work experience and training to teach into the Certificate and Diploma Youth Work Course.

Chapter 10

Regulating Practice

10.1 Introduction

This chapter seeks to outline the measures in place to regulate youth work practice through assuring practitioner competencies and ethical conduct. It looks at how far youth work is regulated through competency/occupational standards, State/national ethical standards, State/national guidelines, and occupational health and safety standards. Additionally, it considers the existence of youth safeguarding guidelines, criminal history vetting and identification/licensing of youth workers.

These regulatory practices are vital for maintaining the quality of youth work, and are a foundational investment that society makes to ensure the accountability of youth work to young people.

10.2 Regulatory processes in youth work

Youth work, like any service impacting on the young and/or vulnerable, requires competency and ethical underpinning that at best is embedded in national policy and human rights. This section discusses areas relevant to regulation because they represent the foundational investment that society makes in youth workers; they are entrusted with the welfare of other people's children. Arguably, the extent to which society ensures safe and effective youth work is equal to the degree to which it has accepted youth work as an indelible element of social care, welfare, youth development and learning, but also the means by which young people might become wholly part of their communities and net contributors to their nations and the wider global culture.

This section looks at the specific criteria below:

1. **Occupational standards for youth work:** Identified and endorsed competencies for youth work practice that are applied practically in framing youth worker education and training and in youth worker competency assessment. Standards generally refer to what is expected of practice.

2. **Competency frameworks:** Refers more specifically to the practitioner's competencies, and therefore focuses more on the practitioner, as opposed to occupational standards, which refer to what is expected of practice.

3. **State/national ethical standards for youth work:** A set of values that drive youth work practice. In the baseline, we have tried to assess the existence of either State ethical standards, or widely endorsed ethical standards (nationally/regionally) where State standards do not exist.

4. **State guidelines for youth work:** Written and endorsed procedural guidelines for the implementation of youth work – these often come in generic form or in the form of guidelines for implementing youth clubs, national youth councils, youth federations, etc. Youth work guidelines, however, need to clearly indicate youth engagement processes and not be limited to programmatic guidelines.

5. **Youth safeguarding guidelines:** A policy that guides youth workers on the protection, safety and security of young people in youth work spaces. This is sometimes included in ethical standards, and is sometimes a standalone document.

6. **Occupational health and safety standards**: A policy that ensures the health and safety of youth workers while on duty.

7. **Criminal history vetting:** Official recruitment guidelines and their implementation for youth workers or those working closely with children and young people that require criminal vetting particularly for child abuse, sexual abuse, etc.

8. **Identification and licensing**: Identification/endorsement that officially ascribes youth worker status to practitioners.

Broad findings indicate that regulatory mechanisms for youth work are still emerging, other than in countries such as the Malta, the United Kingdom, Australia, New Zealand and so on where they were relatively well established, understood and implemented. In other contests, mechanisms were in place, but there were still questions around the broader awareness of them, and lack of mechanisms for training and implementation.

While the baseline has not been able to obtain detailed information on who has participated in developing these regulatory/ethical frameworks, it is nevertheless important in the process of developing these standards that they are owned by youth work practitioners, young people, and State and non-governmental bodies equally.

The Commonwealth's *Draft Code of Ethical Practice for Youth Workers* has been endorsed by the Commonwealth Alliance of Youth Work Associations, which is a potential indication of further commitments to rights-based ethical codes of practice across the Commonwealth.

10.3 Regional trends in regulating practice and practitioner safety

Figure 10.1 illustrates the existence in sampled countries of two key youth work regulatory frameworks – ethical standards and competency frameworks. It is notable that competency standards have been broadly accepted in the Caribbean due to the Commonwealth Caribbean competency standards that are already informing the design of the youth work degree at the University of the West Indies. Ethical standards have emerged where youth workers' associations are in existence, or where regulatory bodies exist for youth work. Overall, much needs to be done to advance regulatory practices around youth work.

Figure 10.1 Regional trends – No. of countries with ethical standards and competency frameworks

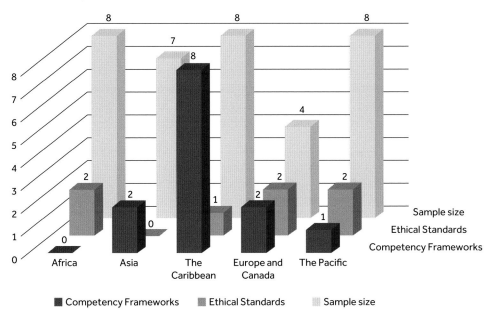

10.3.1 Africa

Evidence available did not demonstrate the broad application of any of the above regulatory supports for youth work in the eight sampled countries, except Codes of Ethics for youth work in South Africa and Zambia.

In South Africa, SAYWA has included the code of ethics in the constitution for their association. To what extent they have been endorsed by the State youth work delivery agencies or youth work practitioners, including the membership, was not clear at the time of writing this report.

Table 10.1 Regulatory frameworks – Africa

Country	Competency/ occupational standards for youth work exists	National guidelines on youth work	Ethical standards for youth work	National occupational health and safety standards for youth work
Uganda	None	None	None	None
Ghana	None	None	None	None
Kenya	None	None	None	None
Malawi	None	None	None	None
Nigeria	None	None	None	None
South Africa	None	None	Yes	None
Tanzania	None	None	None	None
Zambia	None	None	Yes	None

In Zambia, a code of ethics formulated by the Zambia Youth Workers' Association (ZYWA) exists. However, as the Association points out, it is not mandatory for practitioners to sign on to the Code, and disclosure and enforcement mechanisms are yet to be developed.

10.3.2 Asia

No specific ethical standards exist in Bangladesh. There is as yet no provision to license youth workers. The laws and rules guiding youth organisations apply to the individual youth workers, most of whom belong to youth organisations.

In India, while there is no nationally prevalent competency frameworks, a potentially influential competency framework titled 'Challenger Deep – An Outcomes Framework Tool', has been developed for youth workers to self-assess their competency levels and obtain 360-degree feedback from their community of young people and other stakeholders with the help of an assisted coach. This competency framework involves assessment of a youth worker's capacity to instil capabilities in young people under the rubrics of self, society and social change.

The development of this tool was led by ComMutiny – the Youth Collective in collaboration with the Rajiv Gandhi National Institute of Youth Development, Pravah, Restless Development India, and the Commonwealth Secretariat. It is an example of a professional collective spearheading competency frameworks in partnership with a State body. It is a novel approach at competency assessment in youth engagement that tries to capture the nuanced and complex attributes required for youth engagement that supports young people's self-empowerment. Inductions to the tool were being undertaken for members of the Collective at the time of writing.

For Malaysia, all these regulatory frameworks will be formulated as part of the overall framework for youth work that is currently work in progress.

Table 10.2 Regulatory frameworks – Asia

Country	Competency/ occupational standards for youth work exists	National guidelines on youth work	Ethical standards for youth work	Occupational health and safety standards for youth work in State sector
Bangladesh	No	No	No[1]	No
India	No	No	No	No
Malaysia	In process	In process	In process	No
Maldives	No	None	No	No
Pakistan	No	None	No	No
Singapore	Only for working with youth at risk[2]	Yes, for youth at risk social work	No	No
Sri Lanka	Yes	None	None	None

Figure 10.2 ComMutiny the Youth Collective – The Challenger Deep Youth Worker Competency Framework

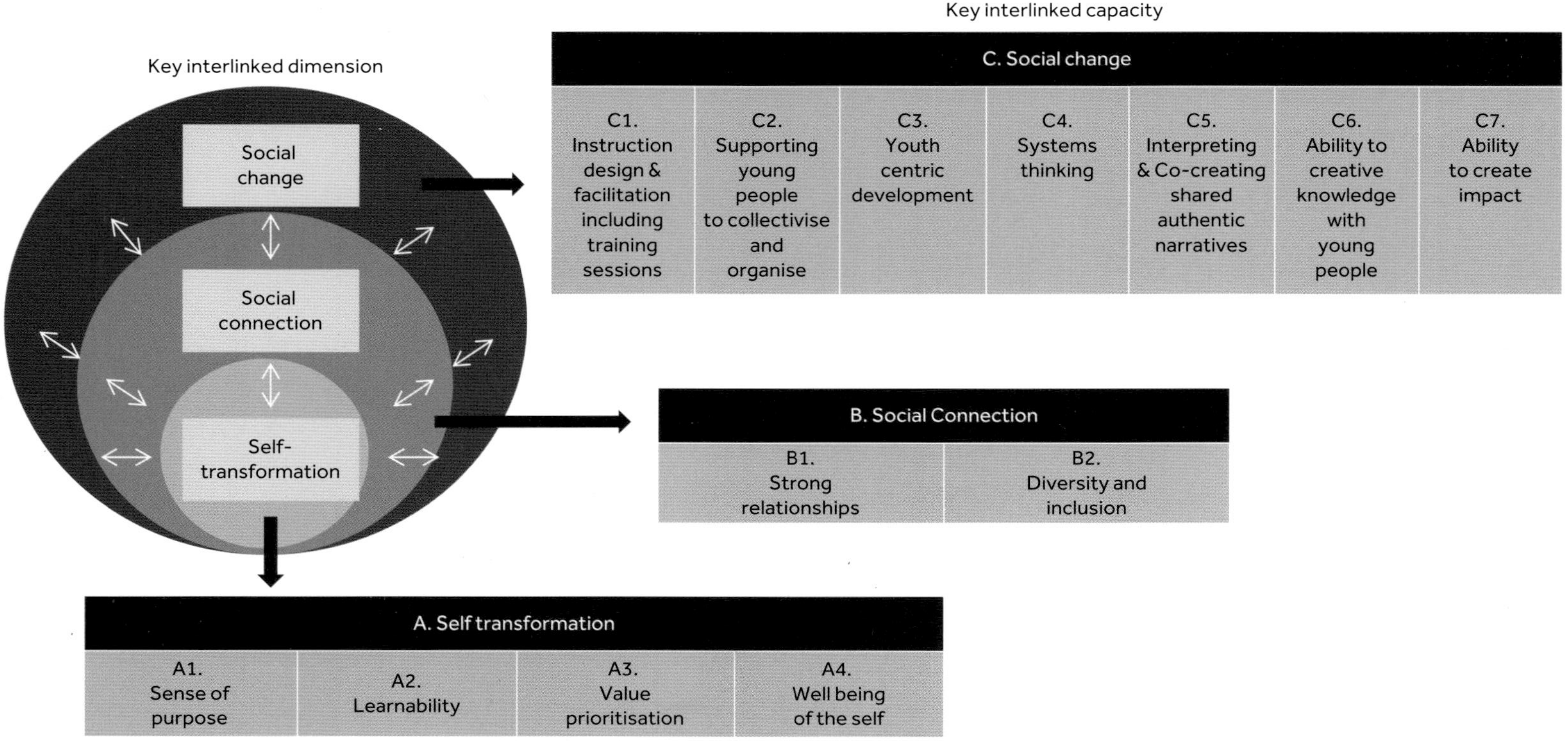

Key interlinked capacity

C. Social change

| C1. Instruction design & facilitation including training sessions | C2. Supporting young people to collectivise and organise | C3. Youth centric development | C4. Systems thinking | C5. Interpreting & Co-creating shared authentic narratives | C6. Ability to creative knowledge with young people | C7. Ability to create impact |

B. Social Connection

| B1. Strong relationships | B2. Diversity and inclusion |

A. Self transformation

| A1. Sense of purpose | A2. Learnability | A3. Value prioritisation | A4. Well being of the self |

Key interlinked dimension

Social change

Social connection

Self-transformation

In Singapore, in order to help youth workers improve their capabilities and provide more effective interventions, the Ministry of Social and Family Development has planned the development of a National Youth Work Competency Framework (NYWCF) by the end of 2017 as a joint initiative between the Central Youth Guidance Officer (CYGO) and the National Council of Social Service. It will set out the specialised competencies required by youth work professionals. The NYWCF seeks to define the specialised and contextualised competencies required by youth work practitioners and clearly chart career pathways and progressions for youth workers – trained and untrained in youth work, social work, or other disciplines. It hopes to give a clearer understanding to youth workers on their job roles and career development.[3]

In Singapore, the category of youth workers includes social workers who work with at-risk youth. This segment of youth work is currently handled by the Singapore's Ministry of Social and Family Development (MSF). The National Social Work Competency Framework (NSWCF) (Ministry of Health, Ministry of Social and Family Development and National Council of Social Service, 2015) was launched in November 2015 through a joint initiative between the MSF and the Ministry of Health to guide social workers across different settings, including those who work with youth. Though it focuses on social work competencies and career pathways for social work professions as well as the knowledge and skills required for various social work roles, there are still some competencies relevant to youth work. The NSWCF references the knowledge and application of ethics and values, and a knowledge of the socio-economic, political and multicultural contexts, all of which are competencies required by both youth and social work. The framework intends to support social workers involved in both direct and indirect specialised practice and includes those who work with key groups, including youth.

The Development framework for Youth Workers (DYW) was also developed by the Ministry of Social and Family Development's as a guiding framework for youth-serving organisations to adequately equip their youth work practitioners with the skills they need to offer services to at-risk youth. The DYW was developed in consultation with youth work practitioners, members of youth work organisations and voluntary welfare organisations (VWOs), the Social Service Training Institute (SSTI) and the Singapore Workforce Development Agency (WDA). The DYW is designed around seven domains.

In Sri Lanka, PYWA has a draft competency framework which includes assessment of competencies for engaging with youth. Even though this process is in line with youth policy commitments to youth work in Sri Lanka, the framework is still to be finalised and adopted by the State youth work sector. The 'Ocean in a Drop' short course developed by the Association for youth workers in Sri Lanka was partially based on the competency framework.

10.3.3 Caribbean

While the picture for the Caribbean is mixed, there are distinctively positive aspects and clear practice that can be shared and built on. In the instances where there is a code of conduct that governs the work of youth workers, it tends to be more specific

Table 10.3 Regulatory frameworks – the Caribbean

Country	Competency/ occupational standards for youth work exist	State guidelines on youth work	State/national ethical standards for youth work	Occupational health and safety standards for youth work in State sector
Barbados	Yes	Yes	Yes	No
Belize	Yes	No	No	No
Dominica	Yes	No	No	No
Guyana	Yes	No	No	No
Jamaica	Yes	No	No	No
St Lucia	Yes	No	No	No
St Vincent and the Grenadines	Yes	No	No	No
Trinidad & Tobago	Yes	No	No	No

to the agency or programme to which the worker is attached than in the case of, for example, Trinidad & Tobago where there is a state code for those working under the Ministry of Education in schools.

Dominica uses the Commonwealth ethics guideline but the actual results of its use have not been clear. Neither has the State endorsed the Commonwealth ethical guidelines.

In Barbados, the ethical standards are based on established General Orders and the Public Servant Code of Conduct but with a strong focus on operational guidelines specific to staff working within the youth development programme – a research-led programme of the Government's Youth Affairs Division. The Barbados code makes provision for staff supervision visits monthly at a minimum and sets out guidance on accountability, integrity, confidentiality and impartiality, and discretionary use of funds – making a clear case of the youth development worker as a service provider. Of particular interest is the section on fieldwork guidelines, which is the only section that speaks directly to the relationship between the worker and the 'client' and speaks to appropriate interactions with the community and clients of the opposite sex.

The former Commonwealth Youth Programme Caribbean Centre's development of the Competency Standards in Youth Development Work for the Caribbean which was endorsed by CARICOM in 2012. This has been accepted by all Caribbean Commonwealth member states and applies to them all.

Box 10.1 Caribbean Competency Standards in Youth Development Work

The Caribbean Competency Standards, developed by the Commonwealth's former regional centre in consultation with stakeholders in the Caribbean, was meant to support the development of competency-based training and education for youth workers. Eighty-two Competencies were articulated for Levels II–V in youth work as is outlined in the Control Document of the competency standards (Commonwealth Youth Programme Caribbean Centre, 2012).

Some member states have been actively using the standards to design job descriptions and codes of ethics, assess youth work practice, etc. (Commonwealth Secretariat, 2014).

None of the sampled countries in the Caribbean has a youth worker licensing processes in place but, as indicated, a few have issued ID cards. It is the perception of youth workers in the field that having an identification card gives the youth workers recognition as legitimate State employees in the sector as this is the norm with other State officials in other fields.

10.3.4 Europe and Canada

The European perspective is generally positive. Youth work is not fully developed in Cyprus so expectations for regulatory frameworks would not be realistic. On the other hand, Malta has a well-developed and socially embedded youth service with clear regulatory mechanisms.

Youth work in Canada is unrecognised at national (State) level and it would be inaccurate to say that the profession is understood in a single specific way nationwide. With no joined-up, national recognition or place for youth work, the profession will not have mechanisms in place to support such practice. That said, the nation has a raft of relevant and appropriate legislation and policy pertaining to young people and professional interventions into their lives. Moreover, child and youth care workers have had a place in the Canadian educational system, working in diverse ways.

There is no specific governmental spending on professionalising youth work in Canada and no accrediting body for youth work education and training.

The occupational standards in Malta are related to the duties of the Malta Youth Work Profession Board, associated with Article 4 of Chap. 533 of the Laws of Malta, as the functions of the Board included the task to:

> Establish and, where necessary, assess existing youth work standards and develop new continuing youth work professional development and other standards, and recommend to the Minister in relation to initial and continuing youth work education, proficiency, experience and other qualifications required for holding a warrant under this [the Youth Work Profession] Act

Table 10.4 Regulatory frameworks – Europe and Canada

Country	Competency/ occupational standards for youth work exists	State guidelines on youth work	State ethical standards for youth work	Occupational health and safety standards for youth work
Canada	None	None	None	None
Cyprus	None	None	None	None
Malta	Yes	Yes	Yes	Yes
UK	Yes	Yes	Yes	Yes

The Board also has the responsibility to:

> Make recommendations to the Minister on the Code of Ethics to be prescribed for the professional behaviour of youth workers, following consultation with the associations and partnerships registered under the provisions of this Act

The following responsibilities are concomitant with this duty:

- Inquire into any allegation of professional misconduct, gross negligence or incompetence by a youth worker;

- Advise, or make recommendations or otherwise express its views to the Minister on any matter on which the Minister is to consult with the Board or on which the Board is to make recommendations to the Minister or on which the opinion or recommendation of the Board is sought by the Minister;

- Make recommendations to the Minister to prescribe in relation to the employment of persons who are in possession of a recognised honours degree or its equivalent but who do not qualify for a warrant under this Act, and who are working under the supervision of a registered youth worker in such establishments or agencies as may be prescribed;

- Perform such other functions as may arise from this Act or any other law, or as may be assigned to it by the Minister.

In the United Kingdom, the National Occupational Standards (NOS) can be used in every part of the UK where the functions are carried out. They are 'Occupational' because they outline the level of functioning that an individual needs to carry out the requirements of the workplace (in terms of their occupation).

NOS are Standards because they are statements of effective performance agreed by a representative sample of employers and other key stakeholders and approved by the UK NOS Panel. The standards are developed for employers by employers through the relevant Sector Skills Council or Standards Setting Organisation.

The NOS for Youth Work are not directly parallel to qualifications, they are deployed to derive appropriate competency-based qualifications for the youth work sector. The Standards, as the agreed standards of performance and knowledge required in youth work practice across the UK, can be used by employers to inform job descriptions, consider skills needs and identify areas of improvement, and can also support individual professional and continuous development.

As the UK Youth Work National Occupational Standards (National Youth Agency, UK (n.d.)) detail, the different contexts in which youth work is practised will have a bearing on how these NOS are applied. The relevant national, regional, local and political context, as well other applicable standards of performance or competence, should be taken into account when reading and applying the Youth Work NOS.

It should be noted that the approach to youth work differs across the four nations of the UK. The NOS have been written to enable the differences to be accommodated and to enable different terminology to be applied as appropriate.

However, regardless of the national context, at the core of all youth work practice are the values of youth work, and it is expected that all those working with young people will work within these agreed sets of values.

The NOS outline ethical standards in a general, rather than a specific way, but expectations for the behaviour and conduct of youth workers is clarified (see National Youth Agency, UK (n.d.))

Both the Institute of Youth Work and the NYA articulate what they understand to be the ethics of youth work that largely mirror, but perhaps more clearly demarcate, what is outlined in the NOS. However, the ultimate underpinning of any such code of conduct is what is required in terms of human rights, law and policy (for example in the UK the Children Act and more broadly the UN Convention of the Rights of the Child).

10.3.5 The Pacific

Apart from Australia and New Zealand, there seems to be little movement in terms of the areas focused on. It might be the case that a regional professional association could play a part in starting to address this situation. The case study in Box 10.2

Table 10.5 Regulatory frameworks – the Pacific

Country	Competency/ occupational standards for youth work exist	State guidelines on youth work	National ethical standards for youth work	Occupational health and safety standards for youth work in State sector
Australia	Yes	Yes Children, Youth and Families Act 2005 (Vic.)	Yes The Code of Ethical Practice for the Victorian Youth Sector. (2007)	Yes Working with Children Act 2005 Child Wellbeing and Safety Act 2005 (Vic) Occupational Health and Safety Act 2004 (Vic)
Fiji	None	None	None	None
Samoa	None	None	None	None
Solomon Islands	None	None	None	None
Papua New Guinea	None	None	None	None
New Zealand	Not for youth work specifically	None	Yes (but not State endorsed)	Not specifically for youth work
Vanuatu	None	None	None	None

describes the background and process undertaken to establish the Victoria Code of Ethics in Australia and its impacts.

Box 10.2 The Victorian Youth Sector Code of Ethical Practice – an Australian success

Dr Tim Corney
Victoria University, Australia
Victoria Youth Workers' Association, Australia

Background

The youth sector in Australia, particularly in Victoria, had a long history of failed attempts at creating and sustaining both a professional association and a related code of ethical practice for youth work (Irving et al., 1995; Grogan, 2004). However, when the Victorian state government enacted new pieces of important youth-related legislation there was a renewed legislative impetus to look again at the professional practice of youth work in Victoria.

As a member of the Commonwealth of Nations, Australia has long been an active supporter of the Commonwealth Youth Programme (CYP). Various Australian state youth councils have consequently recognised the need to develop codes of practice for youth workers in their respective regions, however not all are based in human rights (Griffin & Luttrell, 2011; Grogan, 2004; Corney & Hoiles, 2006, 2007; Corney, 2014). The youth sector in the Australian state of Victoria, despite its best efforts over many years, was without a code of ethics or an agreed statement of good practice for the occupation of youth worker prior to 2007 (Goodwin, 1991; Irving et al., 1995; Grogan, 2004).

The emergence of the code

However, a series of related events, such as the enactment by the Victorian state Labor government of the Children, Youth and Families Act 2005; the Child Wellbeing and Safety Act 2005; the Working with Children Act 2005 and the Charter of Human Rights and Responsibilities Act 2006, all gave legislative impetus to the youth sector to look specifically at the creation of a code of ethical practice for youth work based on human rights considerations (Corney & Hoiles, 2006, 2007; Corney, 2014). Further, debates regarding the professionalisation of youth work and the establishing of a code of practice – long championed by the CYP – were reopened after the appointment of Victoria's Child Safety Commissioner under the Child Wellbeing and Safety Act 2005.

Shortly after his appointment in 2006 the then Child Safety Commissioner, Bernie Geary, gave a significant address to the Annual General Meeting of the Youth Affairs Council of Victoria, in which he called for the sector to participate in the task of addressing child safety by developing a code of practice for youth workers. He outlined the need to protect not only young people, but also those who work with them, stating, 'I strongly believe that youth work needs to come

(continued)

(*continued*)

out of the shadow of aligned professions and a major step will be a strong and proud declaration of a code of ethical practice […]' (Child Safety Commission, 2006b).

This call by the then newly appointed Commissioner, coupled with the incorporation of human rights into the enactment of various pieces of youth-related legislation, led to the convening of a Youth Affairs Council of Victoria (YACVic) working group to explore the potential establishment of a sector-wide code of practice for youth work based in human rights (Corney & Hoiles, 2006, 2007). This occurred alongside the re-establishment of the Youth Workers' Association, a professional association for youth workers in Victoria, and a global push from the Commonwealth contained in communiqués, such as the CYP's PAYE goals (2007), explicitly calling for codes of practice based in human rights to be developed for youth workers across the Commonwealth.

The YACVic code working group was strongly influenced by Commissioner Geary, and its outcome focused on safe practice in youth work, particularly the safety of young people and workers, as well as the human rights of young people.

Debates around the drafting of the code was based on previous experiences from across Australia and internationally. A strong decision was made to draft a separate Victorian code based in human rights (Griffin & Luttrell, 2011; Quixley & Doostkhah, 2007; Corney and Hoiles, 2006, 2007; Corney, 2014).

In 2007, the post-consultation document titled 'Code of Ethical Practice – A first step for the Victorian youth sector' was published by YACVic and launched by the Victorian Government Minister for Youth Affairs Hon James Merlino and the Victorian Child Safety Commissioner Bernie Geary. The code was also subsequently endorsed by the Victorian professional association for youth workers (YWA) and by the Victoria University degree programme in youth work, the largest youth work training programme in Australia.

Content of the Code

The Victorian Code provides agreed statements about what is to be considered good youth work practice, and also provides an overarching frame of reference with which youth workers can engage in awareness raising on a range of human rights and citizenship issues. The Victorian Code, although supported and launched by government and the professional association, is self-regulatory and voluntarily adhered to by youth workers. Both the Youth Affairs Council of Victoria and the professional Youth Workers' Association endorse the Code.

Use of the Code has included

1. Training and induction of the code for the youth sector

2. Development of promotional material by the Youth Affairs Council

(*continued*)

And the Code and subsequent dissemination/publicity has resulted in

1. Degree-level youth work training courses incorporating units on the professional ethics of youth work as a compulsory component of their degree programme,

2. Its human rights basis encouraging youth workers to identify themselves and act as advocates and facilitators of human rights for young people.

3. Many agencies also now define their programmes and practices with young people in human rights terms and elements of their programmes contain human rights outcomes for young people.

Benefits for Youth

The benefits have been incredibly wide ranging and transformative – from the increased safety of young people and for workers, to improved competence and efficacy, through to providing a basis and definition to the role of youth workers. This has served to professionalise the youth sector, enhancing both the training and practice of youth work, the work of agencies and the outcomes for young people.[4]

In New Zealand, youth work is largely a community-based practice. It is not mandated by the State as a primary or preferred mode of working with young people. Despite evidence supporting the need for interdisciplinary teams to collaborate in the support and promotion of positive youth development in contexts like youth health services, the State has not formally endorsed youth work, or created any guidelines or supportive mechanisms that relate specifically to youth work.

Much movement has occurred in terms of guidance and ethics in the organised youth work sector outside of State structures. The sector is currently working to self-determine youth development competencies to underpin the national professional body. The Code of Ethics for Youth Workers in Aotearoa (New Zealand) is a document that was developed with the sector, with the principles of youth development and the Treaty of Waitangi[5] at the centre.

That said, as part of the Children's Action Plan (Ministry for Vulnerable Children, 2017) there are general core competencies for people working with young people, and regulations affecting youth workers that relate to health and safety and police vetting.

10.4 Trends in youth safeguarding and practitioner vetting

Because entrants to the professions will often be trusted with very personal aspects of people's lives, it is not only their skills and academic ability that needs to be assured. Their **attitudinal, behavioural, ethical and moral profiles** need to be considered. This might be ascertained by qualifying institutions and/or professional bodies, although, classically, both might likely be involved in this sort of investigation of background and personal suitability of prospective professionals. Needless to say, in the youth work field this sort of safeguarding procedure should be of high priority, as professional qualification means that in effect practitioners are being licensed by qualification to work with, care and take responsibility for other people's children.

However, the picture in terms of entry to youth work across the Commonwealth seems a cause for concern, with little evidence of explicit youth safeguarding/protection policies, criminal history vetting for youth workers, or youth worker licensing being evident in the countries sampled.

National youth safeguarding policies within youth work were identified Canada, Australia, the UK, Malta and New Zealand, and were also reported in Bangladesh and Barbados. Criminal history vetting was evident where there was successful public sector history vetting with no specific requirements for youth work except in Canada, Malta, UK, Australia and New Zealand, and youth worker identification to protect both practitioner and young person were barely evident except in Trinidad and Tobago, Barbados and Malta.

Table 10.6 Safeguarding and vetting – Africa

Country	Youth safeguarding/ youth protection policies in State youth sector	Criminal history vetting for youth workers	Youth worker licensing/ID card
Uganda	None identified	None identified	None identified
Ghana	None identified	None identified	None identified
Kenya	None identified	None identified	None identified
Malawi	None identified	None identified	None identified
Nigeria	None identified	None identified	None identified
South Africa	None identified	None identified	None identified
Tanzania	None identified	None identified	None identified
Zambia	None identified	None identified	None identified

Table 10.7 Safeguarding and vetting – Asia

Country	Youth Safeguarding/ youth protection policies in State youth sector	Criminal history vetting for youth workers	Youth worker licensing/ID card
Bangladesh	Yes	Yes	None identified
India	None identified	None identified	None identified
Malaysia	None identified	None identified	None identified
Maldives	None identified	None identified	None identified
Singapore	None identified	Vetting is carried out for those involved in certain youth-at-risk and residential programmes funded by the government	None identified
Sri Lanka	None identified	None identified	None identified
Pakistan	None identified	None identified	None identified

Table 10.8 Safeguarding and vetting – the Caribbean

Country	Youth Safeguarding/ youth protection policies in State youth sector	Criminal history vetting for youth workers	Youth worker licensing/ID card
Barbados	Yes	Yes	Yes
Belize	None identified	None identified	None identified
Dominica	None identified	None identified	None identified
Guyana	None identified	None identified	Yes
Jamaica	None identified	None identified	None identified
St Lucia	None identified	None identified	None identified
St Vincent and the Grenadines	None identified	None identified	None identified
Trinidad and Tobago	None identified	None identified	Yes

Table 10.9 Safeguarding and vetting – Europe and Canada

Country	Youth Safeguarding/youth protection policies in State youth sector	Criminal history vetting for youth workers	Youth worker licensing/ID card
Cyprus	None identified	None identified	None identified
Malta	Yes	Yes	Yes
UK	Yes	Yes	None identified
Canada	Yes	Yes	None identified

Table 10.10 Safeguarding and vetting – the Pacific

Pacific	Youth Safeguarding/ youth protection policies in State youth sector	Criminal history vetting for youth workers	Youth worker licensing/ID card
Australia	Yes	Yes	None identified
New Zealand	Yes	Yes	None identified
Fiji	None identified	None identified	None identified
Tonga	None identified	None identified	None identified
Samoa	None identified	None identified	None identified
Solomon Islands	None identified	None identified	None identified
Papua New Guinea	None identified	None identified	None identified
Vanuatu	None identified	None identified	None identified

While the regional baseline surveys informing this document provided information about contextual or relative safeguarding or vetting procedures for entry to employment roles with young people, there was no information about procedures for entry to institutional qualifying programmes, which can include practice placements (unsupervised access to young people).

Overall, of the 35 countries involved, only a small number had any kind of youth-work-specific checks. In the UK, for example, it is a legal requirement for students working unsupervised with young and/or vulnerable people (which includes those undergoing professional training) to be subject to checks by the Disclosure and Barring Service (DBS).

In Canada provincial/territorial law refers to much the same procedures. For example, in British Columbia, the Criminal Records Review Act ensures that people who work with or may potentially have unsupervised access to children or vulnerable adults undergo a criminal record check by the Criminal Records Review Programme(CRRP).

A person whose criminal record suggests they present a risk of physical or sexual abuse to children or a risk of physical, sexual or financial abuse to vulnerable adults will not have access to these groups. However, unlike in the UK, the non-profit sector and volunteer organisations are not covered by the Act, but have volunteers working with children or vulnerable adults. This said, such organisations can have criminal record checks done by the CRRP at no cost. Most organisations, because of risk, reputation and associated funding, will look to carry out such checks.

For-profit organisations not covered by the Criminal Records Review Act that require criminal record checks for employees or volunteers are encouraged to contact their local police.

It is probably not a matter for debate that those working with children and young people at any level should be vetted in relation to safeguarding, as well as for their attitudinal and skill profile. Clearly this is of high priority as part of entry to professional studies, but also in terms of other forms of professional accreditation or certification.

10.4.1 Trust

Professional accreditation, certification and qualification are kitemarks of knowhow, attitude, behaviour, ethical and moral awareness and conduct. As such, they reflect the levels of trust clients, employers and society might invest in individuals and qualified groups.

Very generally (and approximately) professional qualification will denote one's capacity to make professional judgements that can be trusted (and not just follow instructions).

All levels of qualification signify relative 'social trust'. Professional qualification carries with it the highest order of social trust, hence not everybody or anybody can enter a profession. If a profession (for instance by way of qualifying agencies and/or a professional association) gives entry to anyone and everyone, or just makes entry relatively easy, it has given up its gatekeeping role. What then might any trust that clients, employers and society invest in this profession be based on?

10.5 Conclusions

Regulatory frameworks such as ethical standards and competency frameworks catering specifically for the youth work profession were still in their infancy in most sampled countries. The Caribbean competency standards supported by the Commonwealth was an example of a region-wide adoption of standards in the design of competency-based professional courses for youth work. Ethical codes of conduct and competency/occupational standards were relatively well implemented in countries such as the United Kingdom, Australia and Malta, but were still emerging in most other countries. Even where they existed, often, implementation and practised regulatory measures were not that clear. Any member state interested in translating legislation and policy to practice would need to ensure ethical codes of conduct and competency frameworks that are developed collectively by practitioners and receivers of services, young people. All other frameworks need to be developed as deemed relevant to local, national and regional contexts.

Notes

1   There is no specific ethical standard and protection policies for youth work, but it has been manifested different ways in different policies and acts applicable directly for organisations, hence applicable for youth as well, such as the Bangladesh Skill Development Policy 2011, Youth Organisation (Registration and Operation) Act, 2015, Youth Policy 2003.

2   However, for youth workers who work with youth at risk there is a competency framework under http://www.sasw.org.sg/site/national-social-work-competency-framework.

3   NYWC Framework factsheet https://app.msf.gov.sg/LinkClick.aspx?fileticket=iRIwHqWvxpc%3d&portalid=0

4   This case study has been informed by Commonwealth of Nations (2007), Corney (2014), Corney & Hoiles (2006 and 2007), Child Safety Commission, Australia, 2006), Goodwin (1991), Grosan (2004), Griffin & Luffrel (2011), Sercombe (1997), Irving et al. (1995), Surrey County Council UK (2006), The National Youth Agency, UK (2004), Youth Affairs Council of Western Australia (2003), Youth Affairs Council of Victoria (2007), Children, Youth and Families Act 2005. Victoria. Australia, Child Wellbeing and Safety Act 2005. Victoria. Australia, Working with Children Act 2005. Victoria. Australia, Charter of Human Rights and Responsibilities Act 2006, Victoria. Australia, Commissioner for Children and Young People Act 2012. Victoria. Australia, Working with Children Act 2005. Victoria. Australia.

5   The Code of Ethics for Youth Workers provides youth workers with guidance on how they can make a significant contribution to supporting Māori development in every context and community. Bicultural practice in a diverse postcolonial nation is central to youth work in New Zealand.

Chapter 11

Professional Validation of Youth Work Education and Training

11.1 Introduction

This chapter discusses the concept of professional validation and trends in the professional validation of education and training for the youth work profession.

Across the Commonwealth, the validation and professional recognition for degree-level youth work qualifications are usually left in the hands of national governmental and extra-governmental bodies generically responsible for higher education standards and/or individual institutions. Exceptions include Australia and Malta, where youth worker associations have some influence.

Professional validation is important as it connects qualification with the field, which provides the means to keep training and education up to date, aware of changes in and pressure on practice, and so relevant.

11.2 A model of the professional accreditation of youth work

A model of accreditation can be drawn from the practice of the National Youth Agency (NYA) England. It is not put forward as something to copy or emulate; however, it is a thoroughly articulated process that demonstrates the complexity of professional accreditation, as indicated in Box 11.1.

11.3 Replicability of professional accreditation

The procedure described above represents a complex process (relative to the processes involved in non-professional qualifications). Should a Commonwealth member state wish to set up the necessary structures and processes for professional validation of youth work, it is probable that it will take considerable time, effort and meaningful partnerships with institutions carrying expertise for professional accreditation to ensure quality of the process.

11.4 Professional accreditation in Commonwealth regions

Professional accreditation of youth work education and training were only available in the UK and Australia. Other courses only underwent general university certification.

11.4.1 Africa

Overall, findings from Africa indicate that there is no youth work-specific professional accreditation in most countries surveyed except in Kenya. At university

Box 11.1 Professional accreditation process – National Youth Agency, UK

The following provides a brief introduction to the professional validation criteria and processes that are applied by the NYA and the Training Standards Committee (TSC) in its scrutiny of submissions and which form the basis on which all submissions will be judged. The NYA publication 'Professional Validation and Curriculum Requirements 2015' (National Youth Agency, UK, 2015) presents the process through which Higher Education Institutions in England can seek formal professional validation of their programme of education and training in youth work.

The role of the NYS is broadly that which would be adopted by an active and influential professional body in other professions, though it is not itself such a representative body.

In their own words, the NYA is a 'youth intermediary charity', that is it acts as broker (or 'go-between) between the field and institutions such as universities. The NYA's stated turnover of £10 million is, in part, raised by fees paid by these institutions for the NYA to recruit and deploy people from the youth work field as and when required.

On the basis of this role, it identifies itself as 'the national expert on youth policy and youth work' and is responsible for the professional validation of youth work programmes in England only. Wales, Scotland and Northern Ireland have their own professionally validating ETS bodies and requirements.

The NYA argues that it has the responsibility to ensure that youth workers are properly trained and prepared. This might be understood to be effectively translated via the NYA's role in ensuring the fitness for purpose of youth work programmes that develop the knowledge, skills and values of practice. The Requirements cover the management, staffing and resourcing, teaching and learning, professional practice and the quality assurance of programmes. Professional practice is a key element of what makes the professional programmes distinct, putting the students' ability to apply academic theory to the direct work with young people and organisations as crucial to their achievement of professional status.

The position of the NYA and ETS is that the professional validation process is first and foremost designed and run to promote and secure the profession of youth work as a distinct and different approach to working with young people. The requirements expect programmes to be in line with current policy and delivery contexts so that newly qualified youth workers are able to contribute effectively to services for young people and work within multidisciplinary teams. In this regard, programmes should demonstrate how they equip learners to meet the requirements of the subject benchmarks and National Occupational Standards for Youth Work (National Youth Agency, UK (n.d.).

(continued)

(*continued*)

Therefore, the programmes eligible for professional validation are those that have a clear youth work pathway throughout all levels of learning and cover curriculum requirements. The NYA does not accept requests for validation from combined programmes where youth work is only part of the learning. However, the NYA does consider programmes that have a specialised approach to youth work or are contextualised, if in line with NYA guidelines (National Youth Agency, UK, 2016, p. 6).

level, all the courses are approved by the Senate but accredited by the Commission for University Education (CUE). Information as to how such accreditation is arranged and actualised was not accessible.

This suggests that there are minimal measures being put in place to align youth work courses with the current social realities and development challenges affecting the lives of young people. The lack of course lecturers qualified in youth work exemplified a discipline which is 'starved' of adequate competencies – those required to drive it towards achieving its social goals.

This situation can also affect the development of effective, visionary practitioners and policy-makers in the youth sector; the emergence of individuals and groups able to evaluate and anticipate the social changes in the practice environment and make timely strategic adjustments to improve the practice.

Furthermore, there is minimal planning and investment in securing relevant field practice opportunities. This is particularly difficult given that some states do not refer to youth workers' training institutions for graduates when employing youth workers.

11.4.2 Asia

In general, no youth work-specific professional accreditation processes were identified. In the past, quality measures set up by the Commonwealth Diploma in Youth Development were in use, but there is no evidence of the current use of these criteria.

11.4.3 Caribbean

While professional accreditation is said to be delivered by UWI, there is no clarity on how this accreditation works. The Diploma quality assurance guidance is of course available to the UWI.

11.4.4 Europe and Canada

Table 11.1 Professional validation of youth work qualifications – Europe

Country	Nature of professional accreditation of youth work qualifications
Canada	While accreditation is in its infancy in Canada (see Child and Youth Care Educational Accreditation Board of Canada (CYCEA), n.d.), the commitment to child and youth care likely disallows comparative analysis with other contexts. However, it is thought that there are too many processes that have been identified for institutions to work through an accreditation process. First, the focus is on self-study where the programme looks at its various components and discusses them in relation to the field, accounting for the choices they've made, with the assumption that there needs to be an internship component(s) and applied focus. The second process is an emphasis on quality improvement where reviewers appointed by the accreditation board review and assess the programme. As there is no licensing in Canada or regulatory body for youth work/child and youth care, the motivation is to promote the idea that staff from accredited programmes are more competent and have 'higher' qualifications. This has created some tensions in the field in geographic locations where youth work qualifications are obtained via private colleges (e.g., Newfoundland).
Cyprus	There are no accredited courses or accreditation processes relating to youth work practice in Cyprus.
Malta	The Youth Work Profession Act, 2014, gives formal professional recognition and status to youth workers, as well as regulating the profession and determining the qualifications and conditions under which youth workers can acquire such recognition. No specific professional validation of academic courses exist.
The United Kingdom	In the UK, over the last 20 years or so, this generally speaking has required a degree qualification, which is of course academically underwritten by universities. However various agencies, such as the NYA (claiming some degree of representation of youth work as a practice) have been used to provide a professional kitemark for such programmes mostly by way of advice and recommendation. Usually, to gain professional recognition, programmes need to evidence ongoing assessment of practice.

11.4.5 The Pacific

Table 11.2 Professional validation of youth work qualifications – the Pacific

Country	Nature of professional accreditation of youth work qualifications
Australia	Youth Workers Association – Victoria Eligible Qualifications and professional validation process for training courses. Western Australian Association of Youth Workers – Western Australia Eligible Qualifications and Practitioner Experience
Fiji	No information
New Zealand	No evidence of youth work-related professional validation.
Papua New Guinea	No information
Samoa	No information
Solomon Islands	No information
Tonga	No information
Vanuatu	No information

In Australia, the Youth Workers Association – Victoria has a degree course validation process. At this stage, only the degree course at Victoria University has gone through the YWA validation process. The Western Australian Association of Youth Workers plays a significant role in the assessment of practitioner experience, but has no formal course validation process.

11.5 Justifying the professional label

Decisions about professionally qualifying individuals in any profession will usually include ongoing assessment of practice in the field (throughout the programme of studies) by senior and/or experienced peers (supervisors and/or line managers) in appropriate settings. It is hard to see how programmes that do not include this might justify the fitness of a candidate to practice.

Professional qualifications will also commonly be generated, assured and quality maintained calling on advice and input from representatives from the professional field that the qualification serves. Such oversight might most beneficially be facilitated by the appropriate professional association, the membership of which may likely be more objective and representative of the field than say a 'hired hand' brought in by a qualifying institution.

Unless there is this type of assurance it is difficult to understand how prospective employers, students and clients might be convinced that programmes and qualifications (including study content, materials, study tasks, required reading, practice placements, teaching and teacher experience) are 'safe' and relevant (appropriately informed and up to date, etc.).

It seems, to an extent, that the gatekeepers to professional practice throughout most of the Commonwealth are academics located in educational institutions. This is quite contrary to what might be understood by most professions as advisable, desirable or 'safe'.

11.6 Conclusion

The findings above on professional validation highlight the need for the Commonwealth to advance validation processes and support the development of robust professional youth worker associations, with influence and authority in the field, which might correctly and desirably include shared oversight of the conferment of professional status.

Chapter 12

Professional Supervision

12.1 Introduction

This chapter examines the extent to which supervision specific to the youth work profession has been established in member states.

Professional supervision is a formal and disciplined professional conversation between practice colleagues. It is widely used as a means of quality assurance, and is often self-evaluative. It is seen as a management, learning and support mechanism in social work, counselling and psychotherapy as well as in some teaching, medical and policing contexts. This chapter outlines the existence of supervision as a learning and regulatory framework in youth work across the sampled countries.

12.2 What is professional supervision in the context of professional learning and development?

Youth work is understood to require reflective practitioners; people who are able to think about, discuss and justify their practice in order to develop, hone and improve the services they deliver to young people. Supervision is a recognised tool in this process that looks to improve youth work responses, helping to make them more effective, efficient, responsible, relevant and safe.

The practice of professional supervision can be refined in different ways according to aims and contexts, but essentially the work of supervision is focused on the interrogation of practice, which can take place no matter how much or how little experience one might have; it is not limited to those in training or structured education.

Professional supervision is not appraisal in the sense that one person is straightforwardly evaluating the performance of another, although it might encompass elements of self-assessment and, when required, guidance. It is not a debate, although it is an exploration. Neither is it an argument. However, it is enquiring, questioning and even probing. At the same time supervision can't be counselling; it isn't a form of therapy. Neither (perhaps at the other extreme) is it casual chatting.

Supervision concentrates on the development and perfecting of practice, the professional activity of the practitioner. To this extent, it is pragmatic, which does not preclude aims to support, but this is not starting from a deficit assumption about the supervisee; what is being supported is a postulation of asset – that the supervisee has it in them to maintain, refine, progress and/or better their practice delivery with appropriate supervision.

In short, the major outcome of supervision is the development of professional judgement as a foundation of innovation, sharpening, enhancing and improving the functioning of the supervisee and so the offer, capacity and operation of their organisation.

This said, more generally, professional supervision promotes learning, considered action and, within realistic boundaries, facilitate reflective practice. This process is aimed at underpinning client safety, wellbeing and care, which allows for, forwards and confirms the effective and efficient achieving and/or realising of agency aims, professional objectives conduct and attitudes, desired outcomes, goals and purposes. Supervision grounds, consolidates and advances policy and practice, while emphasising ethical and moral service delivery.

12.3 Youth work supervision in the Commonwealth

The baseline indicated little formal supervision processes in the Commonwealth outside the European context. Existing expertise within or outside your region, as indicated in Table 12.1, can be drawn on for the further strengthening of supervision practices in youth work in youth work implementing agencies.

12.3.1 Africa

It seems that some key stakeholders take youth work supervision to be staff appraisal or monitoring via reports. In some contexts it was argued that every institution employed their own methods or frameworks of 'supervision' of staff members to achieve their different goals. However, for the most part it was reported that there was no practice standard or guidelines.

South Africa indicated supervision for students during their service learning or practicum, which is required by specific module requirements included in youth work degree programmes. Nonetheless, there seems to be no supervision for practising youth workers.

Table 12.1 Supervision – Africa

Nature of professional accreditation of youth work qualifications			
Country	Formal supervision exists	Supervision guidelines exist	Qualifications exist for youth work supervision
Ghana	No	No	No
Kenya	No	No	No
Malawi	No	No	No
Nigeria	No	No	No
South Africa	No	No	No
Tanzania	No	No	No
Uganda	No	No	No
Zambia	No	No	No

In Ghana, there is no formal supervision for youth workers, although the monitoring of the Youth Empowerment Agency (YAE) activities through the reports of the implementing agencies is perceived as a form of supervision.

In Kenya and Malawi, it was reported that there are no formal supervision or national guidelines for supervision of the youth officers/workers. It was argued that most key stakeholders in Malawi consider the work of 'supervision' to be conducted by the local youth officers to whom all organisations working with youth are obliged to report. However, there was no practice standard for such 'supervision'.

Nigeria also reported the non-existence of structured supervision.

In Tanzania, the government youth workers are expected to adhere to their departmental legislation and human resources regulations. In the NGO sector supervision is the responsibility of the Registrar of Societies.

Considering the specific goals of youth work supervision, such as enhancing professional growth and development, it is important to ensure that youth work supervision is not generalised or grouped with the general 'line manager staff supervision'. This seems to be the way supervision is understood in Africa, however.

In view of this, there is no significant evidence of the existence of formal or non-formal supervision of youth workers.

12.3.2 Asia

In Singapore, the Youth Work Association (Singapore) has delivered a youth work supervision course with the intention of establishing a Register of Youth Work

---

Box 12.1 Youth work supervision framework, Singapore

John Tan

Member, Youth Work Association (Singapore)

How it all started

The youth work supervision framework was part of our ongoing development as a fledgling youth work association. In the absence of a formal pre-employment track for youth workers in general, it was challenging to establish any form of benchmarks or standards of practice. The Committee of the Youth Workers' Association (Singapore) therefore decided that it would instead be easier and more feasible to kick-start a process of supervision practices so that it can help at least tackle what is already in the field. The assumption was that current youth workers, irrespective of their settings and organisations they belong to, may be helped by a pool of senior youth workers armed with supervision, coaching and mentoring skills

(continued)

(*continued*)

Principles of the Framework

So far, the supervision framework stresses the following principles. They are not exhaustive but express the salient points:

a. **A Strengths-based Approach** – Rather than focusing on deficits and placing our efforts on reducing them, we should also work on one's inherent strengths and talents.

b. **Relationship Building and Contracting** – The dimension of supervision is a relational one and thus thrives on positive relationship elements.

c. **Skills and Interventions in Supervision** – The practice of supervision requires a plethora of skills and techniques that must be honed for greater effectiveness.

d. **Ethics and Values in Supervision** – Supervision must be anchored on a positive basis of solid values and ethical principles.

e. **Collaborative and Peer Group Feedback** – Supervision need not only be approached from a top-down hierarchical angle but should include the lateral dimension of peer collaboration.

f. **Reflective Practice** – To hone professional development, it is essential to conduct regular reflection.

Implementation

Our initial run yielded 24 trained supervisors. The impact of the use of supervision tools, however, is yet to be measured and the YWAS Committee is keen to follow up on this process. This process is aligned to the planned launch of a National Youth Work Competency Framework by the Singapore Government in 2017.

Supervision practice is very aligned to the framework in that it is embedded in the modules pegged for senior and principal youth workers.

Challenges

This is an ongoing process. One obstacle we face is the lack of recognition for the Youth Workers' Association and their power to advise and inform change in practice through the supervision framework. This was also raised by youth-serving organisations that would fall under the supervision guidance framework. This was a legitimate observation. As YWAS is not a regulatory body, we have no teeth when it comes to 'enforcing' standardised practices.

To address this challenge, The YWAS committee then felt it would be more appropriate to approach it as a coaching tool made available for the various youth organisations to tap from, and it is used as such in some contexts.

Our initial supervision course garnered some 24 participants who come from five different agencies. It is estimated that they each have oversight over at least two or three other youth workers in practice.

Table 12.2 Supervision – Asia

Country	Formal supervision exists	Supervision guidelines exist	Qualifications exist for youth work supervision
Bangladesh	None	None	None
India	None	None	None
Malaysia	Drafting	Drafting	Drafting
Maldives	None	None	None
Pakistan	None	None	None
Singapore	Yes	Yes	Yes
Sri Lanka	None	None	None

Supervisors, looking to raise the standards of youth work practice in Singapore. This experience is outlined in Box 10.1.

The general conclusion from the baseline research in Asia was that, with the exception of Singapore, there is no significant engagement in the field of youth work supervision in the region. Malaysia, however, is in the process of drafting supervision guidelines as a part of its emerging framework for professionalising youth work.

Table 12.3 Supervision – the Caribbean

Country	Formal supervision exists	Supervision guidelines exist	Qualifications exist for youth work supervision
Barbados	Rules for formal supervision are mandatory as set out in the Ministry's Performance Review Development System. This is augmented by the guidelines set out in the *Division of Youth Handbook*. In addition, there are assigned supervisors who mentor and validate practice activities of workers.	Yes	Supervisors are qualified by academic qualifications and/or years of experience in the post. The Supervisors in the Division have more than 15 years' practice experience.
Belize	No	No	No
Dominica	No	No	No
Guyana	No	No	No
Jamaica	No	No	No
St Lucia	No	No	No
St Vincent and the Grenadines	No	No	
Trinidad and Tobago	No	No	No

12.3.3 The Caribbean

No youth-work-specific supervision mechanisms were reported, except in Barbados.

12.3.4 Europe and Canada

In Europe, Malta is laying the foundations for the provision of supervision, and the training of supervisors is currently being established. There has been experimentation with Skype supervision (with practitioners in the UK), and one-to-one and group supervision.

Supervision in the occupational context of youth work is relatively well established in the **United** Kingdom. It is a subject requirement of most undergraduate and postgraduate programmes. However, while supervision is seen as fundamental to professional practice in the child care field and was highlighted in Eileen Munro's extensive Government review of child care (Department for Education, UK, 2011) (this document consistently highlights the importance and the necessity of skilled supervision), many full-time youth workers are not committed to the practice, while comparatively few part-time and voluntary practitioners have access to supervision.

Qualifications exist for youth work supervision, but perhaps the most esteemed (as it is validated by Community Learning and Development (CLD) Scotland and as such deemed a professional qualification) is offered by the YMCA George Williams College.

While supervision is widely recognised in fields such as social work, counselling and psychotherapy in Canada, there is no specific emphasis on specialist youth work supervision. This is probably understandable as youth work has no formal recognition in Canada. This said, supervision may well be offered to youth workers involved in organisations that are acclimatised to or deliver social work/counselling services, but this is speculative and there is no structured or devoted supervision for youth workers and as such no guidelines.

As in many other aspects of youth work, in Europe, cross regionally, the access and understanding of supervision varies. It is

- well developed and seen as fundamental to child care in the UK;
- evolving in Malta;
- not obligatory but accessible in Canada as a desirable practice;
- invisible/non-identifiable or not promoted in Cyprus.

Table 12.4 Supervision – Europe

Country	Formal supervision exists	Supervision guidelines exist	Qualifications exist for youth work supervision
Canada	Yes	No	No
Cyprus	No	No	No
Malta	Yes	Yes	No
UK	Yes	Yes	Yes

12.3.5 The Pacific

Table 12.5 Supervision – Pacific

Country	Formal supervision exists	Supervision guidelines exist	Qualifications exist for youth work supervision
Australia	Yes	Yes	No
New Zealand	Yes	Yes	No
Tonga	No	No	No
Fiji	No	No	No
Samoa	No	No	No
Solomon Islands	No	No	No
Papua New Guinea	No	No	No
Vanuatu	No	No	No

Australia has no formal legislated obligation for professional supervision as a requirement for practising as a youth worker, although specific workplace supervision does occur both through management structures and accountability measures in workplaces and through professional networks of supervision. While management supervision resonates more with appraisal and assessment of productivity than professional supervision, there are many formal and informal professional supervision networks that operate around Australia, primarily self-organised by youth workers. The YWA in Victoria, however, have developed supervision resources and provide a voluntary supervision structure including regularly offering professional development seminars, workshops and annual conferences for members of the youth work association and providing support to the informal supervision networks.

In New Zealand, supervision is not widely used as part of the training and development of youth workers in government employment. However, the youth development sector has generated guidelines, although these are inconsistently enacted (largely because of resourcing) in the community sector.

12.4 Developing professional supervision practice

In terms of the development and enhancement of youth work as a profession in the Commonwealth, it would seem central that knowledge about the nature of supervision practice needs to be promoted, and that a skills base needs to be built. This might be facilitated by structured practice/academic programmes such as those offered by the YMCA George Williams College in the United Kingdom (YMCA George Williams College, n.d.).

The programme to be delivered by Agenzija Żgħażagħ, the National Youth Agency of Malta, is a similar case. This programme follows a six-month experiment of international co-operation using Skype supervision, building on a partnership programme (with the YMCA George Williams College) familiarising youth workers in Malta with a good practice model. This was carried forward as follows:

- Youth workers in the UK, with experience of supervision, collaborated with youth workers in Malta.

- Maltese/British pairs of practitioners, alternatively taking supervisor/supervisee roles, conducted regular supervision sessions (six one-hour sessions of supervision over a six-month period – sessions took place at approximately three-week intervals).

- All participants wrote brief but structured and evidence-based self-assessments of learning as supervisors and supervisees.

- Supervisors detailed and evidence the learning and development of supervisees as youth work practitioners from the process of supervision.

- Supervisees looked at their own learning and development as youth workers, calling on evidence gleaned/identified from the supervision process.

Figure 12.1 Development of Supervision Studies in Malta – Introductory Programme

The project will proceed in two phases:

Phase 1–The development and delivery of a six-month pilot programme. This will involve;

a) The nomination of between 8 and 12 candidates for training
b) Three full-day workshops;
- workshop 1 will take place in week 3 of the course
- workshop 2 will take place in the week 12 of the course
- workshop 3 will take place in week 20 of the course
- workshops will focus on participant learning via the sharing of practice and the study materials
c) All participants will be supplied with study materials electronically
d) All participants will undertake 5 sessions of supervision as supervisees
e) All participants will undertake 5 sessions of supervision as supervisors
f) All participants, as supervisees, will provide a satisfactory self-assessment of their learning
g) All participants, as supervisors will provide a satisfactory assessment of their supervisee's learning

Students will be encouraged to keep in regular contact with the tutor via email and Skype. Electronic and face-to-face tutorials will be made available.

Phase 2–Following review and assessment of the pilot programme during a two-day conference, a proposal for postgraduate certificate in supervision studies will be submitted to the University. This will include study materials.

This initial process allowed for the development of skill and insight about the use and conduct of supervision.

Following the completion and evaluation of the introductory programme in Malta, it is hoped that a structured and accredited course might be initiated, perhaps as a partnership between the University and Agenzija Żgħażagħ.

As a first stage of developing supervision practice, it would be advantageous to draw on the experience of those Commonwealth countries where professional supervision is being incorporated in education and training, and where it is practised.

12.5 Core factors in teaching supervision

While supervision gives the task to the supervisee to develop their own conclusions and solutions, the supervisor has an educational and advice function, especially in terms of the supervisee's safety and performance and the safety of the supervisee's clients.

Usually supervision encompasses three areas:

- particular incidents, issues or cases

- situations or contexts (physical workplace and networks, including frustrations with and emotional responses to the same)

- career considerations.

The third area can incorporate such areas as further training, conditions of work, career prospects and career aspirations, retirement, perceptions about how to manage and delegate work.

Sometimes two or all three of these provinces might be touched on in one supervision session. When supervision has an educational emphasis the direction of the encounter is (relatively) more clearly defined in relation to the above areas.

'Vision' is the means to gaze on or look at. Logically, linking 'vision' with the word 'super' implies a sort of 'extra-looking' or 'looking plus'. However, the word 'supervision' tends to be used to refer to one person overseeing another, as a means of checking their performance. But this would be a bit of a dead-end occupation if this scrutiny was not also a means of performance getting better (rather than just a way of maintaining a standard).

Both checking and improving performance are, more or less, encompassed in the supervision process. The extent to which either happens over a number of sessions depends on the context. But supervision is developmental (connected to continuous learning about the management and delivery of practice) and linked to performance (maintaining and improving standards).

12.6 Ways and contexts

There are different ways and contexts in which supervision takes place: peer supervision, education and training and in groups. It can also be more inclined towards support or management.

Figure 12.2 Areas of supervision focus

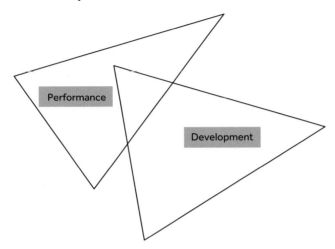

Figure 12.2 shows a diagram that can help practitioners to think about where their own supervisory encounters might be placed. For instance, if they are overtly managerial, more of an appraisal perhaps, one might place one's experience at the extreme right-hand point of the upper triangle. But if what the practitioner experiences feels more like a counselling session, they may feel inclined towards the bottom right hand point.

Although there are commonalities across supervision contexts, youth work has specific concerns and issues arising out of the nature of practice. The welfare/wellbeing, education/learning mix is unique, but it also changes from situation to situation. Sometimes youth workers are involved in igniting, making room for or generating relatively tangential learning experiences. In other spheres and/or points in time, youth workers can be implicated in clearly formalised and directive education, overt guidance, training and instruction – even, given the need – comparatively didactical forms of teaching.

However, in initial training and education, one of the primary concerns of supervision is the student's learning and development as a practitioner. This is second only to personal and client safety, but it might be a much closer second than, say, in an employment situation, where there is necessarily a major focus on performance and effective delivery. While the latter is also a consideration in training, it might not be as crucial (in relation to course requirements) as it could be in a field agency/organisation, given the need, with funding in mind, to ensure that intended outcomes are achieved.

The role of the supervisor in the educational context might be thought of as being much clearer, although it is no less complex. In this context of supervision, the supervisor has a role in supporting the learner on their 'learning journey'. Each supervisee's path on this journey, although having commonalities with study peers, will be unique to that person. As such the supervisor needs to get to know the strengths, areas for improvement/development and aspirations of their supervisee in order to provide effective and timely supervision. At the same time, the supervisee must be able to communicate the same information profile to the supervisor; this cannot be a one-way process.

It is possible to see how aims, contexts and job specifics could require the supervision encounter to be set in particular areas of the above image. But one could also add other triangles, maybe for 'support' or 'guidance', among others.

12.7 Practice without supervision can become malpractice

The above heading is a strong, perhaps shocking statement, but youth work practice without mechanisms to promote reflection, consideration and introspection – the wherewithal to examine, explore, critique and develop responses and services – could be considered 'unsafe', creating prime ground for accidents to happen and mistakes to occur without the means to prevent mistakes, or to learn from them.

Perhaps of all the aspects of youth work in the Commonwealth supervision is the most underdeveloped. Indeed, it appears that knowledge and skills to implement supervision are limited, and in some cases, non-existent. This being the case, it is clear that the Commonwealth, working with expert and experienced partners, might constructively look at developing supervision practice examples internationally as part of a further strengthening the fundamental foundations for effective, efficient, safe, **examined** practice.

12.8 Conclusion

Supervision was less well developed in countries sampled compared to other regulatory frameworks discussed in Chapter 10. While general supervisory practices were evident in some countries, not all of them were informed by the tenets of reflective practice advanced by youth work supervision.

This situation is of concern as youth work supervision is one of the principal means to promote reflective practice, being deployed in order that practitioners might address practice needs, ensuring better outcomes for the youth service users.

The goals and approach of youth work require the consistent enhancement of practice in order that it remains relevant and appropriate. This is part of professional growth and development and supervision is a crucial means of ensuring the same.

The evidence available in the baseline will become useful to countries in identifying knowledge sharing around training and implementing supervision practice in their own countries.

Chapter 13

Financial Investment and Youth Worker Remuneration

13.1 Introduction

This chapter represents the minimal data that was received on a. State investment in youth work and b. youth worker remuneration. It was difficult for countries to assess investment in the profession, i.e. in education and training of youth workers, as well as investment in youth work delivery, due to the fact that it is not recognised as a distinct profession in most member states. Youth worker remuneration was equally hard to assess and compare across regions/member states.

13.2 Investment in youth work

The rationale for the inclusion of this section was to seek to achieve some understanding of investment in the education and training of youth workers, in quality assurance and regulation, and in the implementation of youth work programmes, training and qualifications for youth workers, including partnerships with universities for creating professional routes to practice.

Investment could be taken to refer to financial inputs, but it can also be considered as the deployment of expertise and the creation of relevant structures and mechanisms. Much of the latter considerations have already been examined.

As in other elements of the recognition of youth work as a profession, there was little continuity or evidence around investment in the education and training of youth workers, or investment in youth work programmes, processes and spaces. Few contexts have a clear, delineated or demarcated budget for youth work. Provinces, counties, local authorities, regions, states and even parishes often generate their own finances and/or receive block funding from central national funds, perhaps for all child and youth services. This is then syphoned into delegated areas, one or some of which could include youth work services.

For example, a number of local authorities in the UK have a budget for 'integrated children's services'. However, the definition of this will vary according to needs and the relationship with other services. It can encompass everything from early years (0 to 5), including health visiting and residential care to Child and Adolescent Mental Health services and care-leavers (up to the ages of 21 or 25). This said, much of the youth work footprint in the UK has widely been subject to commissioning and is now in the hands of the commercial sector, while remaining the responsibility of the local authority.

In other Commonwealth contexts, youth work finance replicates some of this, although there is at least as much variation as commonality. Broadly speaking, youth work is underpinned by some State funding, social and charitable enterprises (NGO's), commercial interests and elements of international aid. This said, professionalisation is by and large dependent on State and educational partnerships.

The question asked in the baseline research with regard to budgets was:

> *What percentage of the Youth Ministry/Youth portfolio agency budget is set aside for professionalizing the youth work sector including investments for education and training of youth workers and supporting sustained field practice with young people through youth clubs etc.*

It was, however, not possible to obtain meaningful, systematic data for this question across the sample countries. Therefore, the following narrative will summarise what is possible to elicit from the given data. It should be noted that without knowing the percentage of overall government expenditure on youth work components in relation to gross domestic product (GDP), gross national product (GNP), etc., it is hard to understand the significance of stark figures, and such comparisons have been beyond the scope of this study.

It should also be noted that budgets indicated as for youth activities are not always necessarily devoted to youth work-like activity (i.e. genuine youth engagement).

13.2.1 Africa

Overall, the key stakeholders in both the Government and non-governmental agencies working in the youth sector appear to have limited knowledge about funding allocations for youth work. Budgets allocated to the area of youth development and empowerment services were available in some countries, and in others, budgets allocated to the nodal youth agencies were available. It was not possible to draw conclusions on the adequacy of the budget, or how this enabled quality youth work/youth engagement practices.

13.2.2 Asia

It was stated in the Asian baseline that this data is not available for any of the countries surveyed as there is no separate line item for youth work per se. While, budgets for the youth, youth and sport and other designated ministries with some responsibility for youth were made available, these are general, and not comparable, as each budget covers either a permutation of services, describes services in different ways or combines services in a distinctive manner. In some cases, anecdotal evidence was available, such as that in Sri Lanka the National Youth Services Council, a State youth development implementing agency, allocates funds for the training of their youth officers in the Commonwealth Diploma in Youth Development Work run by the Open University of Sri Lanka.

13.2.3 The Caribbean

While countries such as St Lucia, Dominica and St Vincent and the Grenadines were able to demonstrate budget allocations for youth services, in other contexts only

Figure 13.1 Dominican Youth Development Division Annual Budget - Youth Work

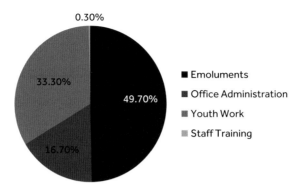

0.30%

33.30%

49.70%

16.70%

- Emoluments
- Office Administration
- Youth Work
- Staff Training

ministerial or department budgets were traceable. Dominica is the only country that specifically indicated budget allocations for youth work. Again, it was not possible to clearly ascertain what percentage of these budgets was actually invested in genuine youth youth/youth engagement practices.

The chart from Dominica shown in Figure 13.1 is the best example of an articulation of spending on youth work as opposed to salaries, administration and training.

13.2.4 Europe and Canada

In some contexts, particularly Europe and Canada, it was difficult to ascertain investments for youth work as this is often seen as an integrated service. Malta presented the clearest example of budgets for youth-related programmes and activities, as well as for grants to the Youth Agency. It would be safe to surmise that the distinct recognition of youth work as a professional category in Malta, and the accordance of legislative status, also creates a greater likelihood of specific budget breakdowns for youth work.

In the United Kingdom, despite local cuts, a relatively large budget has been allocated to the NCS, which is proving successful in removing barriers and providing opportunities for social development to young people in the UK.[1]

13.2.5 The Pacific

Australia spends significant funds on youth support services, education and health for young people and had a separate budget for youth affairs up to the budget period 2013–14. It is not clear how this will be demarcated in future budgets now that the new Cabinet has incorporated the previous Ministry of Youth into the Ministry of Education and the country no longer has a specific youth portfolio, an office for youth, or specific Ministry for youth. In New Zealand, budget allocations existed for the implementation of youth development, the Youth Development Partnership Fund, and service deliver to promote the interests of, and improve outcomes for, young people.

In most of the Pacific small islands, while agency-related budgets were available, it was not possible to obtain specific budgets for youth work.

13.3 Youth worker remuneration

Across the Commonwealth, youth worker salaries are calculated and expressed in a range of ways and numerical data did not allow for any form of adequate analysis.

However, what a youth worker earns is likely to be dictated by their employment circumstances; in some contexts, an NGO will not always provide a comparable salary to State employment, but in others NGOs might be providing higher salaries than the State, particularly country officers of international NGOs. Therefore, there will be disparity between NGOs, not only with regard to their origins (local or overseas) but also according to their reputation and how well they are established.

13.3.1 Africa

Data on the remuneration for youth workers is not available for all the countries. Most of those working in the youth sector have qualifications in the social sciences rather than youth work and there are few systems to guide youth worker practice or salary. Even though South Africa and Zambia have made recognisable progress through the inclusion of youth work in national youth policies, deriving youth worker salaries for these countries has been difficult. This may indicate a need to ensure stronger measures to translate policy into practice.

Ghana reported that the remuneration for youth workers is decided via negotiation between the employer and the employee. This perspective appears to contradict the operations of most Governments, where remuneration in the public sector is pre-defined.

Zambia reported that it was difficult to stipulate youth worker salaries as the country had 'youth workers by default' and not by qualification, in spite of the policy commitments to youth work.

13.3.2 Asia

Again, salary assessments were not possible, and no specific salary issues were raised.

13.3.3 Caribbean

Salary assessments were not possible.

13.3.4 Europe

In the UK for example, the figures quoted below relate to the Joint Negotiating Committee (JNC) for youth and community workers. This body has for many years set the national framework used to grade and pay youth work jobs.

There are two grades within the JNC framework:

- youth support worker

- professional youth worker

The JNC recognises youth and community workers' qualifications which have been professionally approved by the Education Training Standards (ETS) Committee of the National Youth Agency. The NYA endorse youth support worker qualifications and have a process of professional validation for higher education programmes.

Many people work with young people without JNC-recognised qualifications, often with related qualifications or extensive experience of working with young people.

JNC Terms and conditions

The JNC has also negotiated pay and agreed terms and conditions of service. It consisted of an employers' side and staff side and ensures that all views within the youth and community field were represented.

In December 2015 the JNC employers' representatives announced their intention to withdraw from national bargaining through the JNC and pursue the assimilation of youth and community staff to National Joint Council (NJC – the generic local government instrument) terms and conditions. It is likely this will undermine the professional standards of youth work education in the UK and have serious long-term implications for the sector (see National Youth Agency, UK (2017b).

However, many local authorities and commercial employers are abandoning JNC guidelines as youth work becomes more and more a type of temporary and/or part-time form of employment and increasingly the supply of qualified youth workers outstrips employer demands.

The conditions of work and salaries for youth workers in many of these commercial/ entrepreneurial (not philanthropic) manifestations of youth work described elsewhere in this report have been less than satisfactory. Moreover, work is often temporary, part-time and/or relatively derisory.

13.3.5 The Pacific

In Australia, youth workers are remunerated under the Social and Community Services Employees (State) Award (AN120505). Pay rates change from 1 July each year, and rates are applied on 1 December of the same year.

An entry-level youth worker would be paid as a 'community services worker Grade 1' at AUS$731.50 per week or AUS$19.25 per hour. At the top end, a worker would be paid as a 'community services officer Grade 6 – Year 2' at AUS$1701.74 per week or AUS$44.78 per hour. This does not include overtime, shift or penalty rates. Compulsory retirement savings known as superannuation is 9.5 per cent of salary, and annual leave is four paid weeks per year.

In New Zealand rates of remuneration for youth work have decreased against the national average wage over the last 10 years, despite comparative evidence that youth workers are far more qualified than they were in 2006 (see Ara Taiohi, n.d.).

Employment as a youth worker tends to be precarious and short term in nature. The fledgling professional association for youth workers in New Zealand has placed a priority on improving youth workers' pay and conditions alongside general advocacy for the profession.

13.4 Conclusion

There is much more to be done in terms of youth work budgeting and understanding youth development budgets in relation to investments for professionalising youth work considering the eight dimensions referred to throughout this document. There is a greater likelihood, such as is the case in Malta, of definitive budget allocations for specific dimensions of professionalisation such as education and training, support to youth workers' associations, youth engagement practices as opposed to general youth programmes, youth work supervision and professional accreditation, etc., in contexts where there are clear policy commitments to recognising youth work as a profession.

Note

1   To date, more than 200,000 young people have completed the programme, which is not only innovative in terms of course content, but it is also delivered by the third sector, creating valuable partnerships nationally. The UK Government spent £130.4 million on NCS in 2014/15 (figures for 2015/16 are at the time of writing unavailable). It is projected that the NCS will serve 300,000 young people a year at a cost £1.1bn by 2020.

Chapter 14

Conclusions and Recommendations – Way Forward for Professional Youth Work

The research strongly indicates that youth work in the Commonwealth is a diverse and multifaceted practice. While it has commonalities in terms of delivery and intent, it does not conform to any one set of techniques or approaches. This is probably reflective of the character of this 'family of nations', its cultural and historical diversity, as well as the differences in economic and social background. With this in mind, it would seem to be unnecessary to insist on uniformity for its own sake and wise to be ready to promote mutual learning from the richness of response.

However, this poses issues in arriving at some form of unanimity in terms of professionalism. Wants, needs and requirements differ from context to context, even within relatively small nations and geographical areas.

The Commonwealth has, over the years, sourced and expended a comparatively large amount of energy, intellectual labour, time and finance into developing paths to facilitate professional responses. This has led, directly and indirectly, to probably tens of thousands of people taking up training and education at almost every level between basic introductions to practice to postgraduate qualification. The benefits to young people have almost certainly been considerable; it is likely that millions of Commonwealth citizens have grown up in the embrace of youth work; the concern and effort of what Nelson Mandela saw, with reference to the Commonwealth, as an organisation that 'makes the world safe for diversity' has also contributed to this.

Youth work's claims of working with young people in order that they 'fulfil their potential' can sound pretty trite when one asks how one might know when someone has reached that point (or half-reached it). But in defence of those youth workers, why would anyone want a child not to make the best of their potential?

Given the size of the Commonwealth youth population, youth work is likely to have a growing presence, certainly in the light of racial, political, social and economic tensions and divisions, that are replicated in different contexts across the Commonwealth. Youth workers prospectively need to be more than programme providers, being ready to take on aspects of roles such as counsellor, mediator, advocate, activist and educator. As the practice develops, appending new roles and expectations, society and young people will look to youth workers for a range of responses.

In today's context, professionalism for youth workers in the Commonwealth is no longer a luxury or strategy for enhancing the profile or status of the field. Professional expertise is a necessity as practitioners increasingly assume responsibility for the positive development of a massive section of the total population.

In any society and maybe across societies, it would be helpful to have some agreement about the actual and comparative value of youth work. This perhaps might help with regard to establishing what might be the appropriate level of remuneration for youth workers in any given context.

The Commonwealth has found that youth work is fundamental to national development, and may be considered as pressing as other needs, considering issues of social cohesion, economic and social inequalities, etc., for which youth work will have a response related to the delivery of basic health/education services and care. Therefore, the Commonwealth and member states have made efforts to advance youth work as a practice that is professional.

There can be little doubt that the presence and skills of youth workers work as a fillip to any society in terms of the stability and social health of communities. The Commonwealth believes and has shown that it is in the interests of governments to invest in youth work because of its direct and indirect contributions to positive human development and social productivity, to establishing democratic cultures, to social cohesion and a sense of direction for the future of communities, regions, nations and the world. Commonwealth leaders have consistently agreed with this perspective and have unfailingly backed youth work initiatives.

For all this, a significant section of the population of the nations focused on would probably correctly assume that youth work is largely a part-time and/or voluntary activity. The contribution of volunteers in faith-based and uniformed provision across regions dwarfs the full-time workforce. Many of these volunteers have comparatively modest training and support, while an appreciable number do not access any form of training. As such, it is likely that the professional status of youth work may be something of an enigma for most people across the Commonwealth, as it might be for many youth workers who are not in a position (partly because of the lack of training) to understand the complexities associated with the explicit assertion of professional status. The mere claim to professional status, or a level of regard an occupation might command in terms of professionalism, does not mean that the occupation has professional status in any legislative and so indisputable legal sense.

Such considerations need to be thought about with regard to the professionalisation of youth work. Yes, we would logically want youth workers to act professionally; to have the requisite skills, ethical awareness and so on, but to have this must youth work be corralled within a profession? If it is, what happens to the massive majority of youth workers who practise part-time and who are volunteers? If they are not provided with the means to act professionally, having professional awareness and knowhow, how we will be able to claim that youth work is founded on professional values, principles and conduct?

As highlighted above, the Commonwealth has achieved much in the advancement of youth work, but it is clear perhaps that a few fundamental questions might need to be asked or re-asked; 'What must youth work in the Commonwealth be?'

What then, are the 'Musts' and 'Shoulds' for member states aspiring to provide professional, visionary youth work services for young people?

14.1 The 'Musts'

1. **Build a collaborative vision for youth work**

   Build a national vision for professional youth work based on the foundations of a strong, competent cadre of youth workers with attitudes, knowledge and capabilities of professional judgement. Build this in collaboration with all youth work practitioners, those teaching youth work, with youth stakeholders, and especially with young people.

   This would be seen as a vision of an occupation concerned with the rights and wellbeing of young people, that involves practitioner empathy, but unlike certain incarnations of social work or teaching, that which avoids assumptions of deficit – the person in front of me is not necessarily relatively ignorant (generally uneducated) or helpless (broadly in need of help). Youth work is not centrally concerned with 'at-risk' groups but developmental processes aimed at the generic youth population.

   The welfare focus of youth work, its orientation of care for, and concern about, young people – what amounts to the values of the practice – is often forgotten in discussions about professionalism and youth work, and the research related to this is scant (Beker and Maier, 2001). However, this element of professionalism in youth work practitioners risks missing what is perhaps the most intricate aspect of the role; it is related to feelings about and orientations toward social justice and equity, and as such, has a political underpinning. Arguably, this is the foundation for everything youth workers do and determines how they applies their knowledge and skills. This end goal should not be lost in building this vision.

2. **Formalise youth work education and training in qualifications frameworks**

   Ensure that youth work training and qualifications are registered onto the National Qualifications Authority Framework or by a relevant recognised qualifications authority to formalise education and training for youth work.

3. **Obtain professional recognition for the youth work profession**

   Ensure that Public Service Commissions recognise youth work as a profession in the public sector. While many countries have assigned youth service officers/ youth co-ordinators in public sector youth structures, and many countries include functions related to youth work in the role and responsibilities of youth service officers, the formal recognition of the profession would obtain value and recognition for the profession, regularise competitive pay scales and, by extension, strengthen youth worker retention and systematic delivery of asset-based youth work for young people. An evidence-based policy paper that sets out the rationale and approach for the recognition of the youth work profession is usually a good start.

4. **Develop a framework for professionalism considering the eight criteria of the baseline and other relevant national/regional priorities, and implement the framework**

    Assess your country's/region's status in terms of the eight criteria for professional youth work that defines the baseline (The existence of: a collectively formulated and owned definition of youth work as a profession, policy and legislative commitments, professional organisation as youth workers' associations, code of ethics, competency standards and other regulatory frameworks, qualification pathways, professional validation, professional supervision, and investment.)

    Develop a widely consulted framework that brings on board the expertise and interests of all stakeholders highlighted in **recommendation 1**. Where a professional association exists, ensure their participation and leadership in the process as the core organisation of practitioners. In terms of government-led frameworks for professionalism, Malta and Malaysia provide an established and emerging professionalising process, respectively.

    An implementation plan, and monitoring and evaluation of the plan, needs to be built into the process.

    The rest of the recommendations below help articulate directions for recommendation 4.

5. **Set up structures and processes for youth work**

    The ultimate test of the ability to impact young people's lives through youth work practice will depend on how trained and competent youth workers are facilitated with the resources of sustained and effective youth work delivery structures. Many youth club processes and learning processes developed in the youth work sphere would be helpful in planning for and investing in youth work delivery structures and processes. An example is the Commonwealth-Pravah-NYKS pilot *Co-Creating Youth Spaces: A Practice-Based Guide for Youth Facilitators* (Commonwealth Secretariat et al., 2014).

6. **Make youth work delivery accessible and safe**

    This suggests the necessity to have **proficient, trusted practitioners, who are ready and able to engage with young people and foster positive life outcomes** (Astroth et al., 2004). Ensure safety and vetting mechanisms for professionals working with young people so that young people will not be put at risk by allowing significant access to them by those who, both unintentionally and otherwise, might do harm to them.

    Again, conventional filters and checks will not be adequate for such a massive safeguarding challenge. While much might be achievable via the co-operation between police and youth work providers, on the scale we are looking at pan-Commonwealth, innovative forms of vigilance and vetting are needed at a community level.

7. **Ensure continuing education and competency-based programmes to raise practitioner abilities and status**

   Continuous professional development supports the retention of youth workers and enhances their capacity to respond appropriately to young people (Walker, 2003).

   While there is support for professionalising youth work by way of university-level education, others have it that experience-based training and preparation is the best way forward. Regardless of this lack of consensus about the means of professional development, it has been argued that youth work seems to be heading towards more formal professionalism.

   To use an example outside of the Commonwealth (for the sake of comparison), in the USA, there has been a consistent demand for more concentrated and formal training arrangements for youth workers, and a foundational definition of youth development work. Borden and Perkins (2006, p. 101) have it that 'given the complexity of the needs of today's young people, it is both timely and prudent to increase the type, quality, and quantity of educational experiences available to community youth development professionals.'

   The Commonwealth Youth Council has also asked for greater attention to be paid to the practice of peer youth work, where young people themselves attain professional status in order to engage other young people. In a context where research has highlighted the benefits of young professional peers engaging with others of their age group, this is indeed a further area of inquiry and strengthening through adequate education and training.

8. **Establish rights-based ethical standards**

   Develop and ensure the implementation and monitoring of ethical standards for youth work practice in a participatory manner involving practitioners and young people. Ensure the participation of youth service beneficiaries in the monitoring and evaluation of services.

   For youth workers to be professional, these ethical guidelines and professional direction is critical, and is similar to ethics that govern social workers, teachers and other like professionals who are involved with young people.

   For Sercombe (2010), ethics in youth work arises out of the unique character of the relationship between the youth workers and young person that is central to its practice. It is not like the association between a pupil and teacher, or a social worker and a client, although it can involve elements of the same, and of other roles (counsellor, advice worker and so on). Youth workers, while perhaps acting in a friendly manner, are not friends, neither are they or can they be (if they are to remain professional) surrogate parents, or older siblings. Corney (2014), while offering a helpful critique of Sercombe, also provides a unique rights-based framework that provides further guidelines, principles and responsibilities of practice. The Commonwealth Secretariat's Draft Code of Ethical Practice for Youth Workers also highlights a similar rights-based framework. It is this generic but also delineated youth work role that requires unique knowledge and skills; the association needs to motivate trust, but maintain appropriate boundaries.

9. **Develop an evidence-base for youth work**

Evidence is what tells us what works, and what does not. Demonstration of the impact of youth work on young people's lives and on peace and prosperity of countries generally, also promotes trust in the profession, and encourages investment. Evidence also helps youth workers hone their craft.

There have been recommendations by, among others, Azimi (2005) to address the lack of evidence-based tools for to assess youth work and its impact on young people. However, youth work practice remains hard to assess due to the lack of localised, context-relevant models and measures of youth work effectiveness. Without this, it is difficult to see how professional development can be said to be happening. Moreover, in the current context of financial cuts to youth work, there is an urgent need to invest in research that demonstrates a link between professionally trained youth workers and positive youth outcomes (Beker, 2001; Eisikovitz & Beker, 2001). This calls for the development of tools and methods to evaluate youth work.

The upcoming *Transformative Youth Work International Conference: Developing and Communicating Impact*, 4-6 September 2018[1] explores evidence of the impact of youth work in selected European countries. This would possibly lead the way for similar impact assessments in the Commonwealth. While the impact of youth work on youth development, and equality for youth, is not always easy to measure, quantitative and qualitative modes of measuring achievement need to be explored and adapted.

10. **Develop a knowledge base for youth work**

Knowledge creation in the youth work profession was not specifically addressed in this study. There is a significant corpus of intellectual work, both academic, and more practice-oriented, in the Commonwealth that needs to be collated, and shared. Examples of the more practice-oriented work include 'Ocean in a Drop: Inside Youth Leadership', an examination of youth-led youth work and other youth initiatives in the context of India. Additionally, numerous youth work journals, including the *Commonwealth Journal of Youth Development Work*, periodically published jointly with the University of South Africa (UNISA), and the *Journal of Youth Work Ethics* published by Ara Taiohi in New Zealand add to the corpus of knowledge and deliberation around youth work. Such initiatives need to be improved and expanded.

11. **Discuss and formulate competency frameworks for youth work as relevant to your context (Huebner et al., 2003; Quinn, 2004)**

With the professionalisation of youth work comes the need for standards to measuring professionalism. As indicated above, youth work lacks baseline tools for measuring professionalism, comparable to those found (for example) in professions like pharmacy (see Chisholm et al., 2006) or medicine (American

Board of Internal Medicine Committees on Evaluation of Clinical Competence and Clinical Competence and Communication Programmes, 2001 – see http://www.tau.ac.il/medicine/cme/pituach/030210/1.pdf).

Even though a formalised model of professional youth work has not been developed, Davies, Harte and and others have suggested some elements of what can be taken as 'quality' youth work. These include:

- Competency: specific/unique knowledge and skills;

- Integrity: ethics;

- Care/concern: values

Youth work competences are the 'knowledge, skills, and personal attributes workers need to create and support positive youth development settings' (Astroth et al., 2004, p. 27).

As youth work is fundamentally and essentially developmental, to be competent, it would be key for a professional practitioner to be able to show one has the knowledge and skill to work with young people as this is central to the 'quality practice' (Evans, 2008; Sockett, 1996).

The Caribbean Commonwealth competency standards and the UK's occupational standards may be guides to forms of assessing professionalism. At a more granular level of assessing direct youth engagement competencies, ComMutiny – Youth Collective's Challenger Deep assessment tool would also be a helpful guide.

Once again, competency standards need to be developed in collaboration with youth workers' associations, universities, young people and other youth sector stakeholders. This creates a means to evaluate and/or measure professionalism.

12. **Monitor and evaluate youth work**

   Ensure mechanisms that enable youth workers and managers to monitor and evaluate the processes and results of youth work. This evidence helps convince planners and investors of the worth of youth work.

13. **Invest in youth work and develop budget lines specific to expenditure relevant to professionalising youth work**

   Youth work needs investment. Public spending considerations for youth work are vital and the evidenced erosion of public investment in youth work needs to be curbed. At the same time, well-executed plans for funding strategies ranging from equitable and rights-based public-private partnerships, entrepreneurial innovation, bilateral and multilateral partnerships, crowd funding and so on, need to be encouraged.

   In the public sector, clear budget lines need to be set up in ministries and departments for youth work-related expenditure including budget allocated for the education and training of youth workers, for investment in youth work programmes and processes, for the establishment of youth-work delivering youth clubs, and so on.

While adequate funding is crucial for implementing youth work, the quality of the individuals involved in planning, operating and monitoring practice is also key. 'As public investments in youth development programmes continue, the preparation and ongoing development of adults who work with young people in programmes has increased in importance' (Borden & Perkins, 2006).

14. **Focus on quality recruitment**

Invest in, and liaise with professional associations of youth workers in ensuring the recruitment of suitable youth work professionals whose qualifications, but above all, youth engagement competencies, are adequately assessed. Davies (1988 as cited in Harte, 2000) argued that youth workers, to be professional, need a blend of exclusive skills and knowledge. They therefore also need to be **judiciously selected.**

15. **Establish and implement supervision frameworks**

Explore collaborations with professional associations and universities with advanced frameworks and implementation mechanisms as elaborated in the baseline, for setting up supervision standards so that youth workers might preserve and deepen their trained skill.

A great and lively network across our planet is there for the making, and supervision can be the cementing agent holding this together; a massive, dialogical nexus of development, exploration, examination, betterment and learning – a humming, buzzing human dialectic and the collective voice of the young.

14.2 The 'Shoulds'

Having taken just a cursory look at the 'musts' of the kind of youth work we might want, how about the 'shoulds'? At best, what do we want youth work to do?

1. **Make youth work fun**

Young people might look to youth work to be 'fun' and that would seem reasonable to most people; youth *should* be a time for having fun; fun involves play and we know that play is edifying in itself.

2. **Make youth work a learning experience**

As much as youth work is made to be fun, parents and governments may also believe it should offer opportunities for young people to learn. **If learning is to be fun it is going to be related to things one wants to learn.** But does this bring us back to the problem of training? Is it not the case that adults need a good deal of education to be able to work with young people to facilitate their learning? The project of **ComMutiny – the Youth Collective** in India has shown that young people can develop their own learning environments simply with the encouragement (or lack of discouragement) of allied adults. Sugata Mitra's 'Hole in the Wall Project'[2] has confirmed this worldwide. Perhaps his 'granny cloud' could be an inspiration?[3]

This notion does not make professionally qualified youth workers redundant. In fact, it can create a whole new role in youth work in centralised hubs, perhaps sponsored by a range of finance from State grants to crowdfunding and entrepreneurial innovation. The knowledge of graduates can be disseminated effectively from every corner of the globe, but also such work can offer completely novel research possibilities to build on and extend practice.

That these processes are underway in many Commonwealth member states is a positive sign.

As a result of the commitments of the Commonwealth's Plan of Action for Youth Empowerment (PAYE), there have been ongoing calls for the generation of a youth work code of ethics, enhanced practice standards, and the collectivisation and professional organisation of youth work professionals. This was a logical and clear advance toward raising the quality of youth work. Such initiatives have received extensive support, and the Commonwealth commissioned relevant resources such as the draft Code of Ethical Practice, guidance on youth work, as well as guidance on establishing professional associations (Commonwealth Secretariat 2012a, 2012b and 2014). While national-level movement along these lines have begun to be energised, these is yet more to be achieved, and sustained.

Young people are the greatest resource that youth work has (indeed without them there would be no youth work) and it is their collaboration that is the means to make youth work accessible, safe, fun and a means to promote and stimulate learning, and in turn cohesive, prosperous, societies.

Youth work is a growth profession, in a growth sector.

Notes

1   https://www.marjon.ac.uk/courses/our-faculties/faculty-of-education--social-sciences/department -of-social-sciences/transformative-youth-work-2018--developing-and-communicating-impact-/
2   see https://www.ted.com/talks/sugata_mitra_shows_how_kids_teach_themselves?language=en
3   http://www.bbc.co.uk/news/technology-17114718

Annex 1

Identified Commonwealth Youth Workers' Associations

Youth work association name	Country	Association contact	Commonwealth contact
Africa			
South Africa Youth Work Association (CAYWA member)	South Africa	**Address:** 312 Main Avenue, Ferndale, Randburg 2194, South Africa **Phone:** + 27 (0) 11 674 5405 **Fax:** +27 (0) 11 674 5485, **Email:** saywa@mail.ngo.za, goitsiene05@gmail.com	Tamara Mathebula tamara.mathebula@gmail.com
Zambia Youth Work Association (CAYWA member)	Zambia	**Address:** C/o Ministry of Youth, Sport and Child Development, Lusaka Provincial Youth Office, Fairley Road, Ridgeway, P.O. Box 31852, Lusawwka, Zambia **Email:** zywaprofession@gmail.com **Phone:** +260 977 60 36 37/ 979 27 64 93 Facebook: Zambia Youth Workers Association	Andrew Tandeo andrewtandeo@hotmail.com
Asia			
ComMutiny—The Youth Collective (CAYWA member)	India	**Address:** 11/8 Nehru Enclave East, Kalkaji, New Delhi, India **Email:** CYC.delhi@gmail.com **Phone:** http://commutiny.in/	Ashraf Patel ash.pravah@gmail.com CYC.delhi@gmail.com
Youth Work Association Singapore (CAYWA member)	Singapore	**Address:** 28 Pasir Ris Drive 6 #01-21 Singapore 510428 **Phone:** 0065-5833-3481 **Email:** **Website:** www.youthworkassociation.org	Dr John Tan john@care.sg

(Continued)

Youth work association name	Country	Association contact	Commonwealth contact
Professional Youth Workers' Association (CAYWA member)	Sri Lanka	**Address:** Professional Youth Workers' Association, No. 73, 1st Floor, Delkanda Plaza, High Level Road Delkanda, Nugegoda, Sri Lanka. **Email:** pywasl@gmail.com **Website:** www.pywa.com	Dr Shantha Abeysinghe shan99a@gmail.com
The Caribbean			
Jamaica Professional Youth Workers' Association	Jamaica	**Address:** Jamaica Professional Youth Workers' Association, E 39, Geranium Avenue, Hamilton Gardens, St. Catherine **Email:** youthworkjamaica.org **Telephone:** 876-8332132 Facebook: Jamaica Professional Youth Workers Association	Tanya Powell trichpowell@gmail.com
Europe and Canada			
Council of Canadian Child and Youth Care Associations	Canada	**Website:** http://www.cyccanada.ca/	Kelly Shaw kellyshaw@eastlink.ca
The Professional Association for Lecturers in Youth and Community Work (TAG)	Europe	**Address:** 1 Kennington Road, London, SE17QP **Telephone:** 0044-208 787 5830 **Email:** info@tagpalycw.org **Website:** http://www.tagpalycw.org/	Lyn Boyd L.M.Boyd@hud.ac.uk
Malta Association of Youth Workers (CAYWA member)	Malta	**Address:** c/o Agenzija Zghazagh, St Joseph High Road, Santa Venera, SVR1012, Malta **Email:** info.maymalta@gmail.com **Website:** http://www.maymalta.org/	Miriam Tuema miriam.teuma@gov.mt

(Continued)

Youth work association name	Country	Association contact	Commonwealth contact
Institute of Youth Work	United Kingdom	**Address:** Institute for Youth Work, Kemp House, 152-160 City Road, London, EC1V 2NX **Email:** info@iyw.org.uk **Website:** https://iyw.org.uk/	
The Pacific			
Youth Workers Association – Victoria (CAYWA member)	Australia	**Address:** Brunswick West 3055, Victoria, Australia **Email:** info@ywa.net.au **Website:** https://www.ywa.org.au/ **Address:** Leederville WA, Australia **Email:** connect@youthworkwa.org.au **Website:** http://www.youthworkwa.org.au/	Dr Robyn Broadbent robyn.broadbent@vu.edu.au
Western Australian Association of Youth Workers Inc.	Australia	**Address:** P.O. Box 286, Leederville, WA 6902 **Email:** connect@youthworkwa.org.au **Website:** www.youthworkwa.org.au Facebook.com/YouthWorkWA twitter.com/YouthWorkWA instagram.com/YouthWorkWA	-
Ara Taiohi Professional Association for Youth workers (CAYWA member)	New Zealand	**Address:** Level 3, 148 Cuba St, Te Aro, Wellington, New Zealand **Email:** admin@arataiohi.org.nz **Website:** http://www.arataiohi.org.nz/	Anya Satyanand anya.satyanand@arataiohi.org.nz
Canterbury Youth Workers Collective (member of the above national association)	New Zealand	**Address:** 301 Tuam St, Christchurch Central, Christchurch 8011, New Zealand **Email:** penny@cantyouthworks.co.nz **Website:** http://www.cywc.org.nz/	

Annex 2

Baseline Questionnaire

Name of Region ....

Name of questionnaire administrator ....

Email and Phone Contact ....

Stakeholders interviewed:

Country	Name of respondent	Institution

Note: If there is no data available/found for a country, please indicate this in each question as N/A, if there is data, but the researcher has not been able to access it, say 'not accessible'.

1. Trend Analysis: Provide a brief for the eight selected countries for the region in terms of trends in youth work policy and highlighting the most remarkable achievements, the greatest challenges and ways to overcome challenges and ways forward (no more than 500 words).

   ....

   ....

2. National/Regional Youth Work Bodies: Please fill in below core national public body recognized for policy and legislation in youth work, and for implementing youth work.

Country/sub-national/ region	Key national youth work policy body – i.e. Youth Ministry etc.	Key national youth work implementing body – i.e. National Youth Council etc.

3. Policy and legislation: Please fill in the chart below (refer to guidelines)

Country/ sub-national/ region	Current youth policy exists and if so, duration	Current youth policy indicates commitments to youth work	Specific youth work policy exists	Youth Act exists	Youth Work Act exists	Other

Explain all affirmative answers below and attach relevant documents in soft copy form, with a summary observation of salient points in youth work policy and legislation for the region, particularly if qualifications need to be made in relation to data above. *Also mention if youth work is framed in ways that are empowering and engaging young people:*

....

....

4. Guidelines and Supporting Mechanisms in the State youth work: Please tick as applicable and attach relevant documents. Explain answer. (refer to guidelines)

Country/ sub-national/ region	Official definition of youth work	Competency/ occupational standards for youth work exists	State guidelines on youth work	State ethical standards for youth work	Youth Safeguarding/ Youth protection policies in State youth sector	Occupational health and safety standards for youth work in State sector	Criminal history vetting for youth workers	Youth Worker licensing/ ID card as a youth worker

Elaborate on your answers in the matrix and attach relevant documents. Mention all pertinent observations. Also mention if easily identifiable and utilized non-state guidelines and supporting structures as mentioned above exists.

....

....

....

5. No. of youth workers in the state youth sector. This refers to youth workers in the main State body/bodies holding the youth portfolio.

Country	Total population	Total youth population	Male youth workers	Female youth workers	Total youth workers

6. Accredited Courses in Youth Work: These are for courses that carry credits only. Please fill in data below with relevant attachments on youth work education and training. Tick where the relevant qualification exists. Please also indicate names of universities, or training institutes running these courses. (refer to guidelines). Please note that qualifications referred to here have to be youth work qualifications, and not general youth studies qualifications.

Country 1 – 8 Name: (Box per country)							
University/ Institution	Short	Certificate Course	Diploma	BA	MA	PhD	Other (explain)

7. Non-accredited training on youth work: Indicate the most prominent short courses directly linked to developing the skills of youth workers and youth development practitioners that were conducted, or continuously available for the past two years (these can be limited to short courses managed by the relevant State youth sector body, and any other dominant youth sector bodies including UN agencies). This is meant to be an indicative, rather than exhaustive, list.

Country	Name of Course and target trainees (youth workers, youth work managers, policy makers etc)	Training Institute with address, email and phone numbers
Country 1 – 8		
Country 2 etc		

8. Minimum qualifications: Indicate below the minimum qualification required for State youth workers, and any predominant qualification required for non-state youth workers. This does not include qualifications required for youth work management. Indicate where this requirement is mentioned.

Country	Minimum qualification for government youth workers including specification of area of studies (ie general degrees, or do they require specific youth work related degrees?	Minimum qualification for non-government youth workers including specification of area of studies (i.e. general degrees, or do they require specific youth work related degrees?

9. Youth Workers' Associations: Fill in below where active regional, or national or sub-national youth workers associations exist (please tick and attach any supporting documents as relevant) (refer to guidelines). Active=currently operational and has evidence of activity for the past two years.

Country/ sub-national/ region	Active Youth Workers Association exists, if so, name and address with email and phone numbers	Plans underway – if so explain status + plus contact details	Membership			Key Activities and achievements
			Male	Female	Total	
Country 1 Name:						
Country 2 Name:						
Country 3 Name:						
Country 4 Name etc:						
Country 5 Name:						
Country 6 Name:						
Country 7 Name:						
Country 8 Name:						

10. Training of teachers: Teacher training for youth work academics and trainers

Country	Nature of teacher training for youth work academics/Trainers

11. Course accreditation: Fill in below professional accreditation processes for youth work education and training for each country, and highlight good practices (please see guidelines).

Country	Nature of professional accreditation of youth work qualifications

12. State youth work practice: Describe predominant youth work practice methods in the State sector, and if there are any linkages with the non-state sector. i.e. is there sustained engagement with groups of young people through youth clubs etc., through well-defined methodologies? Any strengths? Weaknesses? *Does practice generally reflect empowering, asset-based approaches to youth work?* You can be broad in this answer as this is for a general understanding only. Key informants may contribute to this question.

Country	Existence (or not) of clear empowering asset based approaches to youth work in the State sector, and evidence for this	Existence of partnerships with the non-governmental sector if any in implementing youth work. Explain – name of agency, nature of partnership and nature of work

13. Youth work supervision: Fill in below government supervision processes for youth work if any, and whether supervision guidelines exists.

Country	Formal supervision exists. If so how is this indicated?	Supervision guidelines exists	Qualifications exist for youth work supervision

14. Youth work programmes and plans: Please list and attach links or documents where available of any key programmes and plans for youth work in the country that are not included in the questionnaire above, with a brief explanation. These

could be either governmental or non-governmental initiatives and could be either linked or not linked to existing legislation and policy.

Country	Youth Work Programme/Plan

15. Non-Governmental sector: List any key non-governmental organizations/ institutions recognised as working in youth work in the region/country, with a brief explanation of the work they do, including advocacy on youth work with government, and any significant policy or practice impact they have had in the region.

Sub-National level/ Country/Region	Name of NGO/INGO/ Institution with address, email and phone numbers	Activities at sub-national, national or regional level

16. Government spending on professionalizing youth work: What percentage of the Youth Ministry/Youth portfolio agency budget is set aside for professionalizing the youth work sector including investments for education and training of youth workers and supporting sustained field practice with young people through youth clubs etc. (refer to guidelines). This should be for the last financial year for which a budget is available.

17. Youth worker remuneration:

Country	Average salary of a mid-level state sector school teacher	Average salary of a mid-level state-sector youth worker	Source/s of information

18. Influence of the Commonwealth Secretariat/Commonwealth Youth Programme (CYP): Do any States attribute the gains they have made in professionalizing youth work to the Commonwealth? If so, please indicate in which dimension of the six indicated in 'dimensions of professionalization' above (section 4), and how? (please note that those with adequate institutional memory need to be tapped to respond to this question).

Country/sub-national/region	Parameter of influence by Commonwealth, and how?

19. General trends: Please provide a qualitative analysis of general trends in youth work practice in relation to the empowerment of young people in the region (about a 1000 words). Mention specific country good practice.

   ....
   ....

20. Challenges: Provide a summative analysis of challenges in youth work education and training and youth work policy, legislation and practice in the region (key informants may contribute to this question).

   ....
   ....

21. Overcoming challenges: What, in the consultants' opinion, and in relation to discussions with stakeholders, are key means of overcoming challenges, and moving towards the full professionalization of the sector?

   ....
   ....

22. Challenges in implementing survey methodology/data collection.

   ....
   ....

Annex 3

Baseline Interviewees

Country	Name	Institution
Africa		
Ghana	Stephen Mensah-Etsibah	National Youth Authority, National Youth Authority, Ministry of Youth and Sports (Director of Programmes)
	Emma Ofori-Agyemang	Policy Planning, Budgeting, Monitoring & Evaluation (PPBME), Ministry of Employment & Labour Relations (Director) +233 302 665 797
	Kennedy Ofori	Adult Education and Human Resource Studies, University of Ghana, Legon, Accra (Coordinator CYP) +233 244 535 942
	Alice Attipoe	Human Resource Division, Ministry of Employment and Labour Relations, Director +233 302 665 797 +233 244 206 535
Kenya	Peter Wainaina	Ministry of Public Service, Youth & Gender Affairs; P.O. Box 30050-00100 Nairobi. Tel: +25420227411
	Inspector John M. Mwangi	National Youth Service of Kenya; P.O. Box 30397-00100 Nairobi, Tel: +254208561489
	Mildred Nzau	Youth Agenda Kenya; P.O. Box 10174-00100 Nairobi, Kinanu60@Gmail.Com
	Augustine Gatotoh Mwangi	School of Continuing and Distance Education, University of Nairobi (Officer in Charge Diploma in Youth Work), Tel: +245721291639, Augustine.Gatotoh@Uonbi.Ac.Ke
Malawi	Aubrey Chibwana	Executive Director of National Youth Council of Malawi
	Mphatso Baluwa Jim	National Coordinator of Malawi Girl Guides Association
	Dominic Nyasulu	Executive Director of Youth Platform on Climate Change, Dominicnyasulu@Yahoo.Com, Tel: +265 999 621 845
	Judith Msusa	Deputy Director at The Department of Youth in the Ministry of Labour, Youth and Manpower Development. Tel: +264 999 416 564, Jmsusa@Gmail.Com
	Dr Chiziba Goliath	Africa University of Guidance, Counselling & Youth Development (AUGCYD)

Country	Name	Institution
Nigeria	S. K. Ikata – *Director* M. Nwaogu – *Assistant Director, Alumni of Diploma in Youth Work* K. Mohammed – *Assistant Director* E. O. Ochoga – *Staff, Alumni of Diploma in Youth Work* Madam Beatrice – *Staff*	Federal Ministry of Youth Development & Sports Official, Email: Hmysdirect@ Gmail.Com; Tel: 08076949533
	Nkeiruka Joy Ogbuji	Alumni of Youth Work Course Alumni, Diploma in Youth Work Course, Nkjoy@Gmail.Com, Tel: 08163993644
	Wale Ajani	Youth leader from NGO, Tel: 08032266543; Waleajani@Gmail.Com
	1. Professor Sophia Ogwude 2. Dr Emem Obonguko 3. Habib Yakoob 4. Prof Suleiman	University of Abuja Team, Tel: 08037077944, 08093344454; Soogwude@gmail.Com, Tel: 08036082195, 08055442465; Ememm123@Yahoo.Com, Tel: 08034508527; Hatimore@Yahoo. Com, Head of Legal & Strategic Studies
South Africa	Batlhobogeng	National Department of Social Development, Bathlobogeng@Gmail. Com
	Dr R. Bernice Hlagala	Department of Planning, Monitoring and Evaluation (DPME), Bernirama@Gmail. Com
	Reggie Nel	University of South Africa; Reggienel@ Gmail.Com, Rwnel@Unisa.Ac.Za
	Shantelle Weber	University of Stellenbosch; Shaniweber@ Gmail.Com
Tanzania	Grace Palangioyo	Mwalimu Nyerere Memorial Academy (Lecturer) Spokesperson for the Interview, +255 754 849572
	James Matonfu	Mwalimu Nyerere Memorial Academy (Lecturer in Youth Work Certificate)
	P. Masika	Tanzania Youth Alliance, P.Masika@Tayoa. Org
	Diana Rose	Tanzania Youth Vision Association, Tel: +255759079 297, Tyvvijana@Yahoo. Com, Dianaroselnc@Gmail.Com
	Julius Shulla Tweneshe	PMO – Labour, Youth, Employment and People With Disability: (Principal Youth Development Officer I); Tel: +255 753687094, Tweneshej@Yahoo.Com

Country	Name	Institution
Zambia	Justin Nsomi	Zambia Youth Workers Association; Committee Member; Tel: +260 968 814 245, Justinsomi@Yahoo.Co.Uk
	Kakuwa Musheke	Ministry of Youth and Sport; Senior Youth Development Officer, Tel: +260 977 766 750, Kakuwajr@Yahoo.Com
	Mulako Mwanamwalye	National Youth Development Council, Project Officer, Tel: +260 978 600 985 Mulakom@Yahoo.Com
Asia		
Bangladesh	Md Rezaul Karim Babu	Vice President, National Youth Council of Bangladesh & Country Representative, HOPE '87 Bangladesh
	Arup Barua	UNFPA Bangladesh
	Reja Syed Ali	Deputy Secretary, Ministry of Youth & Sports, Government of Bangladesh
	Ejaj Ahmad	Bangladesh Youth Leadership Center
	Prof. Md. Mostafizur Rahman, PhD	Department of Population Science, and Human Resource Development, University of Rajshahi
India	Dr Radhakrishnan Nair	Deputy Director Nehru Yuva Kendra Sangathan (NYKS), Ministry of Youth Affairs & Sports, Govt. of India
	Roshni Nuggehalli	Director, Youth for Unity and Voluntary Action, Mumbai
	Kavita Ratna	Concerned for Working Children, Bangalore
	Dr P. Sivakumar	Assistant Professor Rajiv Gandhi National Institute of Youth Development (RGNIYD), Sriperumbudur, Tamil Nadu
	Ishani Sen	Director, Pravah Learning Voyages Consulting Pvt Ltd.
	Sayeda Naghma Abidi	Director, Teen Club, Pravah
	Dr Bhagban Prakash	Senior Advisor, Election Commission of India, Govt. of India
Malaysia	Ahmad Huzairi Bin Rawee	Ministry of Youth and Sports Malaysia
	Prof. Dr Azimi Hamzah	Universiti Putra Malaysia
	Dr Siti Raba'ah Hamzah	Universiti Putra Malaysia
	Dr Abdul Lateef Abdullah (Steven Krauss)	Universiti Putra Malaysia
	Shah Romnizam Ramli	Institute for Youth Research, Ministry of Youth and Sports Malaysia
	Prof. Dr Turiman Suandi	Universiti Putra Malaysia

Country	Name	Institution
Pakistan	Tehmina Habib, Deputy Secretary	Department of Youth Affairs, Govt. of Punjab
	Muhammad Afzal Sulehri, Director	Department of Youth Affairs, Govt. of Balochistan
	Arshad Hussain, Assistant Director	Department Youth Affairs, Govt. of Khyber Pakhtunkhwa
	Sadia Atta Mehmood, Program Technical Analyst (ASRH)	United Nations Population Fund (UNFPA)
	Sadia Rahman, Director Society	British Council Pakistan
	Hammad Rahman, Manager, Volunteer in Service Program	University of Central Punjab
	Sabeeha Shaheen, Executive Director	Bargad
	Fsahat Ul Hassan, Chairman	Youth Advocacy Network
	Sana Sohail, National Coordinator	Youth Peer Education Network (Y-PEER) Pakistan
Singapore	Felicia Yong	National Youth Council
	Gracia Ong	National Youth Council
	Michelle Ling	National Youth Council
Sri Lanka	Mrshanthaabeywickrama	Assistant Director, National Youth Services Council, Maharagama
	Niwantha Kanuwana	Assistant Director, Sri Lanka Youth Corp, No 420, Bauddaloka, Mawatha
Europe		
Canada	Dr Varda Mann-Feder	Concordia University, Graduate Program Director Youth Work, Quebec
	Heather Modlin	Key Assets, Children's Services Provider, Newfoundland & Labrador
	Kelly Shaw	President, Council of Canadian Child and Youth Care Associations, Nova Scotia
	Catherine Hedlin	Grant McEwan University, President – Alberta Association of Child and Youth Care, Alberta
	Dr Patti Ranahan	Assistant Professor, Applied Human Sciences, Concordia University, Quebec
Cyprus	Nickolas Christofi	Cyprus Youth Council
	Maria Christodoulou	Youth Board of Cyprus
	Marios Epaminonda	Ministry of Education & Culture
	Anna Dalosi	Trainer for the Cyprus Youth Council, Former Executive Director of The Cyprus Youth Clubs Organisation
	Socrates Socratous	Cyprus Youth Clubs Organisation
	Giorgos Leontiou	Cyprus Youth Clubs Organisation
	Alexis Koutsoventis	Cyprus Youth Clubs Organisation
	Andreas Kofou	Cyprus Youth Clubs Organisation

Country	Name	Institution
Malta	Marvic Debono	Manager Erasmus+ Youth
	Deborah Bonnici	Youth Worker, Youth Catholic Action
	Ramona Cuschieri	Former President of Maltese Association of Youth Workers
	Miriam Teuma	CEO Aġenzija Żgħażagħ
	Dr Andrew Azzopardi	Senior Lecturer & Head of Department, Department of Youth and Community Studies, Faculty for Social Wellbeing
	Gabriella Calleja	Senior Manager, Agenzija Zghazagh
	Jason Zammit	Chair of The Youth Work Profession Board
Pacific		
Australia	Leo Fieldgrass	Chief Executive Officer Australian Youth Affairs Coalition
	Katie Atcheson	Chief Executive Officer, Youth Action
	Robyn Broadbent	Victoria University
	Mel Vella	Youth Workers Association
New Zealand	Anya Satyanand	Executive Officer Ara Taiohi, Peak Body for Youth Development
	Stewart Irwin	Ara Taiohi Pathways to Professionalisation Working Group
	Stephen Bell	Ara Taiohi Pathways to Professionalisation Working Group
	John Harrington	Ara Taiohi Pathways to Professionalisation Working Group
	Jane Zintl	Ara Taiohi Pathways to Professionalisation Working Group
	Trina King	Ara Taiohi Pathways to Professionalisation Working Group
	Ben Parker	Ara Taiohi Pathways to Professionalisation Working Group
Caribbean		
Barbados	Not available	Not available
Belize	Allison Brown-Mckenzie	Director, Department of Youth Services
	Sandra Diaz-Cadle	Counsellor, Edward P. Yorke High School
	Kevin Cadle	Assistant Coordinator, Youth Apprenticeship Program
	Dianne Finnegan	Former Director, Youth Department
	Kera Bowen Polonio	Former CARICOM Youth Ambassador
	Martha Longsworth Arana	Sr. Youth Development Officer, Department of Youth Services
	Deborah Sewell	Chairperson, Love Foundation
	Andrew Munnings	Founder, Guidelight Productions

Country	Name	Institution
Dominica	Lennox Abraham – Director	Operation Youth Quake (OYQ)
	Senator Jahisiah Benoit – President	National Youth Council of Dominica (NYCD)
	John Roach – Chief Youth Development Officer	Youth Development Division Ministry of Youth, Sports, Culture & Constituency Empowerment
	Matilda Popo – Retired Youth Officer	Student of Degree Programme in Youth Development Work – UWI
	Olivia Douglas – Director	Centre Where Adolescents Learn to Love Serve (CALLS)
Jamaica	Michelle Folkes	Director, Jamaica Professional Youth Workers Association
	Terri-Ann Gilbert Roberts/ Kareen Guscott Research Fellow & Degree Programme Coordinator	University of The West Indies Mona
St Lucia	Marcia Dolor Lashley	Ministry of Youth Development & Sports
	Tevin Shepherd	National Youth Council
	Eulampia Springer	UWI Open Campus
	Patrick Mathurin	Ministry of Youth Development and Sports
	Claudia Jn Baptiste	Ministry of Youth Development and Sports
	La Fleur Quammie-Harry	Monitoring and Evaluation Unit Ministry of National Mobilisation
	Gwenneth Anthony	Youth Affairs Division
	Yoland London	Youth Affairs Division
	Kathleen Jeffers	Ministry of Education
Trinidad	Angela Llo – Manager Life Skills Programme	National Training Agency
	Patricia Hinds	Director of Youth, Ministry of Sports and Youth Affairs
	Donna Boucaud	Judiciary Court Project
	Helen Warner	Service Commission
	Carolyn Gloudon	Youth Training Employment Partnership Programme
	Allison Francis	Ministry of Labour

Annex 4

State/National Youth Representation Structures as of mid-2016

As the empowerment of young people is a central task of youth work (according to the Commonwealth definition) an incidental indicator of the impact of youth work (and so part of its potential professional profile) is youth representation in and on adult administrative and policy structures.

The organised influence (direct and indirect) of young people on government and legislation across the Commonwealth is mixed. There seem to be some helpful examples of how young people can guide and inform policy, but at the same time there are examples that appear no more than tokenistic and/or more adult directed than youth oriented.

a. Africa

Table A4.1 Youth and Formal representation – Africa

Country	Youth and representation
Ghana	It is unclear what youth representation structures exist at the national level. According to a 2012 profile on youth and civic participation, youth and student groups were organised under the Federation of Youth Associations in Ghana (FEDYAG). However, there no indication that it is still in operation.
Kenya	The National Youth Council of Kenya (NYC-Kenya) was established in the National Youth Council Act (2009) in response to the election violence of 2008. The Act mandates the NYC-Kenya to co-ordinate youth activities and organisations along with supporting the national youth policy.
Malawi	Act No. 22 of 1996 established the National Youth Council of Malawi (NYCoM). The 2013 youth policy states that its main function is 'to contribute towards youth empowerment and development through the promotion and co-ordination of activities of youth organisations'. The Youth Consultative Forum (YCF) is a confederation of youth organisations in Malawi. As reported in the *Malawi Voice*, in June 2013 the group petitioned the National Assembly to review the outdated 1996 youth policy.
Nigeria	No information
South Africa	The South African Youth Council (SAYC) was founded in 1997 and is an autonomous, non-partisan umbrella association for youth organisations. According to its 2010 report *South African Youth Council: Towards a Coordinated and Integrated Youth Development*, it is governed by a National Executive Committee comprising provincial chairpersons and secretaries. SAYC represents youth in forums including the National Economic Development and Labour Council (NEDLAC), the South African National AIDS Council (SANAC), and the National Skills Authority (NSA).
Tanzania	The National Policy on Youth Development (2007) commits the government to support the creation of the National Council of Youth.
Uganda	The National Youth Council (NYC) is an autonomous body established by the National Youth Council Act 1993 and seeks to be 'the leading organisation in empowerment of Youths'. It acts as an umbrella organisation for young people and youth organisations in Uganda and seeks to 'organise, mobilise and engage Youth in development activities'.
Zambia	The National Youth Development Council Act (1994) created the NYDC to: • advise the Minister on youth development programmes; • co-ordinate youth activities; • assist and encourage youth development organisations and programmes; • Evaluate and implement youth programmes; • initiate, operate and manage youth development projects; • register and monitor youth organisations in Zambia.

b. Asia

Table A4.2 Youth and Formal representation – Asia

Country	Youth and representation
Bangladesh	The National Federation of Youth Organisations in Bangladesh (NFYOB) describes itself as a co-ordinating council of youth organisations.
India	According to the National Youth Policy (2014), youth organisations in India are 'fragmented, and there is little co-ordination between the various stakeholders working on youth'. Various national platforms and party youth wings exist, yet 'there are no systematic channels for engagement between the government and young citizens and no mechanisms for youth to provide inputs to government'.
Maldives	The National Youth Council (NYC) previously acted as 'the national co-ordinating body for youth affairs' and advised the then Minister of Human Resources, Youth and Sports (MHRYS). The NYC was fully appointed by the minister and did not include youth NGOs or other youth associations. However, the MHRYS no longer exits. The current activity of NYC is also unclear.
Malaysia	The Malaysian Youth Council (MYC) was formed in 1948 and is a non-governmental voluntary organisation that is the sole co-ordinating body for youth and student organisations in Malaysia. It participates in the National Youth Consultative Council (a forum for governmental and non-governmental actors to meet and discuss issues relating to youth development), and plays an active role in the implementation and monitoring of the national youth policy.
	Besides the Malaysian Youth Council (MYC), the Ministry of Youth and Sports, Malaysia has been supported by youths represented under the 'Young Friends' or 'Rakan Muda' and 'iMalaysia for Youth' or 'iM4U' programmes. These three important youth representative structures play an active role in the implementation of youth development activities as espoused in the national youth policy.
Pakistan	There is no official youth council, but there are several youth-led groups that operate at a regional and national level. The National Youth Assembly (NYA) aims to educate youth aged 18-30 about leadership, politics and democracy. The Channan Development Association (CDA) aims to build the capacity of young people, and to act as a resource hub for youth organisations. The role of young people in these organisations is unclear, as is their representative nature.

(*continued*)

Table A4.2 Youth and Formal representation – Asia (*continued*)

Country	Youth and representation
Singapore	The National Youth Council (NYC) was set up by the Singapore Government on 1 November 1989 as the national co-ordinating body for youth affairs in Singapore and the focal point of international youth affairs. On 1 January 2015, NYC began its operations as an autonomous agency under the Ministry of Culture, Community and Youth (MCCY) and housed two key institutions: Outward Bound Singapore (OBS) and Youth Corps Singapore. Together, the agency will drive youth development and broaden outreach to young Singaporeans and youth sector organisations. (reference: https://www.nyc.gov.sg/about-us) The NYC, together with the Singapore National Employers Federation in 2012, also co-founded INSPIRIT, a body of 120 persons aged 28 to 35, seeking to bring young adult leaders together to advocate youth interest in national and community issues, and to champion youth causes.
Sri Lanka	The NYSC, known as Sri Lanka Youth, is legally mandated through the National Youth Councils Act of Sri Lanka. It acts as the focal point for youth clubs and organisations. It delivers extensive programmes including youth awards, education, sports, media, international youth affairs, skills and training. It has close links to government ministries and receives government funding. The NYSC organised the World Conference on Youth in 2014.

c. The Caribbean

Table A4.3 Youth and Formal representation – The Caribbean

Country	Youth and representation
Barbados	The Barbados Youth Development Council (BYDC) is a national umbrella organisation consisting of individual and youth groups. An elected National Youth Parliament exists, and a National Youth Forum was launched in 2010 to provide a space for youth participation in the implementation and review of the national youth policy.
Belize	In June 2012, Youth-IN reported that the Department of Youth Services held a meeting of student council representatives nation-wide to begin the development of a National Youth Council of Belize. The NYC's first executive was elected in 2016.
Dominica	The National Youth Council of Dominica (NYCD) was formed in 1970 and, according to the National Youth Policy (2004), is formed of elected representatives from youth organisations and groups across the country. It is mandated 'to co-ordinate the plans and programmes of affiliated groups within eight designated youth districts'. It is considered an 'equal partner and participant' in the policy process relating to young people in Dominica.
Guyana	The Guyana National Youth Council is a legally registered youth led network of youth, youth-led organisations and youth workers formed in 2013 and led by a five-member Board of Trustees. The GNYC is committed to empowering youth and creating a positive environment for youth development, and by extension national development. The GNYC is still in its early stages and is being established as a non-partisan network. The GNYC is a member of the Caribbean Regional Youth Council and the Commonwealth Youth Council.
Jamaica	The National Youth Council of Jamaica (NYCJ) is an umbrella organisation representing local youth clubs that provides 'assistance in the formulation, implementation and evaluation of government policy regarding youth'. The Youth Ambassadors Programme is made up of 22 young people acting as national and international ambassadors. They focus on thematic issues, such as disability, gender and education, and international forums.
St Lucia	The Saint Lucia National Youth Council (SLUNYC) was established in 1985 and was initially government-funded to deliver national participation programmes.
St Vincent and the Grenadines	The National Youth Council of Saint Vincent and the Grenadines (NYC-SVG) was established in 1966 and 'has long spearheaded the cause of young people in St Vincent and the Grenadines'. Its principles include autonomy, political independence and human rights.

(continued)

Table A4.2 Youth and Formal representation – The Caribbean (*continued*)

Country	Youth and representation
Trinidad & Tobago	The National Youth Council of Trinidad and Tobago (NYCTT) is 'a federation of youth and youth organisations' and is 'the focal point for youth'. The National Youth Council Trinidad & Tobago is meant to be the council incorporating the Trinidad Youth Council and the Tobago Youth Council to be fully representative of youth in the twin island state. The collaboration and merger is still ongoing. The Trinidad Youth Council is listed as a founding member of the Caribbean Regional Youth Council, established in December 2013.
Caribbean Regional Youth Council	The Caribbean Regional Youth Council (CRYC) is the collective voice of national youth councils and represents the voice of youth for the Caribbean. It was established at the Third Caribbean Youth Leaders' Summit 2013, with the instrumental support and continued guidance of the Commonwealth Youth Programme Caribbean Centre. The establishment was as a result of the need for a unified regional body to advocate for and advance the development agenda for youth. The CYRC membership includes Antigua & Barbuda, The Commonwealth of Anguilla, Barbados, The Bahamas, Belize, Dominica, Grenada, Guyana, Jamaica, St Kitts & Nevis, Saint Lucia, Saint Vincent & The Grenadines, and Trinidad & Tobago. Strategically, the CRYC is seeking to establish itself as a strategic youth governance and advocacy network/movement working towards regional representation, integration and co-operation as a platform for youth development. It is supported by the Youth Division of The Commonwealth Secretariat.

d. Europe and Canada

Table A4.4 Youth and representation – Europe and Canada

Country	Youth and representation
Cyprus	The Cyprus Youth Council (previously the Cyprus Youth Council for International Co-operation) is a union of Non-Governmental Youth Organisations (NGYOs) in Cyprus. Founded in 1996, its aim is to promote dialogue and co-operation between youth. The 2007 Council of Europe report states that there is a lack of clarity about the Council's role vis-à-vis the Youth Board of Cyprus and other youth organisations. It recommends 'further discussion and urgent clarification' on its identity and status. The Youth Board of Cyprus is made up of seven members, each representing the youth organisations of each political party in the House of Representatives. The Council of Ministers appoints three members. Its aims include the promotion of 'progress and prosperity' for young people, enhancing participation and 'providing effective solutions to current youth problems'. The Ministry of Education and Culture is the liaison between the Board and the Council of Ministers. The Board is a 'Semi-Governmental Organisation'; however, its budget is provided fully by the state.
Malta	The National Youth Council of Malta was established as an independent body in 1993 with the following aims: • promote a cross-sectoral youth policy; • influence youth policy at a regional and international level; • increase the participation of young people and youth organisations in society and decision-making; • promote the exchange of ideas and experience; • promote equal rights and opportunities amongst young people.Projects have included a Charter of Youths' Rights, Youth Parliament, local youth councils, Youth Day activities and the Mediterranean Youth Forum.
UK	The British Youth Council (BYC) is an umbrella organisation made up of over 230 national and local youth organisations, which supports young people 'to influence and inform decisions that affect their lives'. Member organisations elect an annual board of young trustees (aged 16 to 25) and guide all policy and strategic decisions. The BYC delivers campaigns such as Votes at 16, and participation programmes such the UK Youth Parliament and the international UK Young Ambassadors.
Canada	There are no national or regional youth councils in Canada. According to Innovations in Civic Participation, youth participation in civic life is primarily through civil society organisations. For example, the Boys & Girls Clubs of Canada, one of the largest youth-serving agencies in the country, has youth councils where young people serve as ambassadors for other youth in local, provincial and national levels of the organisation. Youth councils also exist in the private sector, such as the Youth Committee of the Canadian Association of the World Petroleum Council, which seeks to bring a youth perspective to the petroleum industry.

e. The Pacific

Table A4.5 Youth and representation – The Pacific

Country	Youth and representation
Australia	The former Office of Youth and the Australian Youth Forum no longer exists.
Fiji	According to the Ministry of Youth & Sports, the original national youth council, established in 1975 was replaced in 2004 by a National Youth Advisory Board (NYAB). The national youth policy (2011) details its objective to 'advise the Minister directly on issues of concern to young people'. In 2013, the *Fiji Times* reported that a new National Youth Council of Fiji had been constituted with UNDP, providing $150,000 to the council to support their five priorities as part of a three-year strategic plan.
New Zealand	New Zealand has a range of participation structures existing under the Ministry of Youth Development. The national Aotearoa Youth Voices network brings together 'young people, government and community decision-makers'. Members of the network can then be selected to the National Youth Advisory Group, which 'provide[s] government and community agencies with timely advice on many different issues'. The annual Youth Parliament also offers a 'mock' Parliament session.
Papua New Guinea	No information
Samoa	No information
Solomon Islands	The Solomon Islands National Youth Congress (SINYC) aims to 'encourage young people to participate more fully in the country's development'. SINYC was established in 1980 and its functions include advocacy, training, developing provincial youth policies and co-ordinating the National Youth Stakeholders Committee. An annual National Youth Parliament takes places at the National Parliament for a mock session. The SINYC is a member of the Pacific Youth Council.
Tonga	No information
Vanuatu	The Vanuatu National Youth Council's mission is to '[s]trengthen and build networks [and] initiate capacity-building to involve and empower youth in decision-making'. The council represents six provincial youth councils. It also oversees the registration, training and capacity-building programmes for youth groups in Vanuatu.
Pacific Youth Council	The Pacific Youth Council is a regional non-governmental youth organisation made up 10 National Youth Councils across the Pacific region. The National Youth Councils include: Federated States of Micronesia, Cook Islands, Nauru, Nieu, Republic of the Marshall Islands, Palau, Solomon Islands, Tuvalu, Tonga and Vanuatu. A General Assembly is held every three years with an elected executive board responsible for the work plan. The PYC is active within a number of United Nations and international processes and is a member of the International Coordination Meeting of Youth Organisations (ICMYO).

Overall, while there are clear gaps in youth representation, the Commonwealth has done much in the past to increase the representation and influence of young people and involve them in the delivery of practice.

Annex 5

Principles Linked to Course Content and Subject Areas

Principle	Descriptor	Content areas either competency-based or curriculum
Include an understanding of the systemic and structural influences that impact on young people.	Young people are marginalised because of the ways in which society is structured. There are systemic structures and influences that are beyond their control. The subject area needs to include content on the theory of these structural influences, the impact on young people and Youth Work practice.	Young people and society/ sociology. Youth Policy/Political economy.
A focus on Empowerment as a practice ethos.	The practice ethos of the course will reflect an empowerment focus whereby youth work is seen as a way of empowering young people to take greater control of their lives both individually and collectively and facilitate their participation in community and wider decision-making.	Community Development. Youth Practice.
Ethics	Distinct course content on ethics including evidence of training in the Youth Work Code of Ethical Practice.	Ethics. Youth Practice. Youth Development. Community Development.
Youth Development	Course content on youth development and the principles of youth development that focus on a strength-based approach. Youth workers see the participation of young people in their community, school and wider society as a focus of their work. The content will reflect a broader understanding of the link between youth development, social inclusion and social capital; as well as an understanding of risk and protective factors that impact on young people's participation in their communities.	Youth Development. Holistic Practice. Community Development.
Cross-cultural communications and practice	Youth Work practitioners need to have an understanding of cross-cultural practice that is respectful of diversity and equips the youth worker to work in a multicultural community.	Cross cultural understanding working with diversity and young people. Communications.
Group Work	Youth workers work with groups of young people in all sorts of settings. A youth work course should include a group work subject that equips the youth worker with an understanding of the different stages of group forming and how to work collectively and collaboratively with groups of young people.	Group Work.

		Field placement/Learning in the Workplace.
Supervised Practice	Supervised field practice for pre-service youth workers is seen as an essential part of an undergraduate course. A minimum of 300 hours in two settings will form the benchmark. Placement is also seen as a way of encouraging students to reflect on practice; an essential Youth Work practice principle.	
Adolescent health	Youth workers understand that adolescence is a distinct period of the lifespan and is influenced by a range of physiological, psychological and social influences that impact on a young person's health and well-being. Within the context of understanding the social and structural influences that impact on young people, subject content must reflect a clear understanding of the range of influences that frame the health of an adolescent. This subject area would also equip the youth worker with an understanding of the critical health issues that face young people currently, such as mental health and well-being, youth suicide, drug and alcohol use, identity and sexuality.	Adolescent Health
Youth Policy	Youth workers are advocates for young people and often act as agents of change agents. Therefore, they must understand how their practice is influenced by the social policy of the Government of the time, as well as understanding how to influence that policy. Youth policy will include an understanding of how policy is developed, the range of mechanisms utilised and how to engage in those mechanisms. The content will also include the range of policy frameworks currently utilised by Government and their relationship to good youth work practice.	Youth Policy
Respecting indigenous community	Many course work programmes neglect to include an indigenous subject or content that provides students with an insight into the indigenous cultures of Australia, the structural challenges faced by indigenous communities and how they can work collaboratively with those communities.	Working with Indigenous Communities.
Collaborative Practice	Working collaboratively with other youth workers and other professionals is essential in good youth work practice. Course content must reflect and equip students with an understanding of how to work in different service provision settings and how to work collaboratively.	Holistic Practice, Community Development, Inter-professional Collaboration, Ethics.

Annex 6

Core Building Blocks for Youth Work Education and Training: An Example from the Youth Workers' Association Australia

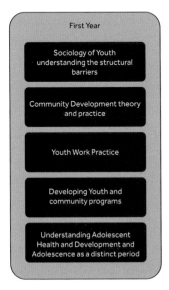

First Year

- Sociology of Youth understanding the structural barriers
- Community Development theory and practice
- Youth Work Practice
- Developing Youth and community programs
- Understanding Adolescent Health and Development and Adolescence as a distinct period

Second Year

- Fieldwork on the job professional placement
- Group Work
- Youth Work Theory and Ethics
- Communication and cross cultural communications
- Political Economy
- Critical Incidents
- Drug and Alcohol

Third Year

- Management of Youth Work/ Human Service Agencies
- Interprofessional Collaboration
- Youth Policy
- Working with Diversity including partnering with indigenous and migrant communities
- Youth Research and Program Evaluation
- Fieldwork on the job professional placement

Annex 7

Graduate Capabilities: Youth Workers' Association – Australia

Graduate Capabilities

Diploma

Diploma of Youth Work graduates should be able to demonstrate skills in the following areas.

1. **Understanding, developing and managing their professional role:**

   - An understanding of, and the capacity to apply and integrate, theoretical frameworks and key concepts relevant to practice in youth work.

   - An informed and critical understanding of their role as facilitators in relation to other professional interventions in the lives of young people and communities.

   - The ability to maintain boundaries in voluntary relationships and in informal contexts.

   - The ability to make informed judgments on complex ethical and professional issues in a disputed field and to act appropriately in line with the Code of Ethical Practice.

   - The ability to operate as a reflective practitioner, demonstrating appropriate professional actions and behaviours.

   - Critical reflection upon, and commitment to, their continuing personal and professional development.

2. **Fostering democratic and inclusive practice:**

   - The ability to build trusting relationships as a foundation for learning.

   - The ability to foster participation and support for young people and adults in playing an active role in their communities, increasing their voice and influence in contexts and on issues that affect them.

   - The ability to create inclusive environments and to identify the power dynamics that are present at both interpersonal and systemic levels.

3. **Maintaining and developing organisations which support practice:**

   - Context-appropriate leadership of individuals and groups.

   - The ability to build trusting relationships as a foundation for learning.

- The ability to foster participation and support for young people and adults in playing an active role in their communities, increasing their voice and role in community governance.

4. **Facilitating personal and collective learning development and capacity building:**

- The capacity to engage with young people and community groups, build relationships and facilitate young people and adults' individual and collective learning and development.

- The ability to support and develop a range of literacies, including emotional literacy.

- The ability to select, plan and evaluate appropriate approaches from a range of intervention methods and techniques.

- A commitment to the learning cycle, both as an individual and as part of an organisation

5. **Networking and multi-agency working:**

- Skills in including young people and community members in partnerships.

- Skills in involving, consulting with, and acknowledging, accountability to stakeholders.

- Skills in developing inclusive networks which do not intensify marginalisation of small projects or minority groups.

6. **Generic Skills**

Graduates should be able to demonstrate:

- An ability to use information and communication technologies.

- Self-management, including the organisation of an efficient and effective work pattern, and working to deadlines.

- An ability to collect and apply basic program evaluation data, as appropriate.

- An ability to present data in different formats, including graphical and tabular.

- Commitment to the improvement of their own learning and performance.

Bachelor Degree

Where a graduate of a Diploma articulates to a Bachelor of Youth Work they are aiming to build on the skills and knowledge gained in that Diploma. For these graduates and for those that have undertaken a single three-year Bachelor degree they should be able to demonstrate skills and knowledge in the following areas.

1. **Understanding, developing and managing their professional role:**

- An understanding of, and the capacity to apply and integrate, theoretical frameworks and key concepts relevant to practice in youth work as identified in the Table of Principles.

- An informed and critical understanding of their professional role as facilitators in relation to other professional interventions in the lives of young people and communities.

- Substantial autonomy in using both conventional and innovative, original and creative methods of planning, delivery and evaluation of youth work programs across a range of practice settings.

- Systematic analysis of relevant concepts, theories and issues of policy, and their use in informing practice.

- The ability to maintain professional boundaries in voluntary relationships and in informal contexts.

- The ability to make informed judgments on complex ethical and professional issues in a disputed field and to act appropriately in line with the Code of Ethical Practice.

- The ability to operate as a reflective practitioner, demonstrating appropriate professional actions and behaviours.

- Critical reflection upon, and commitment to, their continuing personal and professional development.

2. **Fostering democratic and inclusive practice:**

- An understanding of their own approaches to learning.

- An ability to work on their own initiative and in co-operation with others.

- The ability to use their knowledge and understanding critically to locate and influence in contexts and on issues that affect them.

- The ability to create inclusive environments and to identify the power dynamics that are present at both interpersonal and systemic levels.

- The capacity to build practice on an understanding of issues of power, empowerment and the complexity of voluntary relationships.

- The capacity to promote, publicise and share good practice.

3. **Maintaining and developing organisations which support practice:**

- The ability to support and promote the development of productive and sustainable responses and structures, including the support and management of community-based and young people's organisations.

- Skill in safeguarding the health and welfare of individuals and communities through the understanding and implementation of legal and regulatory frameworks.

- The capacity to manage others in the workplace (volunteers, staff, accountability, equality and diversity in the workplace).

- The capacity to provide support, safety and well-being of staff.

- Context-appropriate leadership of individuals and groups.

- Project management skills (monitoring, evaluation, financial management, management of resources, policy development, understanding quality framework models).

4. **Facilitating personal and collective learning development and capacity building:**

- The capacity to engage with young people and community groups, build relationships and facilitate young people and adults' individual and collective learning and development.

- The ability to analyse policies and practices in the light of a range of theoretical perspectives, from the standpoint of participants.

- Effective communication using written, visual, electronic and oral means with individuals and groups.

- Emotional literacy programs, and to devise practice responses with them.

- The ability to support and develop a range of literacies, including emotional literacy.

- The ability to design and implement initiatives, projects and programs using appropriate professional frameworks and method.

- The ability to select, plan and evaluate appropriate approaches from a range of intervention methods and techniques.

- Skill in evaluation of the impact and effectiveness of their work and the work of community-based projects.

- A commitment to the learning cycle, both as an individual and as part of an organisation.

5. **Networking and multi-agency working:**

- Skills in building partnerships with other professionals in education and in health and social care.

- Skills in building partnerships across community groups and young people's projects.

- Skills in including young people and community members in partnerships.

- Skills in involving, consulting with, and acknowledging, accountability to stakeholders.

- Skills in creating effective alliances with both education and health services.

- Skills in creating networks and alliances among and between community groups and young people's projects.

- Skills in developing inclusive networks which do not intensify marginalization of small projects or minority groups.

- Skills in contributing to wider development of young people's services.

6. **Generic Skills**

Graduates should be able to demonstrate:

- Understanding and critical evaluation of research in the field and the ability to undertake small-scale participatory research projects.

- An ability to use information and communication technologies.

- Organisation and articulation of opinions and arguments in speech writing, using relevant specialist vocabulary.

- Self-management, including the organisation of an efficient and effective work pattern, and working to deadlines.

- An ability to collect and apply numerical data, as appropriate.

- An ability to collect, analyse and interpret qualitative and quantitative data.

- An ability to present data in different formats, including graphical and tabular.

- Commitment to the improvement of their own learning and performance.

- An understanding of their own approaches to learning.

- An ability to work on their own initiative and in co-operation with others.

- The ability to use their knowledge and understanding critically to locate and justify a personal position in relation to the subject.

- Skill in reflection on their own and other's value systems and the ability to explore such values in informal contexts.

- Effective communication using written, visual, electronic and oral means with individuals and groups.

- Emotional literacy.

References

Adams, P. (2015), *Mapping Global Youth Work*. London: Cass School of Education, University of East London, online at http://think-global.org.uk/wp-content/uploads/dea/documents/Global%20Youth%20Work%20mapping%20FINAL%20report%20July%202010.pdf accessed March 2017.

Anand, R. (2010), Better India. Prava: Inspiring Youth Citizenship, online at http://www.thebetterindia.com/1555/pravah-inspiring-youth-citizenship/http://www.thebetterindia.com/1555/pravah-inspiring-youth-citizenship/ accessed March 2017.

Ara Taiohi (New Zealand) (n.d.), Analysis and resources page, website http://www.ara–.org.nz/initiatives/analysis-and-resources#stepping.

Astroth, K., P. Garza and B. Taylor. (2004), 'Getting down to business: Defining competencies for entry-level youth workers', *New Directions for Youth Development*, Vol. 104, pp. 25–37.

Australian Youth Affairs Coalition (2014), 'The Values and Ethics of Youth Work in Australia', online at http://www.ayac.org.au/uploads/140424YouthWorkEthicsDPmain.pdf accessed March 2017.

Azimi, H. (1987), *Pendidikan Lanjutan dalam Budaya Kerja Akademik* (Continuing Education in an Academic Work Culture). Serdang: Universiti Pertanian Malaysia Press.

Azimi, H. (2005), 'Helping Malaysian Youth Move Forward: Unleashing the Prime Enablers' *Inaugural Address*. Serdang: Universiti Putra Malaysia.

Azzopardi, A. (2002), *Y-EU?: Young people's perceptions*. Malta: Malta-EU Information Centre.

Nur Fatihah, Bandar A. (2009), 'Budaya Kerja dan Kaitannya dengan Profesionalisme Pengamal Kerja Belia' (Relationship Between Work Culture and Professionalism Among Youth Work Practitioners). Unpublished Master's Thesis. Serdang: Universiti Putra Malaysia.

Beker, J. (2001), 'The Emergence of Clinical Youthwork as a Profession: Implications for the Youthwork Field', *Child and Youth Care Forum*, Vol. 30, No. 6, pp. 363–376.

Beker, J. and H. Maier. (2001), 'Emerging Issues in Child and Youth Care Education: A Platform for Planning', *Child and Youth Care Forum*, Vol. 30, No. 6, pp. 377–386.

Belton, B. (2010), *Radical youth work*. Dorset: Russell House Publishing.

Borden, L. M. and D. F. Perkins (2006), 'Community youth development professionals: Providing the necessary supports', *Child & Youth Care Forum*, Vol. 35, pp. 101–153.

Buontempo, S. (2014), *Youth work as a profession*. Retrieved from Times of Malta website: http://www.timesofmalta.com/articles/view/20140201/opinion/Youth-work-as-a-profession.504996

Burnside, L. (2012), 'Youth in Care with Complex Needs', Alberta, Canada: The Office of the Children's Advocate, online at http://www.childrensadvocate.mb.ca/wp-content/uploads/Youth-with-Complex-Needs-Report-final.pdf accessed March 2017.

CanChild Centre for Childhood Disability Research (2004), *Service coordination for children and youth with complex needs: A report for the Ministry of Children and Youth Services.* Hamilton, ON: McMaster University.

CARICOM Youth Development Action Plan (CYDAP), 2012–2017 (draft), online at http://cms2.caricom.org/documents/13930-cydap_2012-2017_rev.pdf accessed March 2017.

Child and Youth Care Educational Accreditation Board of Canada (CYCEA) (n.d.), Accreditation overview, online at http://www.cycaccreditation.ca/accred-overview.aspx.

Chisholm, M., H. Cobb, L. Duke, C. McDuffie and W. Kennedy (2006), 'Development of an Instrument to Measure Professionalism', *American Journal of Pharmaceutical Education*, Vol. 70, No. 4, pp. 1–6.

Commission for Children and Young People (2006), *A guide for creating a child-safe organisation*, Victoria, Australia: Commission for Children and Young People.

Commonwealth of Nations. (2007), *Commonwealth Plan of Action for Youth Empowerment 2007–2015.* Commonwealth Secretariat, Marlborough House, UK.

Commonwealth Secretariat (1992), Harare Commonwealth Declaration, online at http://thecommonwealth.org/sites/default/files/history-items/documents/Harare%20Commonwealth%20Declaration%201991.pdf accessed March 2017.

Commonwealth Secretariat (2012a), *Establishing a Professional Youth Worker Association: A 12-Step Guide and More*, Commonwealth Secretariat, London.

Commonwealth Secretariat (2012b), Professional Youth Work: A Concept and Strategies, Commonwealth Secretariat, London.

Commonwealth Secretariat (2013a), The Charter of the Commonwealth, online at http://thecommonwealth.org/sites/default/files/page/documents/CharteroftheCommonwealth.pdf accessed September 2015.

Commonwealth Secretariat (2013b), Magampura Commitment to Young People by Heads of Government, Commonwealth Secretariat, London.

Commonwealth Secretariat (2014), Draft Code of Ethical Practice for Youth Workers, online at https://youthworkalliance.files.wordpress.com/2016/06/draft-international-code-of-ethical-practice-2014_v1.pdf.

Commonwealth Secretariat, Pravah, Nehru Yuva Kendra (2014), *Co-Creating Youth Spaces – a Field-Based Guide for Youth Workers*, online at http://thecommonwealth.org/sites/default/files/inline/Co-Creating_Youth_Spaces_web.pdf accessed April 2017.

Commonwealth Youth Programme Asia Centre Youth Work Education & Training Unit (2012), *Establishing a Professional Youth Worker Association: A 12-Step Guide and More*, Chandigarh, India, pp. 6–9.

Commonwealth Youth Programme Caribbean Centre (2012), Competency Standards for Youth Development Work in the Caribbean: Control Document.

CommunityCare (2016), 'Children's social work accreditation risks being "punitive" not supportive, inquiry told'; online at http://www.communitycare.co.uk/2016/04/21/childrens-social-work-accreditation-risks-punitive-supportive-inquiry-told/ accessed 20 April 2017.

ComMutiny, the Youth Collective (2016), The Challenger Deep Youth Worker Competency Framework.

ComMutiny Youth Collective (2017), online at http://www.commutiny.in/ accessed March 2017.

The Concerned for Working Children (n.d.), website http://www.concernedforworkingchildren.org/about/ accessed March 2017.

Corney, T. (2014), *Professional Youth Work: an Australian Perspective.* University of Tasmania, Australia: The clearing House for Youth Studies.

Corney, T. and L. Hoiles (2006), Why the youth sector in Victoria needs a code of ethical practice. *'Yikes' Journal of the Youth Affairs Council of Victoria*, Vol. 4, No. 10, pp. 1–6.

Corney, T. and L Hoiles. (2007), *Victorian youth sector code of ethical practice: Consultation draft*, Melbourne, Australia: Youth Affairs Council of Victoria.

Council of Canadian Child and Youth Care Associations (n.d.) 'Scope of Practice', web page http://www.garthgoodwin.info/Scope_of_Practice.html.

Council of Europe (2005), *Youth policy in Malta.* Strasbourg Cedex, France: Council of Europe.

Davies, B. (1988), 'Professionalism or Trade Unionism?', Ch.10 in Jeffs, T and Smith, M. (1988) *Welfare and Youth Work Practice*, Hong Kong: Macmillan as cited in Harte, S. (2000) 'Youth Workers as Professionals?' Student Youth Work Online, URL: http://youthworkcentral.tripod.com/sean2.htm.

Deloitte and Touche LLP (2007), Professionalism and reputation. London: The Chartered Insurance Institute, online at http://fliphtml5.com/ruqh/ohcd/basic accessed 17 June 2016.

Department for Business and Skills/Department for Education, UK (2016), Post-16 Skills Plan, London: Stationery Office, online at https://www.gov.uk/government/uploads/system/uploads/attachment_data/file/536043/Post-16_Skills_Plan.pdf

Department of Youth Development (n.d.), Bangladesh, website http://www.dyd.gov.bd.

DeVotta, N. (2004), *Blowback. Linguistic Nationalism, Institutional Decay, and Ethnic Conflict in Sri Lanka,* Stanford: SUP.

Eisikovitz, Z. and J. Beker (2001), 'Beyond Professionalism: The Child and Youth Care Worker as Craftsman', *Child and Youth Care Forum*, Vol. 30, No. 6, pp. 415–434.

Ennew, J. (2000), *Street and Working Children. A guide to Planning*, London: The Save The Children Fund.

European Commission (2014), 'Working with young people: The value of youth work in the European Union', online at http://ec.europa.eu/youth/library/study/youth-work-report_en.pdf accessed March 2017.

Evans, L. (2008), 'Professionalism, Professionality and the Development of Education Professionals', *British Journal of Educational Studies*, Vol. 56, No. 1, pp. 20–38.

Fletcher, Adam (2013), *A Short Introduction to Youth Engagement*, Olympia: The Freechild Project.

Fox, C. (1992), 'What Do We Mean When We Say Professionalism? A Language Usage Analysis for Public Administration', *The American Review of Public Administration*, Vol. 22, No. 1, pp. 1–17.

Freire, P. (1970), *Pedagogy of the oppressed*, London: Penguin Books.

Goodwin, V. (1991), 'Youth worker perception of the term "professional": a Victorian study', *The Australian Education Researcher*, Vol. 18, No. 2, pp. 43–63.

Griffin, R. and E. Luttrell (2011), *Future focussed: Youth work in Australia: Reflections and aspirations*. Sydney, Australia: Australian Youth Affairs Coalition.

Grogan, P. (2004), *That old chestnut: The Professionalisation of youth work in Victoria: A discussion paper*. Melbourne, Victoria: Youth Affairs Council of Victoria.

Hargreaves, A. and I. Goodson (1996), 'Teachers' Professional Lives: Aspirations and Actualities', in Goodson, I. and A. Hargreaves (eds), *Teachers' Professional Lives*, London: Falmer, pp. 1–27.

Harte, S. (2000), 'Youth Workers as Professionals?' Student Youth Work Online, website http://youthworkcentral.tripod.com/sean2.htm accessed March 2017.

Hoyle, E. (2001), 'Teaching: Prestige, Status and Esteem', *Educational Management and Administration*, Vol. 29, No. 2, pp. 139–52.

Huebner, A. J., J. A. Walker and M. McFarland (2003), 'Staff development for the youth development professional: A critical framework for understanding the work', *Youth Society*, Vol. 35, pp. 204–225.

Irving, T., D. Maunders and G. Sherington (1995), *Youth in Australia: Policy, Administration and Politics*, South Melbourne, Australia: Macmillan.

Jeffs, T. and Mark Smith (2010), *Youth Work and Practice*, Palgrave Macmillan.

Jenkinson, H. (2000), 'Youth Work in Ireland: The Struggle for Identity', *Irish Journal of Applied Social Studies*, Vol. 2, No. 2, online at http://arrow.dit.ie/ijass/vol2/iss2/6

Krauss, S. E., Idris Khairuddin, Tamam Ezhar, Suandi Turiman, Arif ismail Ismi, Abdullah Bandar Nur Fatihah and Dahlan Dzulhami (2012), 'Exploring professionalism among youth work practitioners in Malaysia: A measurement development study', *Young*, Vol. 20, No.3, pp. 297–322.

Langlands, Sir Alan (2005), 'Gateways to the Professions', online at http://dera.ioe.ac.uk/6459/1/Gateways%20to%20the%20Professions%20Report%20-%20July%202005%20-%20%20FINAL.pdf accessed 17 June 2016.

MAY (Maltese Association of Youth Workers) (n.d.), *Congratulations!*, online at http://www.maymalta.org/

Ministry for Vulnerable Children (2017), Children's Action Plan, online at http://childrensactionplan.govt.nz/childrens-workforce/.

Ministry of Education and the Arts, Malta (1993), *National youth policy*, online at Agenzija Zghazagh website: http://cdn02.abakushost.com/agenzijazghazagh/downloads/National_Youth_Policy_1993.pdf

Ministry of Youth, Malta (2004), *National youth policy*. Retrieved from Agenzija Zghazagh website: http://cdn02.abakushost.com/agenzijazghazagh/downloads/National_Youth_Policy_2004[2].pdf.

Ministry of Youth Affairs (2006), Kenya National Youth Policy: Government Printers: Nairobi.

National Youth Agency, UK (n.d.), Youth Work National Occupational Standards, online at http://www.nya.org.uk/wp-content/uploads/2014/06/National-Occupation-Standards-for-Youth-Work.pdf.

National Youth Agency, UK (2004), *Ethical conduct in youth work: A statement of values and principles from The National Youth Agency.* Leicester, United Kingdom: The National Youth Agency.

National Youth Agency, UK (2015), 'Professional Validation and Curriculum Requirements 2015', online at http://www.nya.org.uk/wp-content/uploads/2015/07/Professional-Validation-Guidelines-2015-final-version-2.pdf

National Youth Agency, UK (2017a), Cuts Watch, online at http://www.nya.org.uk/supporting-youth-work/policy/cuts-watch/ accessed March 2017.

National Youth Agency, UK (2017b), Joint Negotiating Committee (JNC), online at http://www.nya.org.uk/careers-youth-work/getting-qualified/joint-negotiating-committee-jnc/.

New Zealand Ministry of Youth Development – Te Manatū Whakahiato, online at http://www.myd.govt.nz/working-with-young-people/youth-development-approach.html accessed September 2016.

Nicholls, Doug (2012), *For Youth Workers and Youth Work,* Bristol: The Policy Press.

Open College Network Northern Ireland (OCN NI) (2015), Specifications for youth work practice courses, online at https://www.ocnni.org.uk/media/1567/qualification-specification-suite-of-l3-youth-work-practice.pdf.

Panter-Brick, C. (2004), 'Homelessness, poverty, and risks to health: beyond at-risk categorizations of street children', *Children's Geographies*, Vol. 2, No. 1, pp. 83–94.

Parliamentary Secretariat Ministry of Education, Malta (1999), *National youth policy.* Retrieved from Agenzija Zghazagh website: http://cdn02.abakushost.com/agenzijazghazagh/downloads/National_Youth_Policy_1999.pdf.

Parliamentary Secretariat for Youth and Sports, Malta (2010), *National youth policy.* Retrieved from Agenzija Zghazagh website: http://cdn02.abakushost.com/agenzijazghazagh/downloads/National_Youth_Policy_2010_2013.pdf.

Patel, Ashraf, Meenu Venkateswaran, Kamini Prakash and Arjun Shekar (2013), *The Ocean in a Drop. Inside-Out Youth Leadership.* New Delhi: Sage Publications.

Pitts, J. (2007 a,b,c), quoted in Nicholls (2012), *For Youth Workers and Youth Work,* Bristol: The Policy Press, p. 186.

Professional Youth Workers' Association, Sri Lanka (2016), Ocean in a Drop. Short Course for Youth Workers. Unpublished.

Quinn, J. (2004), 'Professional development in the youth development field: Issues, trends, opportunities, and challenges', *Professional development for youth workers: New directions for youth development*, No. 104, pp. 13–24.

Schmied, V., S. Bromfield and P. Walsh (2006), *Models of service delivery and interventions for children and young people with high needs.* NSW Department of Community Services Research Report.

Schembri, S. (2006), *A curriculum for youth workers to implement the national youth policy.* (Unpublished undergraduate thesis) University of Malta, Malta.

Sercombe, H. (1997), *A (draft) code of ethics for youth work (Fairbridge).* Youth Affairs Council of Western Australia.

Sercombe, H. (2010), *Youth Work Ethics.* London: Sage.

Sockett, H. (1996), 'Teachers for the 21st Century: Redefining Professionalism', *NASSP Bulletin*, May, pp. 22–29.

Surrey County Council. (2006), *Code of Conduct*. Surrey, UK: Surrey County Council.

TAG - The Professional Association of Lecturers in Youth and Community Work (TAG) (n.d.), website. 'About the Association', online at http://www.tagpalycw.org/about.html accessed 23 April 2017.

Teuma, M. (2009), Youth work development in Malta: a chronicle. In Verschelden, G., F. Cooussée, T. Van de Walle and H. Williamson (eds) , *The history of youth work in Europe and its relevance for youth policy today,* Strasbourg, Cedex, France: Council of Europe Publishing, pp. 78–83.

University of Malta (2013), *Bachelor of arts (honours) in youth and community studies,* online at http://www.um.edu.mt/socialwellbeing/overview/UBAHYTHPTE-2013-4-O

Walker, J. A. (2003), The essential youth worker. In Villarruel, F. A., D. F. Perkins, L. M. Borden and J. G. Keith (eds) , *Community youth development: Programs, policies, and practices*, Thousand Oaks, CA: Sage Publications, pp. 373–393.

Williamson, B. (1997), *Moral learning; a life-long task*. Stoke on Trent: Trentham Books.

YMCA George Williams College (n.d.), website http://www.ymca.ac.uk/index.php?pageid=35

Youth Affairs Council of Western Australia *(2003), Code of Ethics: A code of ethics for youth work*, West Leederville, Australia: Youth Affairs Council of WA.

Youth Affairs Council of Victoria (YACVic) (2007), *The Victorian youth sector – code of ethical practice*. Melbourne, Australia: Youth Affairs Council of Victoria.

Youth Partnership (2008), *The socio-economic scope of youth work in Europe.* Retrieved fromYouthpolicy.org website: http://www.youthpolicy.org/library/wp-content/uploads/library/2008_Socioeconomic_Scope_Youth_Work_Europe.pdf.

Youth & Policy (2014), online at http://www.youthpolicy.org/factsheets/country/malaysia/ accessed March 2017.

Youth Work Profession Bill (2012), Malta. Retrieved from Justice Unit Cabinet Office website http://cdn02.abakushost.com/agenzijazghazagh/downloads/Youth_Work_Profession_Act,_2012_-_Bill.pdf.

YUVA Youth for Unity and Voluntary Action (n.d.), http://www.yuvaindia.org/about.html accessed March 2017.

Zambia Youth Workers Association (2016), *The State of Youth Work in Zambia.*

National Youth Policies

Australia.   http://www.youthpolicy.org/national/Australia_2010_National_Youth_Strategy.pdf accessed March 2017.

Bangladesh. http://www.youthpolicy.org/library/wp-content/uploads/library/Bangladesh_2003_National_Youth_Policy_eng.pdf accessed March 2017.

National Skills Development Policy. Ministry of Education Government (2011), http://www.ilo.org/wcmsp5/groups/public/@asia/@ro-bangkok/@ilo-dhaka/documents/publication/wcms_113958.pdf accessed March 2017.

http://www.dyd.gov.bd/ accessed March 2017.

Barbados. Ministry of Family, Culture, Sports & Youth (2011), http://www.youthpolicy.org/national/Barbados_2011_National_Youth_Policy.pdf accessed March 2017.

Belize. Belizean Youth Taking the Lead, Ministry of Education, Youth & Sports (2012), http://www.youthpolicy.org/national/Belize_2013_National_Youth_ Development_Policy.pdf accessed March 2017.

Dominica (2004), http://www.youthpolicy.org/national/Dominica_2004_National_ Youth_Policy.pdf accessed March 2017.

Fiji. Ministry of Education, National Heritage, Culture & Arts and Youth & Sports (2011), http://www.youthpolicy.org/national/Fiji_2011_National_Youth_Policy. pdf accessed March 2017.

Ghana (2010), Towards and Empowered Youth, Impacting Positively on National Development http://www.youthpolicy.org/national/Ghana_2010_National_ Youth_Policy.pdf accessed March 2017.

Gibraltar – https://www.gibraltar.gov.gi/new/youth-services accessed March 2017.

India. Ministry of Youth Affairs (2014), http://www.rgniyd.gov.in/sites/default/files/ pdfs/scheme/nyp_2014.pdf accessed March 2017.

Jamaica. Ministry of Youth and Culture, National Youth Policy 2015–2030 http:// www.myc.gov.jm/documents/1436213827National-Youth-Policy-2015-2030.pdf accessed March 2017.

Kenya (2007), Office of the Vice President & the Ministry of Youth Affairs Strategic Plan http://www.youthpolicy.org/national/Kenya_2007_Strategic_Youth_Plan. pdf accessed March 2017.

Malawi (2013), http://www.youthpolicy.org/national/Malawi_2013_National_ Youth_Policy.pdf accessed March 2017.

Malaysia National Youth Development Policy (1997), http://www.youthpolicy.org/ national/Malaysia_1997_National_Youth_Development_Policy.pdf accessed March 2017.

Malaysian Youth Policy (2015), http://www.kbs.gov.my/en/malaysian-youth-policy accessed March 2017.

Malta (2015), Toward 2020 https://education.gov.mt/en/resources/Documents/ Policy%20Documents/National_Youth_Policy_Towards_2020.pdf accessed March 2017.

New Zealand. Youth Development Strategy Aotearoa Ministry of Youth Affairs Action for Child and Youth Development. http://www.myd.govt.nz/documents/ resources-and-reports/publications/youth-development-strategy-aotearoa/ydsa. pdf accessed March 2017.

Children's Action Plan http://childrensactionplan.govt.nz/for-organisations/ accessed March 2017.

Nigeria. Second National Youth Policy Document of the Federal Republic of Nigeria (2009), http://www.youthpolicy.org/national/Nigeria_2009_National_Youth_ Policy.pdf accessed March 2017.

Pakistan. Gilgit-Baltistan Youth Policy https://www.facebook.com/GBYouthPolicy/ accessed March 2017.

AJK Youth Policy https://www.facebook.com/AJK-Youth-Policy-532593863423142/ accessed March 2017.

Papua New Guinea (the report Urban Youth in the Pacific, 2011), http://www. youthpolicy.org/national/Papua_New_Guinea_2011_Youth_Policy_Chapter. pdf accessed March 2017.

Saint Lucia. Ministry of Education, Human Resource Development, Youth & Sports http://www.youthpolicy.org/national/Saint_Lucia_2000_Draft_Youth_Policy. pdf accessed March 2017.

2012–2017 Development Plan http://www.youthpolicy.org/national/Saint_ Lucia_2012_Youth_Sports_Plan.pdf accessed March 2017.

Saint Vincent and the Grenadines. The National Youth Commission (1996), http:// www.youthpolicy.org/national/Saint_Vincent_Grenadines_1996_National_ Youth_Policy.pdf accessed March 2017.

Samoa. Ministry of Women, Community and Social Development (2011), http:// www.youthpolicy.org/national/Samoa_2011_National_Youth_Policy accessed March 2017.

Solomon Islands. Ministry of Development Planning and Aid Coordination Honiara (2011), National Development Strategy 2011 to 2020. Vision: A United and Vibrant Solomon Islands http://www.nationalplanningcycles.org/sites/default/ files/planning_cycle_repository/solomon_islands/cobp-sol-2015-2017-sd.pdf accessed March 2017.

South Africa National Youth Policy 2015–2020. 'We are generation2020. We don't want a hand-out, we want a hand up!' http://www.gov.za/documents/national- youth-policy-2015-2020-8-jun-2015-0000 accessed March 2017.

National Youth Policy 2009–2014 http://www.gov.za/documents/national-youth- policy-2009-2014 accessed March 2017.

Sri Lanka. Ministry of Youth Affairs & Skills Development (2014), http://www. youthpolicy.org/national/Sri_Lanka_2014_National_Youth_Policy.pdf accessed March 2017.

Tanzania. Ministry of Labour, Employment & Youth Development (2007), http:// www.tanzania.go.tz/egov_uploads/documents/fsssssssss_sw.pdf accessed March 2017.

Trinidad & Tobago 2012–17 – For Every Youth a Place, a Purpose, a Plan http:// www.youthpolicy.org/national/Trinidad_Tobago_2012_National_Youth_Policy. pdf accessed March 2017.

Uganda, Republic of (2001), A Vision for Youth in the 21st century http://www. youthpolicy.org/national/Uganda_2001_National_Youth_Policy.pdf accessed March 2017.

Decentralisation Policy, Legal Framework, Local Government Structure and Service Delivery http://unpan1.un.org/intradoc/groups/public/documents/UN/ UNPAN029080.pdf accessed March 2017.

Vanuatu. Ministry of Youth Development (2012), National Youth Development Policy 2012–2022 & Strategic Plan of Action 2012–2015.

Republic of Zambia, Ministry of Youth and Sport – National Plan for Action for the 2015 Youth Policy, http://www.ilo.org/addisababa/countries-covered/zambia/ WCMS_395602/lang--en/index.htm accessed March 2017.

Zambia. Ministry of Youth and Sport. http://www.ilo.org/wcmsp5/groups/public/--- ed_emp/---ed_emp_msu/documents/projectdocumentation/wcms_427020.pdf accessed March 2017.

Children Act (1997), http://www.youthpolicy.org/wp-content/uploads/library/2011_ Uganda_Children_Act_Eng.pdf accessed March 2017.

Ministry of Sport, Youth & Child Development (2006), http://www.youthpolicy.org/national/Zambia_2006_National_Youth_Policy.pdf accessed March 2017.

Legislation – Australia

Children, Youth and Families Act 2005. Victoria, Australia.
Child Wellbeing and Safety Act 2005. Victoria, Australia.
Working with Children Act 2005. Victoria, Australia.
Charter of Human Rights and Responsibilities Act 2006. Victoria, Australia.
Commissioner for Children and Young People Act 2012. Victoria, Australia.
Working with Children Act 2005. Victoria, Australia.

Other web references

American Board of Internal Medicine (2001), Project Professionalism Project Professionalism https://medicinainternaucv.files.wordpress.com/2013/02/project-professionalism.pdf accessed March 2017.
Child & Youth Care Educational Accreditation Board of Canada http://www.cycaccreditation.ca/ accessed March 2017.
Mitra, S, 'Kids can teach themselves' https://www.ted.com/talks/sugata_mitra_shows_how_kids_teach_themselves access March 2017.

National Youth Agency

Getting Qualified http://www.nya.org.uk/careers-youth-work/getting-qualified/ accessed March 2017.
Professional Validation and Curriculum Requirements 2015 http://www.nya.org.uk/wp-content/uploads/2015/07/Professional-Validation-Guidelines-2015-final-version-2.pdf accessed March 2017.
Joint Negotiating Committee (JNC) http://www.nya.org.uk/careers-youth-work/getting-qualified/joint-negotiating-committee-jnc/ accessed March 2017.
Department for Education, UK (2011), The Munro Review of Child Protection Munro review of child protection: final report - a child-centred system https://www.gov.uk/government/publications/munro-review-of-child-protection-final-report-a-child-centred-system accessed March 2017.
OCN Northern Ireland https://www.ocnni.org.uk/media/1567/qualification-specification-suite-of-l3-youth-work-practice.pdf accessed March 2017.
Ministry of Health, Ministry of Social and Family Development and National Council of Social Service (2015), Singapore National Social Work Competency Framework https://www.ssi.sg/SSI/media/SSI-Media-Library/Documents/National-Social-Workers-Competency-Framework.pdf accessed March 2017.
Technical and Further Education Bill (England) https://www.gov.uk/government/uploads/system/uploads/attachment_data/file/536043/Post-16_Skills_Plan.pdf accessed March 2017.
Wakefield, J. (2012), Granny army helps India's school children via the cloud http://www.bbc.co.uk/news/technology-17114718 accessed March 2017.